MY
AUTOBIOGRAPHY

MY AUTOBIOGRAPHY

Davy Russell
with
Donn McClean

eriu

First published in the UK by Eriu
An imprint of Black & White Publishing Group
A Bonnier Books UK company

4th Floor, Victoria House,
Bloomsbury Square,
London, WC1B 4DA

Owned by Bonnier Books
Sveavägen 56, Stockholm, Sweden

– @eriu_books
– @eriubooks

Hardback – 978-1-80418-703-6
Ebook – 978-1-80418-704-3
Audio – 978-1-80418-930-6

All rights reserved. No part of the publication may be reproduced, stored in a retrieval system, transmitted or circulated in any form or by any means, electronic, mechanical, photocopying, recording or otherwise, without prior permission in writing of the publisher.

A CIP catalogue of this book is available from the British Library.

Designed by IDSUK (Data Connection) Ltd
Printed and bound by Clays Ltd, Elcograf S.p.A.

1 3 5 7 9 10 8 6 4 2

Copyright © Davy Russell and Donn McClean 2024

Davy Russell and Donn McClean have asserted their moral right to be identified as the authors of this Work in accordance with the Copyright, Designs and Patents Act 1988.

Every reasonable effort has been made to trace copyright holders of material reproduced in this book, but if any have been inadvertently overlooked the publishers would be glad to hear from them.

Eriu is an imprint of Bonnier Books UK
www.bonnierbooks.co.uk

To my children, their children to come and all of those who might come after, who continue to inspire me to tell stories that matter

Chapter 1

I can see the first fence in front of me. I can see the Melling Road in the sunshine, beyond the Melling Road, and onto the first in that famous line of six fences that takes you up to Becher's Brook and into the teeth of the Grand National.

The size of Tiger Roll: hardly as big as the first fence. And I'm thinking, we could fall at the first fence. It's the Grand National, I tell myself. Big fences. Anyone's race can be over at the first.

If we fall at the first, at least I'll make my flight home.

So we're crossing the Melling Road and I can feel Tiger Roll coming back on his hocks a little underneath me. He knows that something is up, he knows that this is a bit different, and I'm thinking, at least he's paying attention. There are horses around us, but he can see the big spruce obstacle in front of us, he knows that he's going to have to jump over it and he's eyeing it up. I'm looking for a stride and there it is: one, two, three.

I sit still, I don't ask him up. Not really. I just give him a little squeeze, but I let him do it himself. He sees the stride too and he picks up. He clips the top of the spruce, just knocks the top off the fence, but it's fine. Perfect. He lands easily and continues in his rhythm, hardly breaks stride.

Not so bad, I'm thinking. Over the first. I might not make my flight home after all. The second comes up quite quickly and I'm just sitting on his back, relaxed, allowing him to relax. You can't do the running for them, you can't jump the fences for them. The horse has to do all that. All you can do is help them do it as efficiently as possible.

We have a clear run at the second too, and he takes it in his stride. Again, easily, effortlessly, lands running, relax. The third fence is the big ditch, and Saint Are is in front of me, the horse I had ridden to finish third in the race the previous year, Ciaran Gethings on him this time, and I'm thinking, not so bad, he's a safe jumper, he won't cause me any problems. We're eyeing up the big ditch now, it's an important fence, it's important that you meet it on a stride. I see the stride and Tiger Roll sees it too, so I let him at it and up he comes. Sails out over it.

There's a lot going on around us, it's a Grand National, of course there is. You don't tend to see too much of it though, you're concentrating on your own horse, keeping him in his racing rhythm, getting him jumping, conserving energy. Over the fourth, and Saint Are makes a bad mistake just in front of us. I didn't expect that. We weren't directly behind him, we were just to the right of him a little, which was lucky. We could have been into the back of him, our race could have been over. These are the little bits of luck that you need in the Grand National. You don't actually need to be lucky, you just need not to be unlucky.

On to the fifth fence, The One Before Becher's, they call it. Lots of fences have names, Becher's Brook, the Canal Turn, The Chair, Valentine's Brook, Foinavon. This one is called The One Before Becher's, and it's not much bigger and it's not much smaller than any of the others. Tiger Roll measures it up and takes the fence in his stride.

He's enjoying this, he's figuring it out. He's working out the fences. He seems to be realising that he can hit them just below the top, that he doesn't have to jump over the fences' peaks. The spruce on the top is soft, it's just sitting on top of the fence, you can knock it off quite easily without impacting your momentum or your rhythm, and Tiger Roll is beginning to realise that.

Becher's next.

Becher's Brook is not as daunting as it used to be. They have filled in the brook on the landing side that gives the fence its name, and they have raised the ground so that the drop on the landing side of the fence is not nearly as severe as it used to be. That said, it's still a big fence. And it's a tricky fence, because you meet it at an angle, and there is a slight left-hand kink directly after you land, so you don't want to be giving away ground by jumping it too wide.

Our run into the fence is quite good. There's just one horse in front of us, but we have plenty of room around us. As long as the horse in front of us jumps the fence okay, we should be fine.

Again, we meet the fence on a great stride. You don't want to be too long at Becher's because of the slight drop on the landing side. If you meet the fence on a long stride, the drop can be steeper than ideal and it can catch you out. Tiger Roll meets the fence perfectly and he jumps it well.

We have landed before I notice the horse in front of us on the ground. It's I Just Know, his rider Danny Cook thrown clear, but I don't know this at that point. In that instant, he's just a horse. Everything happens so quickly then, I have about 17 thoughts in a fraction of a second. First, I've landed safely, not bad, over Becher's Brook. Then, I'm gone, we're down, we can't avoid that horse, the chance of winning the Grand National gone for another year. Fuck it. I haven't fully formulated that thought, though, when we're clear and upright and intact and moving on.

It had nothing to do with me. It was all Tiger Roll. I was just a passenger, all I had to do was sit still, not mess it up. He had seen the horse falling in front of us before I had. He had taken it upon himself to side-step him, shimmy to his left. Not only that, but he shimmied back slightly to his right again so that I would remain on his back. I didn't really know that he had gone to his left before he was back to his right again and I was still on his back. If he had gone to his left and stayed going to his left to avoid the horse on the ground, I probably would have been out the side door to the right and sitting on the ground.

That's Tiger Roll for you. He's so clever. I don't know for sure that he went back to his right so that I would stay on his back, but I would be surprised if he didn't. Why else would he do that?

For now though, it doesn't matter. There's no time to dwell on it. Foinavon next.

Foinavon is a small fence, the smallest on the course, so named because there was a pile-up at the fence in the 1967 Grand National, which allowed the 100/1 shot Foinavon to win the race. It should be the easiest fence, but it can catch horses out. The fence after Becher's, they are often expecting a drop on the landing side, meaning the ground can arrive at their feet sooner than they are expecting.

Tiger Roll is good over it though. The only problem is that we are wide on the run to the Canal Turn. The Canal Turn, the actual fence, is at a 90-degree angle to the course, so you always like to be towards the inside when you're jumping it, and you always like to jump it at an angle so that you don't go too wide. You could easily lose 20 lengths at the Canal Turn.

I manage to get in a little bit and we jump the fence about three horses off the inside, which isn't so bad. We jump it well too and we land easily, with plenty of space around us as we fan out and face up to Valentine's.

Tiger Roll is low over Valentine's, but he's fine. We're about 11th or 12th as we jump the fences down the side of the course. He's low over the next. He's getting lower with every fence that passes, which is okay for now, he can kick through the tops of the fences, but I just don't want him to get too low. He's higher over the next. He figured out that he was too low over the previous fence, that he needed to get back up a little, so he did. And over the next.

And suddenly we're heading towards the Anchor Bridge crossing and back onto the main racecourse, where we will jump two fences and race up by the stands and jump The Chair and the Water Jump and, all going well, head out on our second and final circuit. There's a nice run over the Anchor Bridge crossing and back onto the main racecourse before you have to jump again, so you can take stock a little, have a look around you, see who's there and who isn't there.

I can see Barry Geraghty and Anibale Fly up on my outside. Jack Kennedy is there on Bless The Wings, just in front of me. David Mullins on Pleasant Company just in front of him. Keith Donoghue is along the inside in his white cap on Valseur Lido, one of the other Gigginstown horses. Rachael Blackmore in the blue Gigginstown cap on Alpha Des Obeaux is just beside him.

I'm happy with how we're going. Tiger Roll is at ease, happy with life, relaxed and settled, enjoying himself, enjoying the jumping, enjoying the fences. We jump the next two fences well, and then we funnel up in front of the stands and onto The Chair. The Chair is a big fence, a wide fence with a big ditch in front of it, so it's important that you meet it in your stride. We're in a little tight to the fence but Tiger Roll just pops over it, gets up a little bit so that he makes sure he jumps out over it.

A horse crashes through the fence just in front of us and comes down. He falls a little to his left, we pass him a little to his right. Again these are the little bits of luck that you need. I see the blue cap out of the corner of my eye as we flash past: Rachael Blackmore, hope she's okay.

The Water Jump is next, it's a fairly simple obstacle, the bush fence is small and the spread of water on the landing side is not very wide, not like the water jump at Auteuil, the Rivière Des Tribunes, which is about eight metres wide. Anyway, we nearly make a mess of the Water Jump. Tiger Roll jumps it a bit to his left and he nearly lands in the water. But we're over it safely, and we're on the inside now as we head for the bend that will take us away from the stands again and onto the second circuit.

I remember Arthur Moore telling me, in the Grand National, be sure to be around the inside as you head out for the second circuit. It's one of the most important parts of the race, and people underestimate it. That bend is so important, he told me. If you are on the inside, you can save ground, save energy, fill your horse up before you start on the second circuit. So I'm thinking, Arthur will be happy with me if he's watching, and I'm sure he's watching.

They used to say that, in the Grand National, you hunt around for the first circuit, survival the objective, and you ride a race on the second circuit, but that's not the case anymore, not in my mind. The race is on from flagfall, and survival is the objective for the whole race. So as we go under the starting gate, one circuit down, one circuit to go, I'm happy with how we're going, I'm happy that we're still in the race, but I'm not thinking about winning. I'm still concentrating on getting Tiger Roll around. I've learned before, in the Grand National, as soon as you start thinking about winning, as soon as you start getting a little bit confident, disaster strikes and it all ends in tears.

He gets low over the second fence on the second circuit, and he gets even lower over the third, the big ditch. That's not a fence at which you want to be too low. He's so low over it that the birch hits my boot and knocks it out of the stirrup. Again, it could have all ended there, but thankfully I get it back quickly enough without losing too much momentum.

He's higher over the fourth and, before we jump the fifth, The One Before Becher's, I can see up ahead that we are going to be by-passing Becher's. There's obviously a horse or a rider being attended to on the landing side, so we're going to be waved around the fence. I notice that earlier than most, so I'm able to angle towards the outside of The One Before Becher's so we can be in a good position to by-pass Becher's without losing our rhythm.

It gets a little tight when fences are by-passed in the Grand National. It used to be the case that you couldn't by-pass fences, the fences would stretch all the way across the course from rail to rail, so there was no option for the field to by-pass a fence, and there was no place for loose horses to escape. There is now, which is good, but, in order to by-pass a fence, the field has to funnel into a fairly small gap. Space is at a premium.

Harry Cobden is on my inside as we move towards the gap and he shouts over at me, asks for room. I could have cut him off, but that wouldn't have been right. You look out for each other.

'Davy, I'm still here!' he shouts over at me.

'Yeah you're perfect,' I say. 'I have you covered.'

So I don't go tight to the wing of the fence as we by-pass it, I leave enough room for Harry to pass it on my inside. He's a good chap, Harry. A very good rider. Unfortunately though, his horse, The Dutchman, makes a bad mistake at the next fence, Foinavon, and unseats him.

That leaves me on the inside on the run to the Canal Turn. I was thinking I wanted to be on the inside anyway, I was travelling better than Harry was, and I was thinking I wanted to get in front of him at the Canal Turn. But his departure leaves it far easier for me. I'm on the inside without having to work for it. Tiger Roll pings the fence and cuts the corner. We pass three or four horses in that manoeuvre and suddenly, with minimal effort, we're fifth on the run towards Valentine's.

He's low at Valentine's. God he's low! He just dives through the top of it and lands running. He'd put the fear of God into you. Over the next and over the next, and I can see Daryl Jacob on one of Gordon Elliott's other horses, Ucello Conti, crashing out to my left.

Jack Kennedy is still there though on Gordon's other horse, Bless The Wings, the horse I had ridden in the Cross-Country Chase at Cheltenham the previous month, just behind me on my inside. Johnny Burke is there up on my outside in the Rich Ricci colours on Childrens List. Brian Hughes is in front of me on Seeyouatmidnight, David Mullins to his left on Pleasant Company, Keith Donoghue just beside me on Valseur Lido.

I see a stride at the third last fence, I ask Tiger Roll up and he jumps it well and lands running. Suddenly we're second, only David Mullins and Pleasant Company ahead of us, but I want to wait. I don't want to go too early.

It's a long run from the third last fence across the Anchor Bridge crossing and onto the main racecourse again before you get to the second last fence, so I need to be patient.

We're upsides Pleasant Company at the second last fence, we're not meeting the fence on a good stride, we get in tight and hit it. Pleasant Company hits it too. Neither of us jump the fence well. But I know that Tiger Roll has plenty of energy left, so I'm sitting and sitting and waiting and waiting and trying to fill him up. Suddenly he falls asleep on me, so I need to wake him up again. We move to the lead on the run to the final fence, I need to make sure he doesn't go to sleep on me again, and we get to the last and jump it in front.

In front over the final fence in the Grand National!

I'm not thinking that, though. I'm just concentrating on my horse. No more fences to jump, but still I don't want to ask him for maximum effort. It may be the Grand National, but it's just another horse race in many ways. You ride to maximise your chances of winning. You don't go for home too early. I know how long it is from the final fence to the winning line in the Grand National.

Many a race has changed in that time. I'm thinking, don't go for him until you get to the Elbow.

So I'm just cajoling him along now, I know he has plenty of energy left, making sure he keeps going forward. Eventually we get to the Elbow, the kink in the rail that takes you past The Chair and the Water Jump that you jumped on the first circuit and up to the winning line, so I drive him forward, ask him for all he has left to give, just green grass between us and the winning line in the Grand National.

Suddenly I feel him stopping underneath me. It's a horrible feeling, you're driving him forward and he's stopping underneath you. Like a car that's running out of petrol, running out of energy. But he's not running out of energy, I know he has plenty left. He's having a look around him, thinking the job is done. He's looking over at the Water Jump and wondering why we're not jumping it. It's obvious to him that the race is over.

I'm helpless on his back. All I can do is keep driving forward, keep kicking and pushing and hope he gets to the winning line. It feels like an eternity. I can hear a horse coming up behind us on our right, I can hear hooves on turf, I can hear the crowd roaring. I can see the winning line, miles away.

I keep driving and squeezing. I'm screaming now! I feel a horse beside us, I see the yellow sleeve on a jockey's arm and then, a few strides later, we're past the winning post. I stand up in the irons, and I'm thinking, fuck it, I saw a lot of yellow there as we hit the line. I saw more yellow on David Mullins's sleeve than I should have seen if we were in front. He was right upsides me. I could have just lost the Grand National.

I pull up and slow to a walk and am still thinking I could have just lost the Grand National. People are telling me I've won but I'm not really listening to anyone. I'm waiting for the result to be called, and I'm worried. I keep Tiger Roll moving, keep him walking. Just keep him on the move.

I'm still waiting. Will I be able to hear the announcement above all the noise? They'll call the number first, I'm thinking, and then I think, what's my number? I don't even know my number! I look down at the saddlecloth, number 13. I'm number 13.

It's taking ages. Why is it taking so long? There are people around me, at the horse's head, at the horse's sides, but I don't want to engage with anyone, not until I know the result. Gordon isn't there. He's obviously staying away from me on purpose until the result is called. I'm just shaking the reins at Tiger Roll, keeping him walking, keeping moving forward, reins in my left hand, whip in my right hand. I could have just won the Grand National. I could have just lost the Grand National.

Why is it taking so long?

And then I hear the voice over the Tannoy.

'Here is the result of the photo finish for first place.'

I have a little look to my right, and then I just look straight ahead of me, and I think, 13, 13, 13.

'First number 13 . . .'

I can't describe that feeling. I feel weak with relief. And ecstasy. I feel like bursting, I feel like crying, I feel elated, I feel deflated, I feel exhilarated, I feel exhausted, all at the same time. And suddenly Gordon is there on my left, grabbing my leg, shouting at me, smiling, laughing. Brian Hughes smacks my hand. Keith Donoghue smacks my hand, gives me a hug. Somebody gives me a bucket of water and I pour it over Tiger Roll's head.

It's all a haze, though. Dreamland. It's unbelievable. Really. The Grand National. I've just won the Grand National.

Chapter 2

What was Youghal like in the 1980s? Economically, on its knees like the rest of County Cork, like the rest of Ireland, but we never saw that. We knew nothing about economics or recessions or depressions. For us, Youghal was a brilliant place to live, and all we knew about was having the craic.

We lived in Sweetfield Estate until I was five, when Dad bought a farm, literally around the corner from Sweetfield. I only have vague recollections of living in Sweetfield, but my cousins and all my friends were there and that was where we played as kids even after we moved. So I had the best of both worlds: living on a farm almost inside the town, and all that goes with that as a kid, the space and the freedom and milking the cows and playing in the hay and riding the ponies, but also playing with my friends in Sweetfield in the town.

Dad was born in Conna in County Cork. His dad was a mechanic, he bought a garage in Youghal, about 20 miles down the road from Conna, and Dad took that garage over. But Dad had a farming background too, his grandfather and his uncles were all farmers, so when he bought the farm in Youghal, he was able to combine the two.

He had a couple of petrol pumps in the garage in the town, and he had an Isuzu dealership and a Citroën dealership, but his main dealership was his Renault dealership. His racing colours are black with a yellow diamond, as close as he could get to the Renault logo in racing silks.

He'd often be going off to Rosslare to pick up a car off the ferry, and I'd always go with him. Or he'd be going around to a customer in the town or just outside the town, and I'd tag along. I loved going with him on those trips. Or if he was off to a match or a point-to-point, I'd be there with him. I'd be like a puppy in the kitchen, as soon as he'd get up off the chair or pick up his keys, I'd be up too, over to the door.

'Where're we going, Dad?'

My mam, Phyllis, was an amazing woman. I never heard her say a bad word about anybody, and I never heard her use bad language, never once in her life. We'd all be cursing and blinding around her, and she'd be giving out to us for using bad language. She did everything for us and for Dad. She worked in the garage, she kept the house, she did all the paperwork, she was everything to Dad and to us. And she was always there for us. She went out of her way to make sure we were all right. She was an angel on earth and I adored her.

She was just a marvellous woman who was always in good form, always happy. And she was the most beautiful woman, always elegant. She never wore much make-up, she didn't have time to put on make-up, she was just a naturally beautiful woman, she had a beautiful smile. And she was a real lady, a fantastic woman. She was just a brilliant person and I miss her every day.

Mam was from Kells in County Meath, so we used to spend large parts of the summer up in Meath, with our uncles and aunts and cousins. My three sisters were a fair bit older than me, and Finnuala was gone early, she went to Cyprus and then to America before coming back to Ireland. Eimear and Aileen were around a good bit when I was a kid, but they were going to college, so I was probably just their annoying little brother who was into ponies.

Diarmuid was around too, but he had his set of friends and we didn't really hang out together outside of the house. So that just left my younger brother Sean. He had his friends too, but we'd often hang out together, especially at home, messing around with the tractor or with the car or with the pony.

We went to the local primary school, and I spent a year in Ring in the Gaeltacht at the end of primary school, Seventh Class, Rang a Seacht, before I went to secondary school. Mam obviously thought it would be good for me, my siblings went to Ring before me and maybe she thought that a year in Ring would take the edges off me. I don't know. But I loved my time in Ring. I made great friends there. You learned how to speak Irish and how to polish your shoes and how to hang your clothes up and how to play hurling and how to kiss girls. I became fluent in Irish, and when I went on to secondary school, I was the best at Irish in the class. I loved Irish class. It was the only class I liked.

I met John Hartnett in Ring. John's uncles played hurling for Cork and he was one of the only friends I had as a kid who was into horses. He had a pony, which made him of interest to me straight away. We got on great, we had loads in common and bizarrely, it turns out his sister was pen pals with a girl from Portumna in County Galway, Edelle O'Meara, who would, many years later in the summer of 2016, agree to marry me.

'Where are you from?'

This was before she even knew I was a jockey.

'I'm from Youghal in County Cork.'

'Do you know Maeve Hartnett?'

* * *

I was always David at home, never Davy. Everybody in Youghal, all my family, all my friends from home, still call me David. My mother never called me Davy in her life, not once. When I started riding, when I started riding a few winners, that's when the Davy thing started, and it stuck. Mam even wrote to the *Examiner* once to tell them to stop calling me Davy! Davy Russell rode a winner. I didn't care, David or Davy, it didn't matter, it was the 'rode a winner' part that was important to me.

We were always doing something, always up to something. And we were allowed get up to something, within reason. Mam loved to see us enjoying ourselves, she wanted us to have fun. Like, if there was mischief to be found, we were allowed to find it.

We were never cheeky, never rude, never disrespectful, but we were always looking for divilment. Sprightly, I'd say is a good word for it. You had a fair idea where the boundaries were though, and if you crossed them, you knew about it. You'd know when Mam would be disappointed with you, and that would be an awful feeling.

'David, you can't do that now David, please.'

The craic with the old car was within the boundaries. This old Sunbeam that appeared on the farm one day. It must have been an old banger that Dad picked up for a song, probably for parts, but it worked, it had an engine and you could drive it, so we did. I was only about eight or nine, but we'd be driving it around the fields, playing cops and robbers, robbing the bank and getting away in the getaway car. About 17 of us and me as the getaway driver.

The craic with the Honda 50 was probably outside the boundaries. A few of us had Honda 50s. I had this banger, the usual, I was about 14 or 15, no tax, no insurance, nothing, and I was out on the roads sometimes, which was wrong. I shouldn't have been near the roads. But it was better craic than going to school.

There was an incident, though, with me and the Honda 50 on the main street in Youghal. I crashed into the back of a car, got flung up against a concrete flower pot! I was fine, I had been wearing a helmet thankfully, but I knew I was in trouble.

A man came and interviewed me after the accident, he must have been some social worker or something. He came to ask me if I was okay, like, if I was having any trouble in my life. It was the opposite; I was having a bonanza. Any troubles at home? Only that I don't have my Honda 50 anymore and that I'm going to have to walk now. Any troubles in school? Only that I have to go at all, that it's getting in the way of me having the time of my life.

Any troubles of any kind? I'm having a beano.

We never really had money as kids, but we never really needed money either. You'd go up to Mass on Sunday, and you'd get 20p to go to the sweet shop afterwards. You'd fill your boots with 20p. A packet of crisps and a bagful of sweets, and you'd be wondering what to do with the rest of the money.

When we got a bit older, we'd work in the garage for a few pounds, a pound an hour or whatever it was, and you'd be rich for the week. I used to think, if you had a fiver in your pocket you could do anything you wanted to do, go anywhere you wanted to go.

You could go to a point-to-point or to a match on a Sunday with a fiver in your pocket. But you had to be ready to leave straight after the final whistle or straight after the last race, or you'd be walking home. Dad would be out the gate as soon as they crossed the line in the last. I can remember running down the hill and jumping into the car with my dad in the queue to leave. I always thought I'd be able to find my way home, always thought I'd be able to get a lift from someone if he did leave me there. He never did, actually, so we never got to find out.

I don't remember ever being sad as a kid. I was always happy, I had such a happy childhood, always having the craic. Summers were brilliant, we had the beach beside us and we had the parks and the funfairs, and the girls would come down from the country and that would be just great craic. And people who I knew from hunting would come to Youghal for the summer.

* * *

I loved hurling. I loved playing hurling, I loved the challenge of it, the skill of it. I wasn't very good at it though. There is this notion going around that I was a very good hurler, but I wasn't.

I loved it though. I played with the local club, with Youghal, my dad was chairman of the club for a while, and I would go to every training session. We had a couple of really good hurlers at the time, no county players but a few top-class club hurlers.

I was just scraping onto the team at corner back. I was a sticky corner back, I wasn't a particularly skilful hurler, and I wasn't the fastest, but I was fit and I could usually stop a fellow from scoring.

John Parker was our manager at the time, the nicest man you could ever meet. He was our next-door neighbour when we lived in Sweetfield, and his daughter Sinéad is one of the kids I used to hang around with in Sweetfield. John actually became one of my biggest fans when I started riding, he'd write me letters and send me texts all the time. 'You're doing great. We're all behind you.'

He and Liam Ó Laochdha, another great GAA man, and a few of the other men from the town used to come to see me ride. Liam was a good friend of Dad's, he was into horses as well, and he was a real Gaeilgeoir. I went to school with Liam's sons. Anyway, when I got riding and got going, John and Liam and the lads would go racing to see me, they wouldn't tell me they were going or anything, they'd never want to be putting me out, they'd just go to support me. That meant an awful lot to me, going racing and seeing a local face in the crowd.

John was a real community man, a real Youghal man, he'd do everything for the community and he'd be involved in everything.

He's a marvellous man. You don't realise the things these people do for the community when you're a kid.

One day, we were playing Midleton. Youghal Under-14s. Now Midleton was always a good club, they'd break your heart, all good hurlers. But they had this pair, identical twins, they were big, they were about a foot taller than everybody else on the pitch, they can't have been under 14 at the time, and they could hurl. Boy could they hurl.

I was marking one of them, and he was tearing me asunder. I couldn't get near him. He was so fast, I was only chasing after him. I couldn't get in front of him, I couldn't block him, I couldn't knock him off his stride.

I was doing my best, it wasn't like I wasn't trying, but my best just wasn't good enough. I was a handicapper chasing after a Grade 1 performer. Your man was killing me. I'm sure John knew I was doing my best, but I'm sure he was frustrated too, and he left a bark at me.

'Come on Russell, he's killing us!'

That was it for me. I'd had enough. I was frustrated that my best wasn't good enough, I was angry at your man who was running rings around me and I was angry at myself for being powerless against him. I was like a horse who was flat to the mat, and you can't get any more out of a horse who is giving his all. John's shout at me was just the final straw.

Before I knew what I was doing, I had caught the hurley and let it fly. I'd had enough. I fired it at John, in John's general direction. I didn't mean to hit him, I didn't mean for it to get all the way to him, I was just exasperated, at my wits' end with all of it, and I was wrecked, chasing around after this lad I couldn't catch. So I fired the hurley at John.

As soon as the hurley left my hand, I knew I was fucked. The hurley was in mid-air and I was thinking, uh oh, this isn't good. So I turned and headed for the changing rooms. I didn't even wait for the hurley to land. It was still twirling around in the air, heading in John's general direction when I turned and headed for the sideline.

I didn't wait to see whether the hurley hit John or not but, thankfully, it didn't. It didn't matter though. It was a crazy thing to do. I didn't go and pick up my hurley, I just left it there, went into the changing rooms, got my stuff and headed home.

A few days later, a letter arrived to our house addressed to me, from the club, telling me I was banned from the club. Proper order. I wasn't surprised. What I did was totally and utterly wrong. Disgraceful. Dad was chairman of the club, but we never spoke about it. He never mentioned it to me and I sure as hell never mentioned it to him! But I'm sure they would have been onto him about it beforehand. I'm sure he knew about it and I'm sure he was on board with it. Like all right-minded people, I'm sure he felt I deserved to be banned.

I was on my way out of hurling anyway really. Horses were taking up more and more of my time, which was leaving less time for hurling and for everything else, and I was only just worth my place on the team, so I wasn't a huge loss. And I deserved the punishment I got.

A few years later, John Parker, in fairness to him, wrote another letter to me, telling me that he thought I had served my time and that I was more than welcome back to the club. That is a measure of the man that John Parker is.

I did go back to the club. I went back to train with the lads a little bit. I wasn't part of the setup or anything, I wasn't part of the team, I was off riding, but I enjoyed going back in to a training session or two, and I think they liked when I came to train with them. That was good old craic. And when the team got to the county final a few years later when I was going well in my career, they got me in to have a chat with the lads.

* * *

Dad's family's involvement with horses goes way back, his uncles had show horses, they won show prizes at the Dublin Horse Show, and Dad was always interested in horses. I used to be on at him all the time to get a pony.

'Dad, I want a pony.'

'Dad, can we get a pony?'

'Dad, when are we getting a pony?'

I had him plagued. There was hardly a day went by that I didn't tell Dad I wanted a pony. Sure the easiest thing for him to do then was to get me a pony. It was far easier than listening to me every day anyway.

I remember the day that Thunder arrived into the yard. It was one of those hot summer days, we were all in the house, messing and blackguarding, under Mam's feet, and Mam had had enough of us.

'Okay, it's a gorgeous day, everybody outside!'

I had this habit of not wearing shoes. In the house, outside the house, in the garden, I rarely wore shoes. I only put on shoes or boots if I was going up to the farm. But I got outside this day, and I saw the horsebox coming into the yard. So I ran up the yard, me and a few of my siblings, no shoes on, I didn't care, Dad dropped the ramp and there was this pony.

'Is he ours?!'

He was bold though, Thunder. He was well named. He took a lot of managing. None of my siblings could manage him, and I wouldn't have been able to manage him I'm sure had it not been for Willie Dalton.

Willie Dalton worked for my dad. Bill Dalton. He did everything around the farm, and he was into horses. He was such a nice man too, he always looked out for us. A lovely man and, when I got older and got going, he followed my career the whole way through.

Before I came home from school, Willie used to tack the pony up, ride him down to get the cows and ride him back up. By the time he'd get back up, the freshness would be gone out of the pony so that I'd be able to ride him. I'm sure that if Willie hadn't done that, every day, I wouldn't have been able to handle Thunder.

Dad got Thunder for all of us, but I was the only one of us who was really interested in riding him in the end, so I had him all to myself. Sometimes I was able to convince Sean to come with me. We'd put up two drums and a pole, that would be Becher's Brook and I'd have to jump it on my pony. I used to get Sean to lie down behind the poles, on the landing side, like a photographer. So he was the photographer and I was the jockey jumping one of the fences in the Grand National. We used to see that on the telly.

Now, there might have been some kind of worth to that if he was an actual photographer, like, if he actually had a camera. He didn't. He was just there pretending he had a camera, because I told him he had to be the photographer! That he had to get a good shot of me and my pony jumping a fence in the Grand National.

And he had no interest in it at all. It was all me, making him lie down on the ground behind the fence. He didn't really know it, but he was taking his life into his hands lying down on the landing side of a pole that my pony was jumping. Thunder was not good to jump, he'd knock as many poles as he'd jump over, and there was my brother, lying down on the ground behind the fence. I didn't care. I didn't think about it too deeply. I just knew that it wasn't real if there wasn't a photographer there.

'You'll be grand.'

Poor Sean was a bit of a crash-test dummy. I'm sure most Irish youngest siblings are. I remember tying a drum to the back of the car and putting Sean into the drum and going for a spin around the fields in the car, with the drum bouncing around the back and Sean in the drum! When I think of it now, it's a wonder he survived. And if he cried, he got no sympathy.

'You're such a baby.'

I'm sure it was good for him, sure it toughened him up for later life.

And we had this dumper, if you turned the steering wheel to the right, it went left. It was back-wheel drive. So there was a knack to driving it. There was a knack to getting it started as well, you had to wind it up, had to fit the knob into the wheel and then spin it. You had to be strong, but you had to have the technique as well, and you had to be fast to get your hand out of there, because if it started before you did, you could lose your hand. We used to spend hours trying to get this thing to start just so we could drive it around the farm.

I didn't really get that much instruction in the beginning on how to ride Thunder, but I loved riding him, so you figured it all out fairly fast. How to tack him up, how to handle him.

When I got a bit older, Dad used to take me hunting. I had to be ready though, I had to have the pony all tacked up and ready to go by the time we had to leave. Dad was never one for waiting around.

I heard his car coming up the yard before I saw it. It was definitely him too, I knew the sound of the engine. Thunder had been ready for ages. Dad stopped the car and reversed it up to the horsebox.

'You ready?'

'Ready.'

Dad headed off down to the house to grab a cup of tea and a slice of toast as I led Thunder up onto the ramp and into the horsebox. As I pushed the ramp back up and closed the catch, Dad was coming back up from the house with his cup of tea still in his hand.

'Let's go!'

I jumped into the front of the car and off we went. I was excited. I loved going hunting with the West Waterfords. I loved the variety of obstacles that Thunder and I would have to negotiate. Clashmore is about 10 miles from Youghal, a 15-minute drive, across the border into Waterford, over the Blackwater, turn left in Piltown and up the road to Clashmore.

There were plenty of people there when we got there, all in their hunting gear, and cars and horseboxes and horses, lots of chat, lots of excitement. Dad pulled up and got out of the car. Suddenly he let a yelp:

'Where's the fucking horsebox?!'

Not there, that's where it was. My job was to tack the pony up and put him in the horsebox. Then Dad would hitch the horsebox to the car. That was my understanding, anyway. Obviously, Dad's understanding was a little different.

More cursing and blinding, I'm sure I got the blame, and it was back down the road again, back home to get the horsebox, which still contained a slightly bemused Thunder. Dad hitched the trailer up and we were back down the road again from Youghal to Clashmore.

There wasn't a lot of conversation on that journey.

Dad didn't ride, but he has always loved horses, he has always loved racing, and he used to go to Cheltenham every year. For me, Cheltenham was this magical, mysterious place that my dad used to go to every year, and every year he'd bring me back a present. A toy or a game or something, but I always knew it was coming back from Cheltenham.

One year at Cheltenham, in the 1980s, my dad made the news. It was the 1982 festival, he was over with the usual gang, staying in John Maycock's house in the Cotswolds, up playing poker all night, the usual. As dawn was breaking and the poker was ending, a bet was struck for Dad to drive John Maycock's tractor lawnmower to the races the following day.

Now, we wouldn't have ever seen a tractor lawnmower, there mightn't have been a tractor lawnmower in Ireland at the time.

'How far is it from here to Cheltenham?' asked Dad.

'About 27 miles,' said John.

'And how fast does your lawnmower go?' asked Dad.

'About 12 miles an hour.'

Dad worked it out: easy money for just over two hours' driving.

So Dad got a few hours' sleep and then headed off, him and John Maycock's lawnmower. It was freezing though, there was frost on the roads and everything, and Dad was freezing, off on his lawnmower on the Cotswolds roads heading for Cheltenham. But he ploughed on, and John Maycock decided to let the local media know so, after a few miles, Dad was being followed by the Gloucester paparazzi.

About five miles from Cheltenham he stopped at a garage to phone Mam, just to tell her what was going on, in case she'd heard something. Lucky he did, because a few minutes after he called her, the *Cork Examiner* called her.

'He'd better cut the grass here when he gets back,' Mam told the *Examiner.*

Dad got to Cheltenham racecourse, drove into the members' car park and parked his tractor lawnmower between a Rolls-Royce and a Bentley.

Chapter 3

I sat down on a bale of hay, wrecked. We were all wrecked. All day spent bringing in the hay, all of us, lads up from the town too to give us a hand. It was a really good summer and it was the best of hay. We had brought in about 3,000 small square bales between us, and we all sat down for a well-earned rest at the end of a long day.

Fizzy drinks weren't really a thing in our house. We didn't really have Fanta or Coke or 7 Up, but on this day, after bringing in the hay, as a treat Mam got a few bottles and brought them up to us in the field. She made tea and sandwiches too, so we were all there, sitting on the bales, drinking Fanta, eating sandwiches, a sense of satisfaction all around at the end of a tough day, but a good day, a worthwhile day, a job well done and completed, the hay all in.

We all sat there for a while, everyone happy, everyone eating and drinking until, one by one, everybody started to leave.

It was one of those long, late summer evenings. The sun was going down, the shadows were getting longer, but it was still bright and it was still warm. It was the summer of 1992, the year of the Barcelona Olympics. Ireland did really well in the boxing, Michael Carruth won Gold, Ireland's first Gold medal since Ronnie Delany in the 1950s, and Wayne McCullough won Silver. If the telly was on in our house that summer, and if there wasn't racing on it, we were watching the Olympics.

Everyone had gone when I noticed a piece of wire on the ground, and I decided it would be a great idea to make an Olympic torch with it. I picked the piece of wire up and twisted it around, so that there was a good long handle on it. I got a piece of cloth and wrapped the top of the wire around the cloth. Then I dipped the cloth in diesel and I lit it. Perfect.

The flames were good, it really looked like an Olympic torch, it looked like I was on my way to light the Olympic flame. I was able to run around with it too and it remained lit, me and my torch, burning brightly, running around the place, on my way to start the Olympics.

After running around for a while, I got a bit tired so I came back to where we had all been sitting to take a break from the important business of lighting the Olympic flame. I was after putting in a huge effort, in fairness to me. I deserved a break, I deserved another drink of Fanta. The Fanta was there on the ground, in between two bales of hay, so I bent down to pick it up with my left hand, Olympic torch still in my right hand, still aflame.

Suddenly, whoosh!

I hadn't noticed but, as I bent down to pick up the Fanta with one hand, the hand that was holding my Olympic torch had touched one of the bales. Before I knew what was happening, the whole bale was ablaze, then the bale next to it, then the bale next to that one. It had been such a good summer, it was so dry, the hay was so good, that it went up like tinder.

I stood there for a few seconds longer than I should have, caught in the moment, not sure what was after happening. Horrified, petrified. I tried to stamp on the flames on the first bale, but I couldn't put them out, and the flames were starting to spread now, way more quickly than I would have been able to put them out.

I watched on for a few more seconds. It was all so surreal. I couldn't believe the place was on fire. The flames were getting away from me now. There was an old car there, a car Dad was using for parts, and the flames were getting close to it. There was a conveyor belt that we used to lift the bales up, to stack them on top of each other high in the barn. There was an old tractor beside that, and a shed beside that, and another shed beside that.

I ran down to the house as fast as I could, calling for Dad.

'Dad! Dad! Dad!'

I shouted before I saw him.

'The haybarn's on fire!'

What the fuck?

Dad ran up to the barn but the fire was raging by then. He tried to put out the flames but he couldn't. Some of the neighbours saw what was happening, the flames were high, they came around and tried to help, it was all hands on deck, but it was no use. The fire brigade was called and everything, but it was all too late. Nothing could be saved. Everything went up in flames, everything was gone, the sheds, the barn, the conveyor belt, the car, the tractor. Everything. All the hay.

I was in bits. Distraught. I couldn't believe what had just happened. It all seemed like a bit of a dream, but it wasn't. I had destroyed the whole year's worth of hay and a few machines along with it for good measure. And I was so embarrassed, running around a hayfield with an Olympic torch in my hand, on my way to light the Olympic flame and start the fucking Olympic Games.

I said nothing though. I kept my head down. I hoped it would all go away. I couldn't tell anyone what had happened. No one asked me, so I didn't say anything. People were asking each other how the fire started, but nobody asked me so I didn't say anything. I was on my own, there were no eyewitnesses, it was just me, and I definitely wasn't going to tell them that I lit the fire with my Olympic torch!

I didn't sleep for days with the worry, but it got a little easier as time moved on. A couple of weeks went by and I kept schtum. A couple of months. I was starting to think I had got away with it, was just starting to relax about it. Then one day I came home from school. I used to come home and fire my schoolbag into the corner, because I wasn't going to need it until the following morning, I wasn't going to be opening it again that evening to do homework or anything anyway. I had far more important things to be doing on a bright autumn evening than homework. Ride my pony or drive the car or try to kill my little brother.

Anyway, this day, I fired my schoolbag into the corner, all set for the evening ahead. But Mam met me at the hall door.

'Go in there,' she said, pointing to the sitting room. 'You're wanted inside.'

'For what?'

I had no idea why I was wanted or who wanted me or why somebody would get in the way of me going back to my perfect life. That's how long after the fire this was, and how little it was on my mind by then.

'In you go now.'

This wasn't good news, I could tell by my Mam. She wasn't happy. And there in the sitting room was the sergeant with my father. Uh oh. Trouble here. Still I didn't cop it. I was trying to figure out which of the many things I had done was coming back to get me.

'How're you doing?'

'Hello David.'

I was afraid of my life now.

'Do you smoke?'

'What?'

'Do you smoke?'

Now, of course I smoked. I was a teenager growing up in Ireland in the late 1980s and early 1990s. It was long odds-on that I smoked.

'No.'

'Were you smoking above in the haybarn there during the summer?'

I was a lot of things when I was younger, but I was not stupid enough to smoke in a haybarn. I knew that was a real no-no, it was drilled into you from an early age, it was just something that you knew not to do. (It's just a pity that nobody ever said anything to me about running around with an Olympic torch in a haybarn.)

I said I wasn't smoking in the haybarn, that I knew not to smoke in a haybarn. But then they kept telling me they knew it was me, that they knew that I had started the fire, and they were concluding that the only way it could have happened was if I was smoking, that it was an accident if I was smoking. They seemed to be saying that, if I wasn't smoking, if it didn't happen by accident because I was smoking, then I must have started the fire deliberately. That it was malicious.

Strangely, none of them thought to consider the possibility that I had started the fire with an Olympic torch.

Now I wasn't going to tell them I had been running around like a fool with a lit homemade Olympic torch. They probably wouldn't have believed me anyway. And the way it was going, I could see that the best option open to me was the smoking option. I'm sure Dad knew I was smoking anyway, so there would be no pain there. And I didn't start it deliberately, and I definitely didn't want them to think that there was even a possibility that I did it out of malice. So I went with the smoking option. It seemed like the least bad option. I was smoking in the haybarn. I'm sorry.

I never said anything afterwards either. I was too embarrassed to tell the true story. To this day, I'm sure my father still thinks I was smoking in the haybarn.

* * *

MY AUTOBIOGRAPHY

I was never into school. I just didn't have any interest in it, and I would get out of it whenever I could. If there was a job to be done, emptying the bins, taking something to another teacher, cleaning out the toilets, I was the first with my hand up. It didn't matter what the job was or how messy it was or how long it was going to take. The longer the better, because anything that got me out of class was a good thing.

I had two homework journals, one for me and one for my parents, and whenever I would be taking some time off, I'd write a note from Mam in my own homework journal. David has a dentist's appointment. David has to leave early today. The teachers must have thought my mam had awful handwriting! My biggest problem was then, when I was taking down my homework, I used to have to take it down twice, once for my parents' journal and once for my own, so I was usually the last one finished.

I was mischievous I suppose as a kid. If there was a bit of mischief going, I was up for it, I was looking for it. I was mad for a bit of divilment. My teachers knew that I was, and I think they kind of let me away with a lot of stuff. They gave me a bit of leeway anyway. We had some marvellous teachers. I wasn't mad about them at the time, and they weren't mad about me, but we came to reach an understanding I think, without anybody ever saying anything.

When the Junior Cert came around, I told everyone I wasn't coming back afterwards. Everyone, that is, except my parents. I had to pass the Junior Cert though. I knew that, if I didn't pass it, there was no chance Mam would let me leave.

I remember going in to get my Junior Cert results, all I cared about was whether I passed or not.

'Did I pass, Miss?'

'Yes David, you passed. Just about!'

I didn't hear the 'just about' part. All I heard was 'passed'. So I went home, job done, sold my books and burned my uniform.

My mother was having none of it though. I feared that Mam might prove to be a stumbling block all right to all my plans.

'You're going back to school,' she said.

'I'm not,' I said.

'You're going back,' she said again.

'I can't. I've sold my books and I've burnt my uniform.'

I did go back though, you'd never win an argument with Mam if she really thought that she was right. I had to go back. But I went back for a day. At the end of the day, the principal called Mam.

'You're going to have to do something with this chap,' he said. 'This is not going to work.'

Dad made a few calls and got me into Kildalton College, and that was brilliant. I was 16, I was the youngest kid in the college, studying Horse Production, and that year in Kildalton College had a huge influence on my career. Timmy McCarthy was there, Timmy McCarthy who won three All-Irelands with Cork. Johnny Doyle was there, the Kildare footballer, top scorer, took the frees, won an All Star award in 2010. Philip Rothwell was there, I ended up riding my first Cheltenham Festival winner for Philip Rothwell.

I found the classes easy. I didn't know it all, but I knew a lot of it, I had done a lot of it. I knew how to plait a horse's mane, I knew what to feed them and how to feed them and when to feed them, I knew how to tack them up. So the first three or four months of the course, what we were learning, I knew it all. But I was interested in it too, and that made the new stuff easy to learn.

Aidan O'Brien's yard in Piltown – Joe Crowley's old yard, where Joseph O'Brien trains now – wasn't far away from Kildalton, and we used to go down there to ride out in the morning before classes. I loved that. We'd do two lots, Aidan would always be there for first lot, we'd tack them up and ride them out, up the hill. Aidan would come down in the Jeep, he'd go, everything okay?, then he'd head off to Ballydoyle, I presume. It was great experience for me, plus it meant that you had a few quid in your pocket to go out at the weekends. If we wanted to go somewhere, we had money to go, and we're back to me having a beano again.

I never drank though. Not really. I drank twice maybe. The first time was when I had a half a can of Budweiser under the bridge in Dungarvan with my cousin, one of my very good friends John Galvin, the night he got his Junior Cert results. I didn't like it though. I wasn't sick, but I just didn't like it, and I figured I could do without it.

The second time was when I broke my wrist in a fall at Fairyhouse, I was going to be out for a while so I wasn't watching my weight. There was a bit of a party going on in a house a few doors down, and they were after running out of drink, so they called to me to see if I had any. Now, you'd get a bottle of champagne every now and again for riding a winner, so I had about 15 or 16 bottles of champagne just inside the door. I ended up going to a night club with Martin Ferris, and getting thrown out.

My dad never drank, and we were never a family for going to pubs. When I was a kid, the Costellos were the Gold Standard. They were so good at what they did, and they never drank. Also, I always wanted to be a jockey, an elite sportsman, and I knew that elite sportsmen didn't drink.

And I loved driving. I was happy to drive everybody home. When I was point-to-pointing, I had no car, the lads would start drinking and I'd be delighted to drive everybody home in one of their cars.

* * *

Dad was chairman of the pony racing committee in Youghal when I was a kid. We had pony races just once a year, around our farm, and it was always a great day. It was a real community event, a fundraiser for the town, with local sponsors and a real buzz around the town on the day.

We decided we would get Thunder ready to run in one of the races one year. He wasn't very fast, we never thought he would have a chance of winning, but just to get him ready to run in it, to be a part of it, that was a big thing for me.

I trained him myself at home and on the beach. I just tried to get him going forward, tried to get him as fit as he could be. And then on the day, to get ready for the race, to put on racing colours and line up on my pony in a race, like a real jockey, that was brilliant. We didn't even get close, but it was some thrill for me, to ride in my first race.

We sold Thunder at Tallow Horse Fair the following year. Tallow Horse Fair is an institution, it takes place on the first Monday in September every year. Dad had Thunder sold early in the morning, but he had his eye on this filly, and he spent all day trying to buy her. The seller wanted £500 for her, but Dad only wanted to give £375, no more. He kept going back to the filly and, at the end of the day, he reached a deal with the seller.

She was a lovely pony, a three-year-old thoroughbred who didn't grow. She was 13.2hh when we bought her as a three-year-old, and I swear she never got any bigger than 14.2hh. I hunted her and I rode her down the beach and I jumped her and I rode her in drag hunts and I rode her in pony races.

Whitebarn Vixen, we called her, and she was a right good pony. I was reminiscing there recently with Robert Widger, who rode Flagship Uberalles to win the Tingle Creek Chase for Philip Hobbs in 2001. (Robert was brilliant to ride showjumping and he had some marvellous ponies.) I had a 100% record on Whitebarn Vixen, she never knocked a pole. Dad ended up selling her for about eight or nine grand, which was a fair price to get for a pony. Actually, a family with the same surname as us ended up owning her, and I went to buy her back recently, I just wanted her to have a home here, to have her here for the kids. Anyway, the phone call didn't go too well, I'm not sure they fully understood me, or they thought that I was messing when I told them my name was Davy Russell. I never got to buy her back, which was a pity.

I did everything on her, Whitebarn Vixen. I'd go pony racing on her and showjumping. I had my first bone-break off her, I got a fall off her in Bartlemy, she was just going so fast to jump, and she was fast that day, too fast, and she came down.

There were great people around then, Ian Hannon, Paul Beecher, Tadhg Beecher. Paul and Tadhg's dad Timmy is a very bright man, and he was always a brilliant man to go to for advice. Before anyone ever had a coach or an adviser, I had Timmy Beecher.

I'd ring him if things weren't going so well, or if you thought you'd given a horse a bad ride, or if you got beaten on one you thought you should have won on, or if someone gave you a bit of stick after a ride. I'd just call him and, whatever way he had about him, you'd feel much better after speaking to him. He'd make you see that you hadn't done an awful lot wrong, that you weren't doing a lot wrong. Twenty minutes on the phone to Timmy Beecher, and you'd think you were Richard Dunwoody again.

I didn't have many rides in pony races, I didn't ride on the pony racing circuit as such. I only had about 20 rides, five or six winners, and most of them were for James Horgan. He was great to me. Whenever he had a runner, he'd be onto my dad: Is David free this weekend? Is David free next weekend?

I rode at Dingle once, the Cheltenham Festival of pony racing. You'd win on a pony in Cork and you'd think you'd be competitive at Dingle, but it wouldn't mean that you would. It was the cream of the crop at Dingle, you had to have a very good pony if you were going to be able to even compete. I didn't get close to winning, I would have been heavy enough too, but I just wasn't good enough.

I remember my first winner well. It was for Dad, on a pony named Chief Raider. He was a fast pony, and I trained him mainly on the beach at home. Dad named him Chief Raider after a horse he had bred, also Chief Raider, a thoroughbred, who won five times over hurdles and fences in Britain. Anyway, the pony Chief Raider was a flying machine, I just had to point and steer him and he did the rest. I probably wasn't a huge help to him, but I still got some kick out of that, my first winner. I think my dad got a few quid out of it too.

Dad had horses in training with Jimmy Mangan at the time. One of them, Free The General, a big horse by General Ironside, was the first racehorse I ever sat up on, at Jimmy's yard. I felt like a real jockey then, and Free The General was so slow, there was never any fear of me getting run away with.

Dad also had horses in training with John Kiely. Any time Dad was going to see one of the horses, he'd always bring me with him. He'd be like, I'm going to John Kiely's, anybody coming? I'd be up and out the door before he had the sentence finished. I would have had the car started and halfway up the driveway if he'd let me.

As I said, I loved going anywhere with my dad. Wherever he went, I wanted to go. People say we're very alike, and I was like an extra limb on him then. Who's coming with me? Me. Where are we going? I can't remember a day when he said do you want to come and I said no.

I loved going to John Kiely's. John is a fantastic man, such a gentleman. I'd wander around the yard on my own, looking at these big National Hunt horses, exploring. Sometimes John would give me a shovel and ask me to move some shavings or something, and I loved that. I loved the feeling that I was working in a racing yard. John would always give me a few quid as well as I was heading off, a tenner or a score, and that was like a million pounds to me. My dad is the same, he'll always give a young fellow around the place a few quid. I try to do the same thing. I think it's such a good thing to do.

I remember when the Kielys' mare Shuil Ar Aghaidh won the Stayers' Hurdle at Cheltenham. John didn't train Shuil Ar Aghaidh, his brother Paddy trained her, but they were just next door to each other so for me it was the same thing.

I remember skipping out of school with my friend Seamus Budds, Ken's cousin, and going to the bookies' office to watch the Stayers' Hurdle that year. You couldn't get into the shop, they were packed deep and spilling out onto the street, so we ended up out on the street and trying to watch the television inside in the bookies' office through the window. And they all backed Shuil Ar Aghaidh, the local horse, the local mare. I had to strain my neck, I could just about see the television screen, Shuil Ar Aghaidh and Charlie Swan coming clear up the Cheltenham hill, away from a horse of Martin Pipe's, Pragada, and a horse of David Nicholson's, Baydon Star, and the roars and the cheers of everyone in the betting shop and everyone on the street. I was thinking, they might hear them in Cheltenham.

This was 1993. Before that year, as far as I was aware, there were never more than two Irish-trained winners at the Cheltenham Festival. We just didn't have winners there. And four years earlier, there were none. Every Irish winner at Cheltenham was a winner to be cherished and a winner to be celebrated.

That year, 1993, there were six in total. Montelado and Fissure Seal and Rhythm Section had won earlier in the week, and Shawiya, Mick O'Brien's horse, had won the first race on Shiul Ar Aghaidh's day, the Thursday, Gold Cup day, the last day of the meeting. And I remember thinking then, you know, a Cheltenham winner is not that far away, it's not that far removed from my reality. If Irish trainers can have winners there, it might be within touching distance. Eugene O'Sullivan had won the Foxhunter with Lovely Citizen just two years earlier. And the Kielys. Sure Dad knew John Kiely well. I was in his yard often. Maybe Cheltenham was not so mystical and so magical that it was out of the reach of ordinary people like me.

I was 11 or 12 when I went to Tramore races with Dad. We were walking out into the car park after racing and this lorry pulled up beside us, a big steel back on it, living quarters in the back and everything, and the driver called out to Dad.

'Is this the chap you tell me can ride a bit?'

Dad always had horses in training with Frank O'Brien. I knew the name, but I had never met the man.

'That's him all right,' said Dad.

Dad was so proud of me, that I was able to ride. I didn't know if I was any good or not, I'm not sure if he knew if I was any good or not, he was just so proud that I could ride.

'Sure throw him in here,' said Frank. 'We'll see if he's able to ride or not.'

So that was it, I climbed into the back of the lorry with Frank and we headed off to his yard in Piltown. Three or four days later, Dad dropped down a bag of clothes, a helmet and a pair of boots, and I stayed there for the summer, in the house with Frank and his wife, who were so good to me, riding out in the morning and working with the horses.

I had a bicycle there and I used to cycle into Piltown with a phone card to phone home, or to phone my cousin John Galvin. I still remember John's phone number. I stayed with Frank and his wife for two months that summer before going back home to get ready to go back to school.

And you started to add to the equipment you had. When I started riding out, I rode out in a pair of wellies and a bare helmet, with a Wavin pipe as a whip. Then one of the lads would give you a pair of goggles, then someone would give you a second-hand whip. Then you'd get a few quid together for leading up horses or for winning a best-turned-out prize or two, and you'd have enough to get yourself a pair of boots. Or someone would be buying a new pair of boots and you'd buy their old ones off them.

Gear was hard to come by. You'd rarely get new gear or see new gear, so when you got some new gear, you kept it, you looked after it. Someone would give you a pair of breeches and you'd mind them. And all the while you'd be trying to get bits and pieces of money together so you could buy gear.

One of the lads at Frank O'Brien's gave me a silk for my helmet, and that was a big deal. They didn't give them out like confetti, and once you got your silk, that was your silk. You didn't change it. Mine was a yellow and silver silk. John Thomas McNamara rode all his early point-to-point winners in the same silk, a red and white silk, until they changed the rules so that you would get fined if you didn't have the proper colours.

When I got a bit older I started going in to the Budds', just a few miles out the road. It was there, with Pat and Ken and Martin, that I started to ride racehorses regularly. Dad would drop me out in the morning, or Ken or Martin would come and pick me up at weekends or on school holidays, and Dad would come out to pick me up in the evening. He was always too early coming to pick me up, I never wanted to leave.

I used to go out to the Budds' during school a little bit too, me and my Honda 50. This was where my second homework journal earned its keep! I'd put on my school uniform and pack my schoolbag with my riding gear. I'd head out the gate on my Honda 50, and I'd get down the road a bit before I'd stop to change into my riding gear. I figured that riding racehorses, mucking out, working around the yard, doing whatever needed to be done, was better craic than going to school. And I was learning more there anyway, more stuff that would be useful to me, than I could ever learn at school. My solo escapades all ended though with the incident with my Honda 50.

I was always looking to go to different yards, I was always wanting to go and work for whoever would have me. I wrote letters to some of the big trainers I knew about, Dermot Weld, Willie Mullins, Jim Bolger. Hello, my name is David Russell, could I have a job for the summer? They all came back to me, so I was so lucky, I was in Willie Mullins's yard for a summer and I was in Dermot Weld's yard for another summer and I was in Jim Bolger's for two summers. That was unbelievable experience for a young fellow to get, with three of the best trainers in Ireland.

We had some craic in Willie's in Closutton. I was riding a horse one day called Ivy Bay. Ivy Bay wasn't a star or anything, he had won a point-to-point and he finished second in a couple of bumpers, but he was a grand horse for a young fellow to ride.

Anyway, I was riding him out one day and one of the lads bet me a fiver that I wouldn't jump off him halfway around the gallop. Now, a fiver to a young fellow in those days was a million pounds. You could get a snack box in the chipper in Bagenalstown for £3.95, and a can was 50p, so you'd have a gorgeous meal for yourself with a fiver, and change. For me, it was a no-brainer.

And the gallop was soft, it was always well-watered. I knew where it was at its softest, it couldn't hurt that much if I jumped off. And Ivy Bay was such a quiet horse, he wouldn't be going too fast and he wouldn't go anywhere anyway after I came off him. He'd probably just stop right there on the gallop and look down at me: what are you doing you fucking eejit?

I was right about most of it.

I picked my spot, about halfway around the big gallop where I thought the ground on the gallop was at its softest. We weren't going very fast at all, so I just took my feet out of my irons and I slipped off. I thought that it would be fine, but it's a long way from the back of a big National Hunt racehorse to the ground, no matter how soft the ground is. I landed with a thud, and I landed a bit awkwardly. It was such a stupid thing to do. It hurt all right, the impact. Thankfully though, I didn't break any bones or injure myself too badly.

It wasn't clever though. You get so many falls as a National Hunt jockey, you get so many injuries, that to jump off a horse on the gallop, voluntarily, to actually go out the side door, for a fiver, for a snack box and a can of Coke, it wasn't one of the cleverest things I did in my life.

The snack box tasted good though.

We used to have to muck out the paddocks in Willie's. One evening, I was doing my job, mucking out the paddocks and putting the muck into the big green wheelbarrow. The wheelbarrow got so full I couldn't move it. I was 14, I didn't have the strength to pick up the big wheelbarrow on my own, so I stayed there and waited for one of the lads to come along to give me a hand. I sat down on the ground beside the wheel of the wheelbarrow and, it being a warm summer's evening and all, and me after working hard all day, I fell asleep.

I woke up quite quickly though when I heard this female voice shouting. Tracy Gilmour, who used to look after Florida Pearl, was head girl in Willie's at the time, and she was shouting at me. She fired me right there and then on the spot.

Disaster. Getting fired from Willie Mullins's. How bad was this? Where would I go now? Who would want me? I decided I wasn't going to tell my dad that I was fired anyway, that was for sure. I decided I wouldn't tell anybody. Even so, I was sure that any chance I had of making it as a jockey was over.

I went up to the top yard to get my stuff, and Willie was there.

'I'm very sorry, Mr Mullins,' I said. 'Thanks very much for the opportunity, I'm very sorry about today.'

I hardly even looked at him.

'What are you talking about?'

'I'm going home now,' I said. 'Tracy isn't happy with me.'
Willie looked at me for a second.
'You stay where you are now,' he said to me.
'Ah I'd better get on my way,' I said. 'The summer is nearly over and I have a few things to sort out at home before I go back to school.'
I went to leave.
'Well, you're more than welcome back here at any time,' said Willie. 'You come back here whenever you want. Okay?'

I couldn't believe that, Willie Mullins telling me to go back to him whenever I wanted. I had so much respect for that man after that. He was like a god to me then. And, it took me a while, but I did get to go back in to Willie's later in my career when I was going in to ride the Gigginstown horses.

* * *

Jim Bolger's office called me back. I remember Mam coming into me, Jim Bolger wants you to go and start work there on Monday. So I got my clothes together, got my boots and my riding gear, and Dad dropped me up to the gate of Jim Bolger's the following Monday morning.

I probably should have been nervous, but I wasn't. Not a bit. I was just excited. I'd had plenty of experience before that, I thought. I'd be well able for it.

I spent two summers in Jim Bolger's, and I stayed with Mrs Murphy during my time there. Jim had houses and digs and families all around Glebe House for his staff. It's very rural around there, accommodation for staff wouldn't be easily found. Jim says he often got lost shortly after he and Jackie bought the place when they were trying to return home. He says that if anyone ever calls in to see him and says they dropped in because they were just passing, they are lying.

Mrs Murphy's was closest to the front gate of Glebe House and I obviously didn't have a car – I was too young to have a licence despite the fact that I had been honing my rally-driving skills around the fields – so that was where I stayed. Mrs Murphy put me in the bed that Paul Carberry had slept in while he was in Jim's, and I thought that was class!

I used to work in the bottom yard, so you wouldn't see the boss very often, but it didn't mean you weren't on your toes all the time just in case he would appear. You'd make sure the yard was tidy and the gravel was raked and the concrete path was brushed. The horses had to look their best too obviously, brushed, groomed, hooves painted, so that, if Jim did appear, everything looked good.

I liked the evenings there, because I usually had the yard to myself, I could go around making sure everything was in order before I headed off for the evening. And I learned so much there. You couldn't but learn how to ride properly on Jim's gallop. It was a wonderful gallop, but you had to get your horse balanced and settled, you had to get your speed right.

And you could only learn from the people who were there. Some of the best people in racing have been through the gates at Glebe House and back out again. Aidan O'Brien and A.P. McCoy and Peter Scudamore were obviously before my time, Paul Carberry was before me, David Wachman was before me, Seamie Heffernan was before me. Paul Nolan had just left before I arrived, as had Willie Supple. But Paddy Brennan was there while I was there, and Joey Elliott and Kevin Manning and Brendan Duke and Ted Durcan and Dick Dowling.

And Jim himself, you'd learn so much from the boss if you paid attention. And what we went on to do together, setting up the Hurling For Cancer Research charity, the work he did for that, the effort he put into setting it up, the energy he puts into it every year, the money that has been raised for cancer research. He's an unbelievable man.

Hurling For Cancer Research has its origins in a game of hurling they used to have between the professional jockeys and the amateur jockeys. Actually, it was more an excuse for a piss-up than anything else. It was good craic though, and we used to travel around to different clubs, Holycross and Newmarket-on-Fergus, and we used to raise a few quid for charity.

It had kind of run its course though, when Jim said to me one day, you know, our staff could play the jockeys. I wouldn't have known Jim very well at the time, just that I worked for him, and I'd see him at the races. I suppose I would have said in interviews and the like that I had cut my teeth at Jim's. He was never anything but very nice to me, very good to me, very friendly towards me. But we started this thing anyway, we had the first match in 2011, and it turned into a bit of a monster.

It's all Jim by the way. The amount of work I do for it is minimal compared to the amount of work Jim does. Anyway, it's always a brilliant day, we always get some of the top people from the world of hurling and the world of horse racing involved. People are so generous with their time. It's still going strong and, to date, over €1.5 million has been raised for cancer research.

We had great craic in Jim's, and we had great craic in Dermot Weld's. It was a big change for me too when I got to Dermot's. Being part of a big trainer's outfit on the Curragh was very different to anything I had experienced before, and riding on the Curragh was different too. Before that, I had been riding around fields and in circles, in point-to-point yards, in pony races. Always turning. In Dermot's, on the Curragh, you got to ride in a straight line, and that was different. The gallops on the Curragh are so vast, the Old Vic is a straight mile up the hill. It's a different ballgame.

I broke my collarbone for the first time on the Curragh, riding out for Dermot. There was a horse there, Galloping Guns, I'll never forget the bastard. He was no good, he ran seven times for Dermot, and he never won. He was never even placed. But he was free and keen, it was very difficult to settle him.

We used to ride him in a gag, and he started to settle better in the gag, so much so that, one morning, we decided to let him go without the gag. Turns out, that wasn't a great idea. He ran away with me, I couldn't hold him, then my reins broke up by the Fox Cover gallop and I fell off.

I remember the pain, I felt the pain in my shoulder and I felt this sickness in my stomach. Even so, I didn't know that my collarbone was broken at the time. In fact, I didn't get it seen to straight away. I actually went to a hurling match that evening, but still I felt this constant pain. My sister kept telling me to get over it, that there wasn't much wrong with me. So I was kind of happy enough when I went to get it seen to the following day and they told me it was broken. I was delighted to get back home with my arm in a sling. I got plenty of attention that summer, plenty of sympathy, back at home and back to school with my arm in a sling.

* * *

I was so lucky, as I was making my way in the early stages of my career, that I came across so many people who looked after me so well.

The O'Briens were so good to me, Frank and Marie, they were beautiful people, they looked after me like I was one of their own. That's probably why I never really got homesick when I was away from home. I loved my home, I loved being around home, but I was so lucky that I had so many people looking after me when I was away from home that I never got too lonely when I was away.

It broke my heart when Frank passed away. I was still in school at the time. I remember my dad being very upset. Frank was a brilliant fellow, one of the nicest men you could ever meet. I still visit his grave.

And Frank's son David is just like him. It was really nice that I could ride a few winners for David. That was a recurring theme through my career, and I loved that it was, that I was able to ride winners for a lot of the people I was with when I was starting out. People like David O'Brien and Michael Griffin and Denis Ahern. I rode ponies for the Aherns.

I didn't ride in many pony races, I wasn't like Brian Crowley or Colm O'Donoghue or Jack Kennedy, they were brilliant pony racing riders, it was like they were moulded to the pony. Or Barry Keniry. Lovely rider. He could go out and ride two or three winners pony racing on Saturday, then jump a double-clear show jumping on the Sunday.

The Budds' home was like a second home for me. Pat a great man and Breda a fantastic woman. Breda used to make dinner for us, and when I say dinner, mother of God the dinner we used to get was savage, and you couldn't get up from the table if you didn't clear your plate.

I'd go to the Budds' for the weekend during the winter, Ken and I would ride out on the Saturday and then we'd go to a point-to-point on the Sunday. I'd stay with Ken on the Saturday night, he'd have a small house party or we'd go down to the local village to play pool with the locals or to hang out with the local girls or to kiss them out the back. Ken's girlfriend at the time had a sister who was my age, and she was probably my first real girlfriend. But it was all about having the craic. We were just living our best lives.

I used to pal about too with a fellow called Tommy Hart. Tommy was in my class at school, he was one of the only people in school who was into horses, so we hit it off straight away. Horses can be a lonely pursuit when you're the only one who's into them. Your friends are off doing the normal things teenagers do, while you're off with your horses.

I used to go to drag hunt races with Tommy. I loved drag hunt races. There were obviously lots of different hunts around different parts of Cork and Waterford. There was one in Dungarvan and there was one in Bartlemy and there were lots in West Cork. I hunted with the Uniteds and the West Waterfords mainly. I'm an honorary member of the Uniteds now. I also hunt with the Woodstown Harriers.

I have always loved going hunting. It's a great day out, it's a real family day, the kids are looked after so well, and they're run by brilliant people. You'd always be in touch with people that you meet hunting all the way along, from childhood to adulthood. People like Mike Long, Ken's uncle, and Tommy Fitzgerald, and Tommy's uncle Pat Fitzgerald. I rode for them. And Dennis Ahern and Alan Ahern, top men, and Robert Widger, who rode against me in pony races. And then Robert Tyner and Liam Burke and Pat Doyle, top trainers who provided me with so many point-to-point winners. And obviously Frank O'Brien, and his sons David and Tony and Kevin. I was so lucky, all the contacts I made early in my life, they were all so important to me in later life, in my career.

The drag hunt was basically a race across open country, from one point to another point about two and a half or three miles away. It would be over banks and hedges and through forests and streams and rivers and any other obstacle that nature would put in your way.

There was a course all right, and you walked the course in the morning before the race, but it was really up to you what route you took. Barry Keniry had a pony for the drag races, Liam Keniry had a pony, Tommy Hart had a pony, Tommy Fitzgerald had a pony. The Budds' had this pony though, a brown and white pony, Sandy, and he was dynamite at drag hunts. He was a little bullet, he was so fast over the banks. Ken and Martin won drag hunts on him, then Martin Fitzgerald won drag hunts on him, then Tommy Fitzgerald got him.

I got on him a couple of times, and it was some thrill when I did. He'd frighten the life out of you, the way he jumped. His speed over a bank. He'd jump these banks as if they were hardly there, the size of him. Up, one stride, down again. Or no strides if the bank was narrow enough. Just up and straight down again. You'd put your finger into the neck strap, point him in the right direction, and you'd just hold on. You could even drop the reins if you wanted to.

Tommy Hart was a genius at plaiting horses. So Tommy would plait them and I'd brush them and we'd get the stencil and brush diamonds into their quarters, make their coats shine, paint their hooves, and we won loads of best-turned-out awards doing that. And once you were there at a point-to-point you always had a chance of picking up something. Somebody would ask you to lead one up, and you'd be delighted to be asked to lead a horse around the parade ring, such as it was. You'd be delighted just to be involved.

We'd go out into the country, off down the back straight, and lie down underneath the fences down the back straight, well away from everyone so that nobody could give out to us or stop us from doing it. We'd lie down in under the fence on the landing side, and we'd wait for the horses to come crashing over the fences.

And we'd wait for fallers, we'd try to catch the loose horses and ride them back in. We loved doing that, catching the horses and riding them back in, no helmets or back protectors or anything. You wouldn't be able to do it now, health and safety regulations wouldn't allow it but, back then, it was good for everybody.

For the horses' owners and handlers, they were happy to have their horses back in. For us, we were just delighted to be there, living our best lives.

Chapter 4

It was some feeling, walking into the weigh room. Tom Lombard was there, and William O'Sullivan, and Eoin Gallagher and Ken Whelan and James Motherway. Jockeys, real jockeys, lads I'd usually be watching riding in point-to-points, my heroes, and here I was, in among them, getting ready to ride with them and against them.

I wasn't nervous. Not really. I wasn't really daunted by all of it. I had done lots of schooling in Ken Budds', so I wasn't worried about jumping the fences, and I had my pony racing experience, going into the weigh room and weighing out and riding a race. I was just excited, like, I couldn't believe I was about to ride in my first point-to-point.

Whitebarn Cailin was no world-beater. We had bred her ourselves, by Buckskin out of a Deep Run mare named Russells Run, but she was a racehorse who had been placed in point-to-points the previous year. Jimmy Mangan trained her, but she had her issues, so we had her at home for a while, I was riding her out every day on the beach at home and up the hills. Then, in March 1996, Dad said I could ride her in the point-to-point at Skibbereen.

The Skibbereen point-to-point course was around the hurling pitch, so it was a tight track and the ground was usually fast enough. Ken had another runner on the day, so he just threw Whitebarn Cailin onto the horsebox with him, and off we went. I had to get the lend of Martin's saddle, I didn't have a saddle of my own, and I just wore the helmet that I used to ride out in and I used the whip that I used to ride out with.

I walked the track beforehand, found out where the start was. That was important, to know where the start was. That was way more important for me than knowing where the finish was. You could worry about where the finish was later, if it came to that.

I thought I was ready, I thought, with all my riding out at home and all my schooling and all my pony racing, that I was ready to ride in a point-to-point, but I wasn't. Not even nearly.

This was a four-year-olds' and older mares' maiden, it wasn't the Gold Cup, but even so, the speed they went. I had never gone as fast in my life before. We went hammer and tongs the whole way, from start to finish, for six minutes, flat out from flagfall.

I was wrecked afterwards. Muscles aching, I had never been as happy as I was to get to the winning line and slow to a walk. It all happened so quickly too, we were off and then it was over. I loved it though.

We finished fifth.

My first ride in a bumper was different again. That was about three months after my first ride in a point-to-point, in June 1996 at the old Tralee racecourse. Pat Budds had this horse, Percy Hannon, a son of Sheer Grit, who had run in a couple of point-to-points. Martin was due to ride him at Tralee, but he got suspended for excessive use of the whip at Tipperary the previous week, he was beaten a short head in a bumper on a horse called I'm A Chippy. So Pat said that I could ride Percy Hannon in his first bumper.

It was some thrill for me, to be going to the races with a ride in a race, the second last race on the day. The weigh room at Skibbereen was a marquee, a tent. At Tralee though, it was a real weigh room, a real building.

DAVY RUSSELL

It was a mixed card that day at Tralee, there was flat and National Hunt racing. Charlie Swan won the first race on a mare for Aidan O'Brien, and Tommy Treacy won the handicap hurdle on a mare for Paddy Mullins, Notcomplainingbut, who had been one of the best juvenile hurdlers in Ireland the previous season.

I was in good company in the weigh room before the bumper. Some of the top amateur riders in the country were there. John Thomas McNamara was there, Barry Cash, David Marnane. Gordon Elliott was there, T.J. Nagle, James Nash. Well, if I thought they went fast in the point-to-point, this was a different league altogether. No fences to slow you down, no obstacles, just flat out for over two miles. Again, I was wrecked at the end of it, every muscle in my body was burning, but, again, it was exhilarating. And again, we finished down the field.

* * *

I got my first car when I was 17, a 1978 Toyota Starlet. It was a year older than me, with mould on the inside and rust on the outside and – as I discovered when I got it home – a little pool of water on the floor under the passenger seat. I didn't care though. It got me from A to B and it opened up a whole new vista for me. It meant that I was able to get around on my own, that I was able to drive to trainers' yards myself.

I spent that summer in Jimmy Mangan's and James Sheehan's. I'd go into Jimmy's in the morning, a half day, I'd be in at half seven and I'd leave at lunchtime, and I'd spend the afternoon at James's. James only had 10 or 12 horses, but he was always very good to me and I was delighted to go there in the afternoons.

Jimmy could have 10 or 12 runners at a point-to-point on a Sunday, and you'd be dying to ride one or two of them. Of course, we didn't know what was running when, but you could tell when the farrier arrived, Jimmy O'Leary. You'd be asking him, which horses are getting the steels for Sunday?

I don't know what the other lads did, but I'd be onto the farrier and then I'd be onto Jimmy. All I wanted to do was ride. I'd try to make sure that I schooled the horses who had got the steel plates on, and you'd be making sure you were on your toes when you were schooling. You'd be hoping that Jimmy would go, hey Russell, you can ride him on Sunday.

There were a couple of dodgy jumpers there, a couple of useless horses, a couple who would run out through the wing as easily as jump the fence, but I didn't care. I just wanted to put on the colours and put on the boots and go out to ride.

I was at Watergrasshill one day when a fellow asked me if I would come to West Cork to school a horse of his. He told me that he was a really nice horse, a half-brother to Mr Mulligan.

This was massive for me. Mr Mulligan had recently won the Cheltenham Gold Cup, he was the best staying chaser in Britain or Ireland at the time, and here was his half-brother, another horse out of his dam Miss Manhattan – or so I presumed, because that's what a horse's half-brother is, another horse who is out of the same mare – somewhere in deepest West Cork, and this fellow was asking me to go down and school him. This was where it was all going to start, I thought. My ticket to the big time.

I wasn't mad about Mr Mulligan's sire, Torus. He was known for being kind of angular and bad-tempered, but if this fellow was a half-brother to Mr Mulligan, by a different sire obviously (because if he was by the same sire, obviously, he would have been a full brother) then he could be a very exciting young horse.

It was about a three-hour drive to this place in West Cork. I would have gone anywhere though to sit on a good horse. I would have gone to the ends of the earth. This place wasn't quite at the end of the earth, but it wasn't far off it, West Cork is far from everywhere. The place was fine, no Easyfix fences or anything, but that was normal then. Just a couple of bales of straw with Christmas trees stuck into them. The horse was a big, narrow horse, not completely unlike Mr Mulligan himself. You could definitely see the similarities.

But he wasn't great to jump, and he didn't give me a great feel. I was disappointed, I was starting to think that maybe this fellow wouldn't be my catapult into the big time after all, but you never know. Mr Mulligan himself was a slow enough burn, it took him four attempts to win a point-to-point and he fell on his first run in a novice chase.

I went into the house for a cup of tea afterwards with this man and his daughter, and we started talking about pedigrees. I was already big into National Hunt pedigrees at the time, I always have been.

'So what's this fellow by?' I asked. 'Who's his sire?'

'Torus,' said yer man.

'Torus?' I checked.

'Yes, Torus,' he said, appearing to get a bit agitated.

I lit up.

'Sure he's not a half-brother at all then,' I said, getting excited at this stage. 'Mr Mulligan is by Torus as well. He's got the same father and the same mother. He's a full brother.'

This seemed to cause even more agitation.

'No, he's only a half-brother,' he said.

I was confused.

'He doesn't have the same mother. He just has the same father.'

Now, everybody knows that, when you talk about half-brothers or half-sisters, you mean that the horses have the same dam, the same mother. You mean that they are out of the same mare. You don't say that Tiger Roll is a half-brother to I Am Maximus because they are both sired by Authorized. Tiger Roll is a half-brother to Austrian School, they are both out of the mare Swiss Roll. Or he is a half-brother to Ahzeemah, winner of the Lonsdale Cup. Nichols Canyon is also by Authorized, as is Goshen, and Echoes In Rain, but you'd never say that Tiger Roll was their half-brother.

So I was after travelling three hours down the road into West Cork to sit on a horse by Torus, a decent stallion, he sired Bradbury Star as well as Mr Mulligan, and Therealbandit, but a stallion that I wasn't really mad about. More importantly, I wasn't really mad about the horse himself, he didn't strike me as a future champion anyway. I finished my tea, politely said goodbye to the man and his daughter, and drove the three hours home again.

I would have done anything to get on a good horse then, and that was a thread that ran through my whole career. I would have gone anywhere to sit on a horse I could ride in a point-to-point. To be honest, I'd have ridden anything in a point-to-point. I just wanted to ride. When I'd go to a point-to-point meeting, I'd want to ride in every race, and I'd ride anything.

There were two brothers, good point-to-point handlers, Paddy and Roddy Daly, Dad had a few horses with them. They'd have runners every Sunday and they'd never have riders booked. They'd go to the meeting and they'd walk into the tent, the weigh room, and they'd go down the list looking for riders. They'd start with the best riders, see if they were available, then they'd go down as far as they needed to go.

I'd be dying to ride. Pick me! Pick me! I'd be like Donkey in the movie *Shrek*. Pick me! But they usually wouldn't want their horse to be ridden by a young fellow who would just keep going, full of enthusiasm, who wouldn't know to stop if the horse got tired. Most of their runners were mares, who would get fitter and fitter as the season developed. At the start of the season though, they'd need a rider who would know when to stop if they weren't getting home. Their horses could jump though, God they could jump, they were always really well schooled, everybody wanted to ride them, and at some stage in the season they would click, they would run themselves fit and they could rattle up a sequence.

Tom Keating used to arrive at a point-to-point or at a school, and I'd be onto him always. He mightn't have a rider for every horse they were going to run or school, and I'd be on at him. I'd be hitting the whip off the side of my boot, just to let him know I was there. When are you ever going to let me ride for you Tom? It took a while, but I got there in the end.

I spent a year with Eugene O'Sullivan. As I said before, I was so lucky, the people who looked after me when I was a young fellow. I lived in the house with Eugene and his wife and family. His daughter Maxine, who rode It Came To Pass to win the Foxhunter at Cheltenham in 2020, was only a kid – makes you feel old – and his son Owen wasn't even born, which makes you feel older.

Eugene and his family were brilliant to me. Again, it was another home from home. And I learned so much. You'd be schooling horses and you'd be breaking horses and you'd be feeding and brushing them as well as riding them work. Then you'd be into the house for dinner in the evening. There was a kind of a separate part of the house where I used to stay, but I'd be in the sitting room in the evening too watching television with Eugene and Mrs O'Sullivan and the family.

It was always a real family-run operation, with Eugene and Mrs O'Sullivan, and Eugene's brother William, who rode Lovely Citizen to win the Foxhunter at Cheltenham in 1991, and then Maxine and young Michael, William's son, Eugene's nephew. Michael is doing really well these days himself as a jockey, he is based mainly with Barry Connell, he rode Marine Nationale to win the Supreme Novices' Hurdle at Cheltenham in 2023. And a lot of their owners were local people, they'd be in around the yard all the time. There was just always a great atmosphere around the place.

Of course, I'd be riding short, I'd tuck my irons up as short as I could, thinking I was a real jockey.

'Leave down your irons!' Eugene would shout at me. 'Drop them down two holes at least.'

The more rides I got, the more experience I got and the more rides I got and the more experience I got. It just evolved. I'd see Tom Keating schooling or at a point-to-point meeting, or I'd see Thomond O'Mara at the annual point-to-point dance.

'Would you ever give me a ride?' I'd say to them.

'When are you going to give me a ride?'

It was a great community though, you'd see everybody there, at the meetings, at the schooling session, and then at the annual dance. There were lots of links between point-to-points and hunting and pony racing, lots of people involved in all the different areas. And if you weren't a complete prick, you'd fit in with everybody.

Interestingly though, there was never a point in my life where I said, I'm going to be a jockey. There was never a moment when I decided I wanted to be a jockey, that I wanted to make a living out of riding horses in races. It just developed like that. I never decided I was going to try to make it as a professional jockey, I never decided that was going to be my career.

I didn't think about things like that too deeply when I was younger. I never sat down and planned, I never said, right, if I'm going to be successful as a jockey, I need to do this or that. I just loved riding horses, that was all I ever really wanted to do. I just kind of went where the flow would take me and I ended up where I ended up. I wanted to ride in every single race, always. I never thought I wouldn't ride horses, to the point that I never considered what I would do if I didn't. And all I ever really thought about was the next horse, the next ride.

I went to Lismore in March 1998 to ride a mare that Jimmy Mangan trained for Dad. I'd ridden her a couple of times before, at Carrigtwohill and at Kildorrery, but she was very good this day at Lismore, we finished second to a mare called Glacial Trial. That was the closest I had got to winning, and I remember Ken Budds coming running over to me to tell me to be sure to weigh in. I wasn't used to weighing in, you only weighed in if you finished in the money, so it wouldn't have been on my mind really, with all the excitement about finishing second. Ken took me and actually guided me over to the scales to make sure.

* * *

The point-to-point season ended at Kinsale every year. Two days at Kinsale, and then done for the season. The year funnelled into Kinsale, all the championships were decided there if they hadn't been decided beforehand, usually in good late-spring or early-summer weather.

I hadn't ridden a winner by the time Kinsale rolled around in the spring of 1997, but there was no way I wasn't going to Kinsale. You never knew what you'd pick up, you'd always get to lead one up and I always brought my gear with me, because you never knew what was going to happen, you never knew where you might pick up a ride.

I went down in the car with Martin Budds. Lord rest Martin, I was stone mad about him, I was obsessed with him, he was a great fellow, he was always bringing me everywhere with him. I loved hanging out with Martin. He had this red Ford Fiesta then with a blue driver's door. That was not unusual then, if you had a car that needed a door, you'd just take whatever door you could get, you wouldn't go trying to match the colour or anything.

Of course, we headed down to Kinsale with nowhere to stay. There was no such thing as Airbnb then obviously, and we couldn't afford to stay in a hotel, so we just headed down, assuming we would find somewhere to stay on Saturday night.

We hadn't found somewhere to stay by 3am. I suppose we hadn't been trying that hard. (In our defence, our efforts were diverted elsewhere.) We were freezing though, and we knew that some of the lads were staying in a B&B. We had a fair idea where it was, so we made our way there. Of course, the house was all locked up when we got there, it was three o'clock in the morning after all, and the lads were asleep, but we managed to find their bedroom and we tried to get in through their window. There was a bit of a kerfuffle, a bit of messing. I was halfway in the window when the lights went on in the main house and I heard this big booming voice shouting at me.

'Here, what's going on there?!'

Martin and I scarpered, back out through the window I had been half-in through, back down onto the ground and down the road. Your man didn't chase after us, but the Gardaí did, for some reason. Lights and sirens and everything, a squad car chasing me and Martin Budds down the road just outside Kinsale.

The Gardaí were fine, they saw the incident for what it was: two lads just having a bit of craic. We asked them if they would arrest us, put us into a cell for the night, it had to be warmer in the cell than it was outside. But they wouldn't.

'What do we have to do to get ourselves arrested?'

'Off you go now lads.'

We headed off down the road, Martin and me, freezing, looking for somewhere to sleep. It's all a bit of a blur now, but we found a rubber dinghy somewhere, in a field I think. The rubber dinghy looked comfortable, but it wasn't. No matter what angle we lay in, we couldn't get to sleep. I had this pain in my neck, whatever angle I was at, and it was freezing.

So we abandoned the dinghy and walked down the road for another little while until we came to this derelict building. It was starting to get bright at this stage, but we were freezing and we were wrecked. We had to try to get into this building, which had this steel pipe running across the pebbledash. Martin went first, and he got across okay. Then me, but as I caught a hold of the pipe, it started to come away from the wall. As I dropped, the pipe caught my hand and ripped it, all the way from the top of my finger to the base of my hand. I still have a scar on my finger now.

Eventually we got into this building. It's actually a new, refurbished hotel now, but back then it was an old derelict hotel. But it was dry and it was warmer inside than it was outside, and I found this big long couch, and we took the curtains from the windows and used them as blankets. At least we got a couple of hours' sleep.

I remember that night well, because it was the last night I saw Martin. The point-to-point dance was on a couple weeks later, Martin would normally go to it, so I couldn't believe it when he told me he wasn't going. Everybody went to the point-to-point dance.

I went of course, had the craic, then I headed off for the summer, so I wasn't around, I wasn't hanging around with Martin or in the Budds' for the summer.

I'll never forget when I heard about Martin's car crash. Late August 1997, he was on his way back from Mill Street after showjumping. I couldn't believe it. It was so sad, I was so sad. Martin meant the world to me. Sometimes afterwards, when I rode a winner, when I rode a big winner, I'd look up to the skies and hold out my arms like an angel's wings. That was for Martin, that was always for Martin.

I cried the day Martin died. I remember the date well, because it was the same night Lady Diana was killed in a car crash in Paris: 31 August 1997.

Chapter 5

You never knew where your opportunity was going to come from.

I went to Boulta one day in late January 1999 with James Sheehan. James was schooling a couple of horses, so I went up with him for the spin and thinking, you never know, there might be someone there stuck for a rider. And, sure enough, Pat O'Connor was there, he had a couple of horses to school, but he was short a rider for one of them so, right place right time, he was happy to allow me to school him.

I thought no more of it until, the following week, at a point-to-point meeting at Tallow, Pat had two horses in a race that didn't divide. Usually, if there were enough horses declared for a race, they would divide and, if a handler had two horses in the race, they'd put one in the first division and the other in the second division. This race didn't divide though, so Pat needed a rider for Spanish Castle. Again, right place, right time.

I got some spin off Spanish Castle that day. I went down the inside, and I asked him up at every fence. I didn't know it at the time, but he had to go long at his fences, he wasn't very good at going in tight and popping, and that suited me grand, given that I was firing him at every fence. I didn't know anything at the time, I didn't know anything about strides or pace or fractions.

I'd had plenty of rides at this stage, and I had gone close, I had ridden a couple of seconds and thirds, but I had never ridden a point-to-point winner. Until that day, when I booted Spanish Castle home, no horse between me and the winning line, just green grass, and 10 lengths back to the runner-up Glenview Rose.

It was some thrill, to ride my first point-to-point winner. I was 19 years old now, I was old enough, I'd had 40 or 50 rides, so it was time for me to ride a winner. I was so happy though. You see the photographs of me afterwards, and you'd be thinking, why is that young fellow so happy. Dad was there, which was brilliant. I have a photo of me and Dad after the race.

I was so grateful too to Pat for giving me the opportunity. Although he did say to me afterwards that he didn't know I hadn't ridden a winner before and that, if he had known, he wouldn't have put me up!

I was starting to get noticed a bit then though. Sean Ahern was very good to me then, he obviously liked the way I rode. Lots of people were good to me then, Michael Hickey, Michael and Fiona O'Connor, John Kiely, Paul Lenihan.

Michael Hourigan was always good to me. He'd rock up with a lorry-load of horses, he wouldn't have riders sorted, and he'd be very happy to put me up. I rode Beef Or Salmon to win his maiden point-to-point at Clonmel in February 2001, just before foot-and-mouth hit, and I rode him on his racecourse debut, in the big Goffs Sales Bumper, the Land Rover Bumper, at Fairyhouse in May 2001, just after racing had resumed.

I got some feel off this horse and he ran a big race for me at Fairyhouse. He stayed on well to finish third behind a horse of David Wachman's named Tuco, who was also making his racecourse debut.

Two significant things about that Land Rover Bumper. Firstly, Beef Or Salmon went on to be Beef Or Salmon, the superstar steeplechaser that he was, winner of 10 Grade 1 races, including three Lexus Chases and three Hennessy Gold Cups, the third of them in 2007 when he was 11 years old. He was never at his best at Cheltenham, he never won a Cheltenham Gold Cup, and he probably didn't get the recognition he should have got as a result. But he was some racehorse, he was some steeplechaser, and his career was brilliantly managed by Michael Hourigan.

I don't think Michael was too happy with the ride I gave him in the Land Rover Bumper though. I was sick that day. I remember going to the races with Paul Tobin, and stopping three times along the way to get sick. So maybe I wasn't at my best on Beef Or Salmon that day, maybe Michael was right. Either way, I never got to ride Beef Or Salmon again. Philip Fenton rode him when he won on his next run at Clonmel the following November.

The second significant thing about that Land Rover Bumper, the 2001 Land Rover Bumper, is that the winner, Tuco, David Wachman's horse, he was owned by Ryanair supremo Michael O'Leary. He was the first racehorse O'Leary owned, and it sparked his interest in racing. It was the genesis of the emergence of Gigginstown House Stud as a racehorse owner, one of the most significant racehorse owners in National Hunt racing. And that was obviously going to have a massive impact, not only for me personally, Gigginstown was such a huge part of my career, but also for Irish National Hunt racing in general.

Paul Lenihan had a horse called Careformenow, who had been running on the track. He only ever won once on the track, he won his beginners' chase at Kilbeggan in July 1997 when he was trained by Aidan O'Brien, but he had finished placed in lots of bumpers and maiden hurdles for Pat Flynn. He ran in 13 bumpers and finished second in eight of them. And he won a point-to-point at Ballingarry in May 1997.

I got to ride him in an Open Lightweights, and that was brilliant for me. You just didn't get rides in Open Lightweights, all the rides were taken up by the horses' owners or by the senior riders. But I rode Careformenow in an Open Lightweight at Ballyragget in March 1999, and we won. And I rode Careformenow again in another Open Lightweights at Dundrum the following week, and we won again.

I actually rode a double that day, my first double. Kevin O'Sullivan was a brilliant rider, he rode lots for Charles Byrnes then and he rode for Robert Tyner and Tom Foley and Thomond O'Mara, but he didn't have a huge amount of interest in it. He was due to ride a mare for Mike Condon earlier in the afternoon, Linda's Leader, and he just decided not to. He didn't even ring Mike, he just gave me the colours and said I might get to ride a few for Mike. Of course, I was delighted. So I won on her, the second division of the six-and-seven-year-old mares' maiden, then I won the Open Lightweights on Careformenow, the last race on the day, and I was made up. My first double.

I went to Dundrum House Hotel afterwards, walking on air after my double, and I met Philip Fenton for the first time there. I had seen Philip lots of course, in the weigh room before and after races, but I never went up to him. You wouldn't dare. Philip was one of best amateur riders around at the time. He was after riding a treble that day at Dundrum, the final leg in a division of the six-year-old geldings' maiden on Up For The Game, a lovely horse by Roselier, in the J.P. McManus colours. You'd be in awe of these things.

Up For The Game was a full brother to The Grey Monk, a high-class staying chaser for Gordon Richards in England, he won the Tommy Whittle Chase and he finished third in the Irish Grand National. Up For The Game turned out to be good on the track too, trained by Edward O'Grady for J.P. McManus, he was only just beaten in the William Neville & Sons Novice Chase, now a Grade 1 race, at Leopardstown's Christmas Festival that year.

Anyway, that was another big break for me, meeting Philip, maybe even a bigger break than riding a double on the same day. Maybe they complemented each other, maybe Philip had a bit of regard for me because I had ridden a double. For whatever reason though, Philip was brilliant to me. We started going racing together a bit after that, like, if we were going up the country to Bellewstown or Kilbeggan or somewhere, I'd meet Philip on the road somewhere and he'd take me to the races. If I was going racing, I'd always ring Philip.

Philip was in great demand, he'd have his pick of three or four or five horses in the bumper at just about every race meeting. Talented rider though he was, he could only ride one of them at a time, so he'd be looking for lads to take the other rides for him, and he was happy to put me in for the next best. He wouldn't want to be letting one go to Tony Martin or one of the other top amateurs, because he might not get that one back if he did!

I was getting a few rides on the track as well then, in bumpers and in amateur races. I'd be ringing around for rides. You'd get the entries for the bumper on teletext, you'd go down through them as close to 12 o'clock as you could, just before riders had to be declared, and you'd chance your arm. I remember ringing Pat Hughes looking for a ride in the bumper and he laughed at me! He was probably right, Philip Fenton was riding for him and Philip was king.

I'd had about 12 or 13 rides on the track before Michael and Fiona O'Connor put me up on Right'N'Royal in an amateur riders' handicap hurdle at Gowran Park in May 1999. He wasn't a bad horse, by Good Thyne, he had won his maiden hurdle over two and a half miles at Gowran Park a few weeks earlier. He had been beaten in a handicap hurdle at Punchestown in the meantime, but he was stepping up in trip to an extended three miles, and he was going back to Gowran Park, a track he obviously liked.

I didn't care, I didn't really know too much about the horse, I was just delighted to be getting a ride in a hurdle race on the track. It was different going to the track, different to going to a point-to-point.

You'd put on your good slacks, you'd shine your shoes, you'd look the part going in.

Right'N'Royal was great that day. He settled nicely for me just behind the leaders, and he jumped well. We moved to the front at the third last flight, which is far enough out at Gowran Park, but he stayed on well to see off Paul Moloney on a horse of David Wachman's.

That was brilliant, my first winner on the track.

I did well in point-to-points too between then and the end of the season, and I ended the season with eight winners, which was enough to see me tie the novice riders' championship with Simon McGonagle.

There was a scholarship going for the leading novice rider, a trip to England to stay with one of the top trainers in Britain then and still, Nicky Henderson, and to have a session with Yogi Breisner, who's brilliant at getting horses to jump and at helping riders to improve.

We were level going into Kinsale, Simon had already booked his holidays and he asked me if I wouldn't ride at Kinsale, if we could tie the championship. I was grand with that, it meant we'd both win the title and we'd both get to go off to Nicky Henderson's. They got wind of our arrangement though, and they told me that, if I didn't ride at Kinsale, I wouldn't get the scholarship. So I did, I rode at Kinsale, I had six or seven rides over the two days, but I didn't ride a winner. I had a few seconds, but no winners. So Simon and I tied the championship.

That was massive for me. Not just because of the accolade, but also because it got me noticed and, most importantly of all, it got me up onto the stage for an award at the annual point-to-point dance! Before that year, 1999, you'd be at the dance and you'd be looking up at the stage thinking you'd love to be up there getting an award. Then I was, me and Simon, joint champion novice riders, and I was on my way.

* * *

Strange thing. You can scratch around looking for rides, begging for rides, and you're at nothing. Then, you ride a winner, you ride another winner, you ride a double, momentum builds and suddenly, you are in demand.

That's what happened to me. I never thought I was a particularly good rider, I never really stopped to consider that I might be all right. I didn't take the time to try to think about how good or how bad a rider I was. I just knew I wanted to ride, I wanted to ride everything, all of the time.

I have Gerry Hogan to thank for my initial association with Pat Doyle. Gerry is now a top-notch bloodstock agent but, back then, he had come back from a spell in Britain and was riding out for Pat Doyle. He obviously regarded me as a rider, because he kept telling me I needed to be going and riding out for Pat Doyle, and he kept telling Pat Doyle that there was this young lad from Youghal who he should have riding for him.

So I started riding out for Pat Doyle and I started getting point-to-point rides for him. The Doyles were only about four miles out the road from me, and it became like another second home. Even when I wasn't in there riding out in later years, I'd just go up for a cup of tea. I didn't know it back then of course, but my association with Pat Doyle was probably a big factor in me getting the job with Gigginstown House Stud in 2007. Pat was training a lot of the young Gigginstown horses then, and it can't have been a negative for me that I had such a good association with Pat.

Pat Doyle was instrumental too in launching the career of Rachael Blackmore, in a kind of indirect way. It was February 2011, Rachael was at college in Limerick at the time, she was friendly with Pat's daughter, so she was in riding out at Pat's. Rachael just happened to ask me one day if I knew of any rides going in lady riders' races or in bumpers or in amateur riders' races, if I could put in a word for her.

As luck would have it, it was on the same day, or maybe the day after, that Shark Hanlon called me wondering if I knew of a good lady rider who could ride Stowaway Pearl in the lady riders' handicap hurdle at Thurles that Thursday.

'This will win,' Shark says to me. 'But I don't have a rider!'

'I have the very one for you,' I said. 'A right good pilot.'

I didn't know Rachael very well at the time, but I had been impressed with her. She was a lovely rider, and she was as brave as a lion. It wasn't just her riding ability though, it was her attitude as well, her enthusiasm. She was plucky, nothing seemed to faze her. But if she hadn't said anything to me, I probably wouldn't have even thought of her when Shark asked me if I knew anybody. Just shows you, timing, opportunity, asking the right question at the right time.

I didn't even know if Rachael had a licence to ride or not. I didn't know that she had never ridden a winner before, but I think I still would have recommended her even if I had known that. Your first winner has to come from somewhere. Everybody needs an opportunity. Like, when I won my first point-to-point in Spanish Castle, and Pat O'Connor told me that if he had known I hadn't ridden a winner before, he wouldn't have given me the ride.

Anyway, Rachael won that lady riders' handicap hurdle at Thurles on Stowaway Pearl, and the Rachael Blackmore story began. Gold Cups and Champion Hurdles and Grand Nationals and fairy-tale endings. She's brilliant, she has been brilliant every step of the way, she deserves everything she has got, all the success, all the accolades. I'm very proud of all that Rachael has achieved. I'm sure she would have got there anyway, but I'm happy I played some small part in giving her the leg up that her talent deserved.

At the time that Pat Doyle was starting to give me rides, Liam Burke started giving me rides, Robert Tyner started giving me rides.

Aiden Murphy put a group of horses together, the bloodstock agent, father of trainer Olly, they were being trained by John

Dineen, and he asked me to go and school them. There were some really talented horses among them, it was an exciting group of young horses. But one stood out for me, a horse by Risk Me, bred to go five furlongs, called Follow Me Boys. He was some horse to school, he was so fast over his fences.

I remember the first day he ran, it was in a five-year-olds' maiden at Killeagh. He was fresh and keen with me going to the start, I was only a young fellow, so I wasn't sure what to do. I was only a novice rider, still trying to learn. I remember asking Tom Lombard for advice.

'I'm in a bit of trouble here Tom,' I said. 'What should I do?'

'Is he a nice horse?' Tom asked me.

'He's as good a horse as you'd ever throw your leg across,' I said without hesitation.

Tom thought for a second.

'Jump off wide,' he said. 'Let him see his fences. Once he sees his fences, he'll settle for you. Then just ride your race.'

That was a measure of the man Tom Lombard. He was riding in the race against me, and still he told me what to do. My plan had been to try to get cover, settle Follow Me Boys in behind horses, try to get him settled that way. If I had done that, he probably would have raced too keenly, expended too much energy. Tom knew that just by looking at him on the way down to the start, and he was happy to give me that advice.

We won. I started Follow Me Boys out wide, just as Tom had suggested, and he settled and jumped, just as Tom had said he would. He was so fast over his fences, he travelled so well for me, and we won well. We came home three lengths clear of Enda Bolger's horse Gunther McBride, with John Thomas McNamara on him, and he was 15 lengths clear of the rest. Gunther McBride turned out to be a very good horse, he won the Racing Post Chase at Kempton a couple of years later for Philip Hobbs.

More than what Follow Me Boys beat though, it was the way he did it. The feel he gave me. I had never had a feel like that off a horse, and I have rarely had it since.

Follow Me Boys was to run in a bumper shortly after that. Philip Fenton was actually due to ride him in the bumper. I understood that. I was only a seven-pound claimer. Philip could ride whatever he wanted in bumpers, but Edward O'Grady had a horse in the race, so Philip had to ride him.

I went down to John Dineen's to ride Follow Me Boys in a piece of work a few days before the bumper and, I'm not joking, if I thought that the feel he gave me in his point-to-point was good, he was even better then. He was after improving again for his point-to-point win.

After I rode him work, they said I could ride him in his bumper. This was massive for me. He was definitely the best horse I had ever sat on up to that point, and, it may be because I was young at the time, but he was one of the best horses I ever sat on in my career. And maybe he was the best.

I never got to ride him in that bumper. Sadly, I never got to ride him again. The day before the bumper, he fractured his pedal bone and had to be put down. I was distraught. We'll never know how good he could have been. The only time he ever raced was in that point-to-point at Killeagh.

Aiden Murphy was very good to me. He took me over to Goodwood that summer, the summer of 2000, to ride a horse that his wife Annabel trained, Open Arms, in an amateur riders' race. That was brilliant, to ride on the flat at Goodwood. We finished third, just a short head in front of a horse of Gary Moore's, Stoppes Brow, with his young son riding him, a fellow called Ryan Moore, who was claiming 5lb at the time. Tom Scudamore won the race on a horse of John Gosden's, and he often reminds me about that when I see him.

I met Aiden and Annabel's son Olly then for the first time, he was only a kid at the time, but he was a lovely kid. I'd always have a chat with him after that when I'd see him at the races or at the sales and, strange the way life works out, he would have a big impact in my career later on when he started working for Gordon Elliott.

* * *

If you had been able to pick three point-to-point handlers to ride for back then, Pat Doyle, Liam Burke and Robert Tyner would have been high up on every list, so it was some stroke of luck for me that the three of them wanted me.

It took a lot of juggling though. You wanted to avoid clashes. Like, you didn't want a good horse of Pat Doyle's taking on a good horse of Liam Burke's or of Robert Tyner's. That would have been no good to me because, of course, I wanted to ride them all. And if I didn't ride one, if I couldn't ride one, they could get John Thomas McNamara to ride it, and the last thing I wanted to do was give away a good horse for nothing to John Thomas. He didn't need extra help from me!

You couldn't tell the handlers that though. You couldn't tell Liam Burke that you wanted to ride a horse for Pat Doyle, that he should run his horse on a different day. You'd have to do it another way. You'd have to convince him that it might be better running the horse the following week, or the previous week. In many cases, Pat Doyle's horse was probably going to win anyway. there was no point in taking him on, but he could win a different race if you waited a week.

The brilliant thing about riding for Pat Doyle was he'd have his horses targeted at races four or five weeks in advance, so you had four or five weeks to try to figure it out. Liam Burke was similar. Robert was a bit different, he wouldn't be letting you know five weeks out, but when he wanted you, he wanted you, you knew he wanted you, and you made yourself available.

Races were often divided, and you could have horses split up through the divides too. Jim Hickey used to sort the entries in those days. Jim and his wife Mary. They'd get the entries in on Sunday, and they'd be going through them on Monday. Jim would get the list of declarations in and, depending on how many there were, he would decide if there would be two divisions or sometimes even three divisions. Each handler's horses were grouped together so that, if they had more than one horse declared for a race, if there was more than one division, a handler would have a horse in each division. That made sense.

Pat Doyle's horses were always first for some reason. It's done alphabetically now but, back then, Pat's horses were on top of the list. They were always number one on the racecard. So, say Pat had two horses declared for a race that was going to have two divisions, they would be together at the top of the list, and Jim would go down the list: Division 1, Division 2, Division 1, Division 2. Or, Division 1, Division 2, Division 3. Pat's first horse would be in Division 1 and his second horse would be in Division 2 and, if he had a third horse and there were three divisions, his third horse would be in Division 3. Same with every other handler who had more than one horse declared for the race.

That was grand. If I was riding for Pat, I'd get to ride each of his horses in each of the different divisions. The problem was when Liam or Robert had horses entered too that I wanted to ride. So I'd ring Jim on Monday and ask him to keep this horse away from that horse, to put them in different divisions if he could. I'd ask Jim to put Liam's horse or horses in under Pat's, so they would be in a different division to Pat's horses. Same with Robert's horses. If Liam or Robert had a fancied horse, I'd try to get the horses ordered so he would be in a different division to Pat's fancied horse or horses.

It wasn't easy to organise, and it became more complicated when there were other horses entered that I wanted to ride. I remember

Denis Murphy had a really good horse, a horse by Torus (Mr Mulligan's sire!) with a lovely pedigree, a horse named Therealbandit, who was running at Kildorerry one Sunday. I rode a winner for Tom O'Mahony on the Saturday, and he said to me afterwards, you're riding that horse for me tomorrow, right?

'Of course Tom,' I said. 'I wouldn't want to ride anything else.'

Now, this was news to me and, disaster, he was in the same race as Denis Murphy's horse. The horses probably weren't beside each other in the list, so there was every chance that they would end up in the same division, which would have been really bad news. I had to ride Tom's horse, but I had to ride Denis's horse as well. I had committed to both.

So I got Martin Ferris to sit at the declarations table when the divisions were being sorted, I got him to keep an eye on how the divisions were shaping up and, if it was looking like the two horses were going to end up in the same divisions, to declare a horse in between so that it would knock the other horse into the other division.

Martin did that, which was grand, but the problem then was, there was a horse declared for the race who was never going to run in it. I remember, we were waiting for ages before the five-year-olds' maiden and they were shouting for Number 33.

'Would Number 33 get their horse into the parade ring please?!'

But there was no Number 33. Of course, I couldn't say anything. I couldn't say that Number 33 was a ghost horse, put in there by Martin Ferris just to knock Therealbandit into the other division of the race!

Everyone was walking around for ages, waiting for Number 33. It felt like a lifetime. I felt bad, but needs must. I couldn't have let down Tom O'Mahony, no way, he was such an important person, and I couldn't have let down Denis Murphy. And I felt bad for Jim Hickey, who had everything arranged perfectly. He wouldn't have allowed it, I had to do it without him knowing. Eventually, they concluded that Number 33 wasn't coming, so they got on with the race.

And it all worked out, the two horses got into different divisions, I got to ride both of them, and they both won. They were lovely horses too, Therealbandit and Coolnahilla. Coolnahilla beat a horse of David Wachman's that day, Knock Knock, who would go on to finish second in the Irish National, beaten a head by Timbera. (More about Timbera later.) Therealbandit went on to win a Rowland Meyrick Chase for Martin Pipe and David Johnson, and to finish second in a Pillar Property Chase. Coolnahilla went on to win a Tim Duggan Chase for Liam Burke. It was good to see those two horses both going on to fulfil their potential.

It wasn't easy juggling everything, but it was all a part of it. Trying to keep everybody happy while, at the same time, trying to ride everything, trying to ride all the good horses I could ride. Robert completely understood, he was a true gentleman about it all, he just wanted me to ride all the horses I could ride for him, and to do my best on them all. And if Pat or Liam had a better horse in the same division, he'd understand if I rode their horse instead.

Pat and Liam were a bit trickier. But if Pat would be giving out about me riding one for Liam, I'd have to try to point out to him how it was good for him too. Of course, I was trying to split them up because I wanted to ride both horses, but I was doing Pat a favour too, getting a fancied one of Liam's out of the way for his fancied one!

I remember riding a mare in Bruff for Liam in the mares' maiden, a mare called Mandys Gold. She ended up being okay, she won a bumper on the track and she won a beginners' chase and she went on to be the dam of Ten Ten and Sizing Gold, both good chasers.

Anyway, this was in March 2000, I was well on my way to my second novice riders' title, I was very happy with how things were going. Mandys Gold was having her first run, and Liam just wanted me to get her settled, do as well as I could do, but the main objective was to get her around and get her home safely.

She was as green as grass, she bucked with me all the way to the start, and she bucked with me on the run to the first fence. She was grand after that though, once I got her settled and nursed her around, she was going okay. But there was a dolled-off fence halfway around, the rest of the field went outside it, but I went inside, saved ground. So I went from about 11th or 12th to third without using up any energy. The problem with that though was, once you were there, once you had made your ground, you couldn't give it away. You want to set off in a race where you are setting off, and you want to be improving your position all the way to the winning line. You don't want to be giving away ground you've just made. That's no way to ride a race.

We turned into the straight, and we were hammering. She had a squeak now, so I gave her every chance. We were hammering down to the last, she was tired, but I saw a stride. Two strides before the fence though, I could feel her getting drunk under me. But we were in too deep, there was no going back. I hoped she had the energy in her to get up and over the last, but she didn't. She crashed through the fence and came down.

I feared the worst, she was on the ground for about 20 minutes afterwards but, thankfully, she was just tired. She got up eventually and she was fine. She actually ran again in Liscarroll two weeks later.

That didn't mean that Liam was happy though. Quite the opposite. He started giving out to me as soon as I got back into the weigh room, into the tent, and he was still giving out to me 10 minutes later.

He was pointing his finger at me and giving me both barrels. All he wanted was for the mare to get home safely, he was telling me again, for me to mind her, make sure she enjoyed herself. If she won, she won, but the main thing was to get the mare home safely. And what did I do? I hammered her over the last three fences, fired her at the last, nearly killed her.

'I'm putting in a hundred per cent here,' he was saying. 'I'm giving this everything I've got, and you're just messing it up!'

I was just sitting there and listening to him. I said sorry a few times, but it didn't seem to be having any impact on the ferocity of the barrage I was getting. I did what I thought was the right thing to do, I was saying. I thought she had a chance of winning. I just took it all though, I didn't fight back. I couldn't be falling out with Liam Burke. He had too many nice horses.

The mares' maiden was always the last race on the day, so I had nowhere to go. I started getting changed, and still Liam was giving out to me. They started to take the tent down around us, and still Liam was giving out to me. It was all a bit strange, just me and Liam in the tent, half-dismantled, him shouting at me, me changing out of my gear. Me with my breeches down around my knees and your man still there roaring at me!

We were there until they had fully dismantled the tent, and we were left there, just the two of us, tent gone, just the bales of hay on the ground around us. Eventually, Liam concluded that he had given out to me enough, that I had got the message and, maybe, if I hadn't got it by now, I was never going to get it.

I put on my jacket and went to join the others in the pub.

Chapter 6

Pat Fahy called me one day, in the spring of 2000, out of the blue. I had never met Pat before, don't think I had ever spoken to Pat before. I knew who he was though. He was Nuaffe's trainer. He had won some of the good staying handicap chases with Nuaffe, the Thyestes Chase and the Troytown Chase, and he had won a big handicap chase at Haydock with him, the Greenalls Gold Cup. Pat had also won the Heineken Gold Cup at the Punchestown Festival with Butches Boy, who had beaten Idiots Venture and Front Line and Harcon to win it.

Pat must have made the connection with me through Sean O'Donovan. Sean used to work for Pat, he was Nuaffe's regular rider for years, he rode him to win all those big races, the Thyestes Chase and the Troytown Chase and the Greenalls Gold Cup. I was very good friends with Sean when we both worked at Jim Bolger's. He used to have me around to his house, his wife would make me dinner, and he'd joke that, when the time came, at the top of my gravestone they'd write, D.N. Russell, 7lb claimer.

Pat was running a horse in the Grade 2 bumper at Aintree's Grand National meeting, Quadco, and he wanted me to ride him. Quadco hadn't run for Pat Fahy before then, he had won a bumper at Sligo in June the previous year, 10 months earlier, when he was trained by his owner John Doyle, but he hadn't run for Pat since he had got him.

I was delighted to be asked, and I wasn't going to turn down an opportunity to ride in a Grade 2 race at Aintree on Grand National day.

Knife Edge was running on the same day, Michael O'Brien's horse. He was a high-class hurdler, he had finished third behind Istabraq in the Irish Champion Hurdle earlier that season, and he had won on the flat at the Curragh on his last run before Aintree. Quadco breezed with Knife Edge on the morning of the race, and he breezed really well with him. All the lads were talking about him before the race, about how good a chance he had. Even so, he was allowed to go off at 33/1.

None of this registered with me too deeply, I was just delighted to be there, to be riding at Aintree. The bumper was the last race on Grand National day, but it had been a great day for the Irish before that. Ruby Walsh had won the Grand National on Papillon for his dad Ted, just the second Irish-trained horse to win the Grand National since L'Escargot, a year after Paul and Tommy Carberry had won the race with Bobbyjo. As well as that, Philip Carberry had won the opening handicap hurdle on Sharpaten for Pat Hughes. It was big, because this was in an era in which there were relatively few Irish-trained winners in Britain.

Quadco was brilliant. I just sat in mid-division, wherever I could, got him settled. Down the back straight and he was travelling, around the home turn and still travelling, and I'm thinking, this could happen. When we got to the two-furlong marker, I couldn't hold him any longer so I just let him go, and off he went. He came away from his field like a horse who was just in the wrong grade. That was some feeling, coming away from the field as easily as that in a Grade 2 race, the last race at Aintree on Grand National day. We won by 16 lengths in the end.

The next time I rode Quadco was in an amateur riders' maiden on the flat at Clonmel the following May, and we won that too. I rode him in the GPT, the big amateur riders' handicap at the 2001 Galway Festival later that year, I fancied him too, but he slipped on the tarmac coming out of the parade ring, and that ended his chance really. He got fierce upset, he didn't run his race, and he still finished fifth. He won the GPT the following year, Peter Fahey rode him. I was committed to a horse for Noel Meade in the race, Carlesimo, but I wasn't surprised that Quadco won.

I was annoyed I wasn't on him, but I was delighted for Pat. Pat was so good to me all my career, he'd always be on at me to ride for him. He'd always fill you full of confidence. He was a great man to ride for. I thought I was going to win the Grand National for him too in 2016 on Morning Assembly. Crossing the Melling Road on the run back around to the second last fence, we were travelling so well. But Morning Assembly just didn't fully stay the extreme trip, he emptied from there.

Rule The World won the Grand National that year for Mouse Morris and Gigginstown House Stud. If the ball had hopped a little differently, I could have ridden Rule The World. Mouse asked me if I wanted to ride him, but I had already committed to Pat, to Morning Assembly, and I wanted to ride Morning Assembly. I thought he had a right chance in the race. Rule The World carried just 10st 7lb, and that would have been a light-enough weight for me. But if I hadn't had a ride in the race, I would have got down to 10st 7lb all right, and then I might have ridden my first Grand National winner two years earlier than I did.

* * *

I had my first ride at Cheltenham in 2000. Ferdy Murphy was aiming a horse named Toni's Tip at the Kim Muir at the 2000

Cheltenham Festival, a race for amateur riders, and he wanted me to ride him.

It was Tom O'Mahony who put me in for the ride. Tom was always really good to me, I owe a lot to Tom, a great man. He had been a key person in Adrian Maguire becoming stable jockey for Ferdy Murphy, and he obviously thought enough of me to suggest to Ferdy that I should ride his horse in the Kim Muir at Cheltenham.

Toni's Tip was running at Carlisle three weeks before Cheltenham, so I went over to ride him in that. He ran well, he finished second to a horse of Jonjo O'Neill's who was actually ridden by Adrian Maguire.

That was a good experience, going over to Britain to ride at Carlisle, but it obviously wasn't a patch on riding at Cheltenham, in the Kim Muir. As I said before, Cheltenham was like this magical place for me. So to actually go there, to ride there. I had never been to Cheltenham before 14 March 2000, when I rode Toni's Tip in the Kim Muir.

I remember thinking the place was massive. It was all new to me, and it was all so big. In later years, when riding at Cheltenham was an annual thing for me, it didn't seem big at all. You know what you're doing, you know where everything is. But I was only 20 in March 2000, and I was a bit star-struck by the place. Toni's Tip gave me a good spin, he just tired in the home straight and finished sixth.

I won the novice point-to-point riders' championship on my own in 2000. That meant a lot to me. It was brilliant to share it with Simon the previous year with eight winners, but I rode 36 winners in 2000, and that was a whole new level.

That was a record for a novice rider. It was a record then, and it's still a record now. Barry O'Neill came close to beating it in 2009/10 when he rode 33 winners, but my record still stands today, and I'm proud of that.

DAVY RUSSELL

There was no autumn point-to-point season back then, there were no point-to-points from early summer until the following January, but you'd still always be tipping away. They were brilliant years for me. You'd have an odd ride in a bumper on the track, I was riding a bit for Noel Meade, so you might be riding in the bumper at Bellewstown one day, then you'd go and stay in Athlone, and you'd have a ride in the bumper at Sligo the following day. And you'd be looking for a good ride in the GPT at Galway, or you'd pick up the odd spare ride in a handicap hurdle.

I was living my best life. I had no responsibilities, I had a car and a few quid in my pocket, and I just went wherever I needed to go. And you'd always be busy, you'd always be up to something. You might be trying to buy or sell a horse, or you'd go to the sales, see if you could pick up something, or some fellow would want you to ride a bit of work, and you'd stay in a hotel or in one of the lads' houses, and you'd be back to the local pub, play some pool, have a few drinks, have the craic, back to Paul Carberry's house, and off you'd go again.

Then the winter would kick in, and you'd be back going point-to-pointing every weekend. We'd share a car if we were going to a point-to-point up north, four or five of us. You'd be up at four o'clock on a Saturday morning, and you'd be on the road. We'd meet up in Slane, Gordon Elliott, Norman Geraghty, the Healys, the photographers, Pat and Liam. John Thomas McNamara would come with us sometimes.

The north was always lucky for me, I'd rarely leave the north without a winner or two. I rode lots of winners for James Lambe up there, and for Colin McBratney. Then you'd be back down the road, you might stay up around Meath, maybe with Gordon, or if one of the lads was having a party you'd go there, or I'd come back down the road as far as Cashel, maybe stay with Ken Whelan.

I was always meticulous about my gear. Whatever I was doing on Saturday night, parties or pubs or pool, it didn't matter, I always had to have everything sorted for the following day before I did it. I'd have to have my gear washed, saddle clean and all wrapped up, boots cleaned and polished. I'd always be afraid that, if you didn't clean your boots properly, the dirt could get stuck in the zip, and then you'd be scratching around on Sunday morning looking for tape to do makeshift repairs. I wouldn't have been into that.

But it was some craic. I could leave home at four o'clock on Saturday morning and not come back until Tuesday.

Foot-and-mouth disease hit Ireland in the spring of 2001. It had a massive impact on all walks of life in Ireland, and it had a devastating impact on agriculture. Racing was cancelled, the Cheltenham Festival was abandoned for the first time since World War II, and the 2001 point-to-point season was severely curtailed.

They stopped the season in March. I had ridden 19 winners by then, John Thomas McNamara had only ridden nine, so I was crowned champion that year for the first time.

I was intent on winning the title again in 2001/2, and it developed into a brilliant toe-to-toe with John Thomas McNamara. John Thomas was a legend. He dominated the point-to-point scene for years. He had won the national title four times by then, and he ended up with 602 winners between the flags. He had this aura about him too, like he was the best and he knew he was the best, and he knew that everybody knew he was the best. And if we were all going up north to a meeting, if we were all meeting and going up in one car, there could be any number of us, me, Gordon Elliott, Norman Geraghty, Simon McGonagle. If John Thomas was coming with us, he'd have to sit in the front seat!

He never went professional, he never wanted to go professional, but he proved time and again that he was able to compete with the best professionals. His association with Enda Bolger was massive, he won five La Touche Cups over the banks at Punchestown, three of them on Spot Thedifference. The injury that he suffered at Cheltenham in 2013 was desperate, and it was so sad when he passed away in 2016.

In 2001/2, just like in all of the previous years that I was riding in point-to-points, John Thomas set the standard. He was the person you most wanted to beat. He was that good. I was full of respect for him, but he was the standard, he set the bar, and I was desperate to get up to that standard.

That was some season. Because of the fact that the 2001 season was cut short because of foot-and-mouth, they introduced an autumn element to the new season. They started the season in the autumn of 2001, and it ended as usual in the spring of 2002. It was only supposed to be a temporary measure, to make up for the shortened 2001 season, but it was so successful they decided to leave it as a permanent part of the point-to-point season. That meant more racing, more races to ride in, more races to be won, and that suited me grand.

I started riding winners in the autumn, and I didn't stop. I was riding winners every weekend. I was riding good horses and I was riding for good people. I just kept riding winners. But every time I rode a winner, John Thomas would ride a winner. If I rode a double, John Thomas would ride a winner or a double or a treble. The competition between us for the title started early, and it ran all the way to the end of the season.

The season ended in Ballingarry that year, and our battle went all the way there. Going to Bartlemy, two weeks before the end of the season, I was four behind John Thomas, but I knew that I had a really good book of rides at Bartlemy. On the same day, a great friend of mine, Paul Tobin, was riding a good horse for Pat O'Connor in a race in which I didn't have a ride. Pat O'Connor will always have a special place in my career, he is the man who provided me with my first point-to-point winner, Spanish Castle, but I wasn't really riding for him then. There was no falling out or anything, not at all, I was just so busy trying to get around all the yards, it was difficult to do it all.

Anyway, this day, Paul Tobin, the type of person that he is, suggested that he get off the horse and let me ride him, help me in my battle with John Thomas. Pat was good with that. I won on four of my original rides that day, and I won on Pat O'Connor's horse. I had three seconds as well on the same day, and a third, in the second division of the four-and-five-year-olds' maiden, which Paul actually won! Nine races, and I was placed in eight of them. That was one of the rare days too on which John Thomas didn't ride a winner, so I went from four behind to one in front in one day.

We went to Dromahane the following week and it lashed rain. I remember the muck, you could hardly see the aprons on the fences, they were black with muck. They actually called off the races after the sixth race. Before they did though, I had ridden a winner and John Thomas had ridden a winner. I won the first race, the Confined Maiden, on Shoot The Pigeon. John Thomas won the Mares' Open on Yerville's Dream. So I was still one ahead.

I remember the two of us were sitting in the weigh room when the announcement was made that the rest of the card had been abandoned.

'Here John,' I said. 'How about, you ride another winner, and we'll call it a day then. We'll tie it.'

'Grand,' said John Thomas. 'Let's do that.'

So it was off to Ballingarry for the final day of the season. Or, it was off with John Thomas. I didn't even go. That was stupid, I should have gone. I was at home, tidying, ironing my shirt for the dance that night! I should have gone to Ballingarry, just to be there in case something unexpected happened.

And, as it happened, something unexpected did happen, or almost happened. John Thomas finished second in the opening contest, but the 'winner' had gone the wrong side of a bale, it was obvious to everyone that he was going to be disqualified.

But the stewards ran out of time between the first race and the second race, so they decided they wouldn't have the enquiry until after the second. I got a phone call to tell me to get myself to Ballingarry, that there might be an issue. But Ballingarry was two hours away, I wouldn't have made it in time for many races.

John Thomas was riding the favourite in the second so, obviously, if he went out and won on that, and then got the first winner in the stewards' room, that would have put him one ahead of me. He would have won the title on his own, and me at home ironing my fucking shirt.

But John Thomas, the man that he was, the integrity that he had, the authority and respect that he commanded, he just said no, we'll have the enquiry now. It should have been a formality anyway, the 'winner' went the wrong side of the marker. Automatic disqualification. The stewards were very good too, they saw the bigger picture, they knew what was going on. Instead of going by the rule book, by the letter of the law, they went by the person, they helped out the person. They were good people, genuine point-to-point people. So they held the enquiry, disqualified the winner, gave the race to John Thomas.

John Thomas went out after the stewards' enquiry and drew stumps on the day, on the season. That was it, championship tied. He said he was sick, that he couldn't ride for the rest of the day, and that was it. Championship tied, 56 winners each.

That was a record at the time, and we both got a great kick out of it. The lads have broken that since, Jamie Codd and Barry O'Neill and Derek O'Connor, they are great riders. Derek rode 113 winners in 2008/09.

Derek was actually just starting to get going when I was coming towards the end of my time as an amateur. He rode his first winner at Killaloe in 2000, he was just building momentum in 2001 and into 2002. He seemed to be following in my footsteps a bit, like everywhere I was, he seemed to get in there too. Pat Doyle's, Robert Tyner's. He seemed to be tracking me through.

Derek was always a fantastic rider, and he has broken all sorts of records in the point-to-point field. He rode 100 winners or more for three seasons in a row, and he has ridden more point-to-point winners than anyone else, ever. He is over the 1,300 mark now. That's an incredible total.

There was never any great rivalry as such, because I had turned professional before he had really got going, but there might have been if I had stuck around. He would have been serious competition. There was one day, we were both in Eugene O'Sullivan's, we both went for the same brush. It was a new brush, new bristles, it did a better job than the old brush, and we both went for it at the same time. It's funny now looking back on it, we laughed about it later, but we nearly came to blows over that brush! I often wonder would Derek have pushed me out of some of those good yards and out of some of those good rides if I had remained as an amateur.

But they were different times back then, I was very proud of the fact that I was able to ride 56 winners in a season, that I tied with John Thomas, and that the two of us were up on the stage again at the dance that evening!

* * *

You never knew where the rides were going to come from, where the breaks were going to come from. I remember in March 2001 getting a call from a trainer in Lambourn, Ralph Smith, asking me if I would ride a horse for him, Tuska Ridge, in the Fox Hunters' Chase at the Aintree Grand National meeting.

I didn't really hear the name of the horse. I didn't care what the horse was. To be asked to ride in the Fox Hunters' at Aintree, over the Grand National fences, I couldn't believe it. This was for real, this wasn't me gathering the grass at home and jumping through pretend spruce fences on my pony. This was real, real fences and real horses and real cameras.

Turns out, Tuska Ridge didn't have much of a chance. He had ability, he had won a couple of bumpers when he was with Frances Crowley when he was a five-year-old, but that was three years previously, and he hadn't done much since he had gone to England. I didn't care, all I wanted was to ride over the big fences and to get on the telly!

I wanted to be up there with the leaders early on, so that the BBC cameras would pick me up, but I couldn't get close to the leaders. The Fox Hunters' is run over two miles and five furlongs, so the start is at the top of the home straight, not at the Grand National start. You jump the first two fences, the fences that are the second last and last fences in the Grand National, and then you are on to The Chair. The Chair is the third fence, you don't have much time to warm up.

So I'm gunning Tuska Ridge down over the first two fences and on to The Chair. He's okay at The Chair, he slows a little going into the fence, but he jumps it okay among horses. Then he slows a bit going into the water jump too, and around the bend that takes you away from the stands. I'm flat to the boards, but I can't get close to the leaders, I'm buried in the middle of them and I'm thinking, there's no way the television cameras will be able to pick me up!

We come to the junction of the courses, where you would turn left if you were on the Mildmay course, but you go straight to take in the line of fences that lead you all the way up to Becher's Brook. Two loose horses at the head of the field decide to turn left and follow the Mildmay course, and they take some of the leaders a bit to their left. For a second it looks like they might be carried out onto the wrong course, but the riders manage to get back inside the loose horses, and get back on the track. They lose a bit of ground though and they lose momentum, so I take the opportunity, I give Tuska Ridge a squeeze and he goes forward and, for a few strides, were are in front! That only lasts for a while though, maybe for a hundred yards, from the Melling Road until the approach to the first fence on the second circuit. Tuska Ridge slowed again going into the fence, and we're buried in mid-division again.

How did that end? We fell at Becher's Brook, but it was a soft enough fall and I was able to get up and catch him before he was able to run away again. So I remounted. I figured, why not? He seemed fine, and I was thinking I would never get the chance to ride over the big Grand National fences again. We went on to Foinavon, the next fence, and he refused. He just didn't enjoy the spruce fences at all.

I rode Tuska Ridge again in a hunters' chase at Fakenham two weeks later. Ralph Smith asked me if I would come over again to ride him, and to ride two other horses for him on the day. It was all a little surreal, me going to Fakenham back then for the day. I was booked for another horse too, a horse for Lisa Williamson called How Ran On. I didn't know I was booked for the ride until I arrived at the track in the morning. He raced in the colours of Halewood International, who would own the 2004 Grand National winner Amberleigh House. How Ran On didn't trouble the judge.

Looking back on it now, it almost feels like that day wasn't real, like it could have been a dream, but it was real all right. Tuska Ridge slowed going into the first fence and unseated me. I never rode Tuska Ridge again. But the two other horses, Ralph Smith's two other horses, I won on both of them on the day. I rode Kingsdown Trix to win a handicap hurdle and I rode a horse called Dick The Taxi in the novices' handicap hurdle, and he won easily.

* * *

I had never ridden Timbera before the 2002 Cheltenham Festival. I knew the horse all right, Dessie Hughes trained him, he had won his last four races before the 2002 Cheltenham Festival, four handicap chases, the last three at Fairyhouse, ridden by the late and much lamented Kieran Kelly in all three. But he was going for the National Hunt Chase at the Cheltenham Festival, and the National Hunt Chase is a race for amateur riders, so Kieran couldn't ride him in it.

Timbera was owned by a fellow called Ted Breen, and my good friend Martin Ferris's sister worked in Ted Breen's office. So maybe that's where the owner got the idea into his head that he wanted me to ride his horse in the National Hunt Chase.

I wouldn't have had a ride lined up in the race at the time. There weren't that many Irish-trained horses in the race back then, and the trainers who had runners, they had their own amateurs. Alan Crowe was riding a horse for Christy Roche, Tony Martin was riding Oa Baldixe for Noel Meade. And some of the other top Irish amateurs had been snapped up by British trainers, Philip Fenton was riding for Richard Rowe, Tom Lombard was riding for Jonjo O'Neill. John Thomas McNamara was also riding a horse for Jonjo O'Neill, Rith Dubh, owned by J.P. McManus.

Timbera was a little keen for me early on, but I just tried to get him switched off and travelling, along the inside. He was a bit to his right over the first fence, but he was better over the second and third, he jumped his way to be just behind the leaders before we turned at the top of the track. After that, it was just a case of getting him into a rhythm in that position, getting him jumping, conserving energy.

He was out to his right at a few of his fences, and when he went to his right over the third last, I could feel another horse coming up on my inside. I was happy enough though, I didn't want to ask Timbera for his effort until as late as possible. I was all the while trying to slow him down, and it's not very easy, slowing down a slow horse. He was out to his right a little over the second last too and, as we headed to the home turn, I could see that it was John Thomas on my inside on Rith Dubh.

He was travelling well, but we were travelling well too. It was probably a strange sight in a four-mile chase, the two of us going down to the final fence, both of us holding on to our horses. Neither of us really wanted to be in front.

I saw a stride at the last and asked Timbera up. He pricked his ears and pinged the fence. Then I asked him to go on, but he kept his head up in the air. John Thomas was still swinging away on Rith Dubh beside me, but I knew that Rith Dubh didn't find much when he hit the front either, so I kept pushing and cajoling. Eventually, John Thomas went for Rith Dubh but, sure enough, he didn't find much.

The two of us then, pushing and coaxing the two horses, asking and cajoling, through the final 100 yards up to the winning line. Rith Dubh hit the front, Timbera fought back. But Timbera was happy just to stay about a head behind the other horse. If we had gone around for another circuit, I'd say he would have stayed a head behind him. It was a fascinating race to watch I'm sure, and it was a great ride by John Thomas, to cajole his horse to victory like that, but I was gutted. I was thinking, that's it now, my chance of riding a Cheltenham Festival winner, gone. I might not get another one.

Over a year later, Dessie asked me if I would ride Timbera in the Irish Grand National. Timbera hadn't won since the 2002 National Hunt Chase, but he hadn't run badly in a handicap chase at Cork on his final run before the Irish National, and he was down to a handicap rating of 130, 6lb lower than he was when he fell at the second last fence in the Irish National the previous year.

He was definitely going there with a chance, I could see that, but I was riding for Ferdy Murphy at the time in Britain, and Ferdy wouldn't let me go. Easter Monday, busy day, he needed me in Britain.

Timbera won the Irish National that year, with Jim Culloty on board. I didn't know then of course that Jim Culloty would provide me with my Cheltenham Gold Cup winner but, even if I had known, I probably still would have been gutted. I remember calling Ferdy.

'That horse won the Irish National,' I said.

'Well,' he said, 'wasn't it nice to have been asked to ride him?'

Dessie Hughes was always really good to me. I remember ringing him from Cork Airport one day when I was on my way back to England. I was coming towards the end of my time in England, and I was looking for a way out.

I just wasn't settling. I know that the over-and-back to Ireland wasn't helping, I wasn't giving myself a chance to settle, but I was enjoying coming back to Ireland so much, I was riding plenty of winners when I was coming back, it was getting more and more difficult to go back to England. I never really thought about staying for the long term. My mind just wasn't there. For example, I don't remember ever thinking I should look into buying a house in England.

I called Dessie from a pay phone in the airport in Cork, and I asked him if he would give me a job. Just a job, riding out or something. I had lots of contacts in Ireland, I was getting plenty of rides, I wasn't looking to replace Dessie's stable jockey, the late Kieran Kelly, or anything like that. I just wanted a base, a reason to come back to Ireland.

Dessie told me that I should stay in England, that I should stick it out a little longer. He was right, he could see the bigger picture, the opportunity I had at Ferdy's. Dessie was such a wise and thoughtful and generous man. He could see what was best for me at the time, he could see that the job I had in England was better than any job I could have got at the time in Ireland.

I went back to England then, I got on the plane in Cork. I rode a double for Ferdy the following day.

* * *

It wasn't easy keeping everyone happy, but I tried very hard to, and I found that, if you were straight up with people, if you were honest with them, they'd respect you for it and you wouldn't fall out with them. For the most part anyway.

I was riding at Clonmel one Sunday, in October 2001, but I was set to go and ride a horse for Pat Doyle in the bumper at Naas, the last race on the card, a newcomer by Accordion named Friend's Amigo. I didn't think that the race in Clonmel would divide, but it did, which was a disaster for me, it meant that the second division was a half an hour later than I thought it would be. I had to leave Clonmel after the first division if I was going to make it to Naas in time for the bumper, so it meant I couldn't take my last ride. That was on a horse for Aidan Kennedy, who was training him for an English owner, Bob Bishop.

That wasn't ideal, I hated letting people down and I hated missing rides, especially on young horses who had the potential to be very good. Aidan was great about it though, and so was Bob Bishop, even though he had flown over from England to see his horse run at Clonmel. I obviously didn't know it at the time, but this was Bob Bishop who, with his wife Jean, would own Cue Card, winner of nine Grade 1 races, including the Champion Bumper at Cheltenham and the Ryanair Chase and the Ascot Chase and the King George. The Bishops had some lovely horses, Mount Oscar and Theatre Guide and Royal Vacation as well as Cue Card.

I rode another horse that Aidan Kennedy trained for them, Tacin, in a point-to-point at Kildorrery in February 2002, and I rode him in his first race under Rules, in a novices' hurdle at Kempton the following January when he was trained by Brendan Powell. We finished a close-up third behind Fork Lightning, a subsequent Cheltenham Festival winner.

Bob was a lovely man. He passed away a couple of days after Cue Card won the King George in 2015.

Anyway, back at Clonmel, I felt desperate, but I went out and met Bob and told him I had to go to Naas. He completely understood.

'If we run him at Bruff next week instead,' he asked me, 'will you be able to ride him there?'

'I will,' I said. 'One hundred per cent.'

'That's what we'll do then,' said Bob.

He was so sound about it.

'And this horse at Naas,' he said. 'Should I back him?'

'You could have a few quid on him if you wanted,' I said. 'We really like him.'

Friend's Amigo won the bumper at Naas.

Chapter 7

I was driving into Boulta as Tom O'Mahony was driving out. He rolled down his window.

'I need to have a chat with you,' he said.

I had a bit of an inkling what it might be about. Tom had been instrumental in Adrian Maguire's move to Britain. Adrian was a top-class jockey, he was a top-class amateur in Ireland before he moved to Britain, he won the Kim Muir at the 1991 Cheltenham Festival on Omerta for Martin Pipe, and he won the Irish National the following month on the same horse, beat Charlie Swan and Cahervillahow in a driving finish, the pair of them miles clear of the rest.

Adrian won the Cheltenham Gold Cup on Cool Ground for Toby Balding in 1992, soon after he moved to England, and he formed a great relationship with David Nicholson through the years, he rode some of the best National Hunt horses of that era, Viking Flagship and Barton Bank and Mysilv. He had been riding for Ferdy Murphy for the last couple of seasons. He had ridden Sibton Abbey for Ferdy to win the Hennessy Gold Cup back in 1992, just getting home from the Gold Cup winner Jodami, but, more recently, he had won the 2000 Scottish National on Paris Pike for Ferdy, and the Maghull Chase at Aintree's Grand National meeting in 2001 on Ballinclay King.

MY AUTOBIOGRAPHY

But Adrian had had a really bad fall at Warwick the previous March. He had tried to come back but, in the end, he had to admit defeat. In the autumn of 2002, he had just announced his retirement from the saddle. I was thinking that Tom's wanting-to-see-me was to do with that.

I didn't think too deeply about it though. This was early November 2002, the new point-to-point season was just getting going. It was a Wednesday, I was riding at Boulta at the weekend, and I wanted to go up and walk the track beforehand. Boulta was always a good schooling ground, but holding point-to-points there was new.

Tom rang me then on the Thursday to ask if I could go to the Silver Springs Hotel on Friday. He said it might be a good idea to take my dad with me.

So I went up to the Silver Springs Hotel with Dad, and it was as I suspected. Tom was there and Ferdy Murphy was there. Ferdy was a great trainer and a great man. He rode for Paddy Mullins and he was private trainer for Bill Durkan, he was there when Anaglog's Daughter won the Arkle at Cheltenham in 1980, before he moved to Britain and took on the same role as private trainer for Geoff Hubbard. He took out his own licence and he trained Sibton Abbey to win the Hennessy Gold Cup, driven to victory by Adrian. He won the Triumph Hurdle in 1996 with Paddy's Return, who also won the Champion Stayers' Hurdle at Punchestown and the Long Walk Hurdle at Ascot, and he won the Sun Alliance Hurdle in 1998 with French Holly, as well as the 2000 Scottish National with Paris Pike and the 2001 Maghull Chase with Ballinclay King.

Ferdy didn't say much. He just said to me, it's there for you, the job as my stable jockey. They're all there for you, all the horses, every horse is yours to ride.

Ferdy had some lovely horses at the time. Ballinclay King and Historg and Tribal Venture and Inn Antique and Coole Spirit. And, of course, Truckers Tavern. And they were all there for me.

I was going to have to turn professional if I was going to take the job, and that was obviously going to be a big step. It was a big decision: to turn professional or to remain as an amateur. As an amateur, you can ride in point-to-points, you can ride in bumpers, you can ride in all those amateur races. You're riding against amateurs, you're consistently one of the best riders in the field and, consequently, you are in demand. But you're not riding every day. To go professional, it's a whole new level. You're competing against the best. I always thought I wouldn't turn professional unless I had a hundred horses to ride.

I loved my life at the time, I loved tipping around and doing a bit of everything, and I loved riding in point-to-points. I loved riding good horses and I loved riding lots of winners. But you couldn't ride every day as an amateur. Point-to-points were only on essentially at weekends, and amateurs can only ride in 21 professionals' races on the track every year. If I could have ridden every day as an amateur, I wouldn't have even considered turning professional.

Some lads told me not to turn. You're a big fish in a small pond, they said. It'll be a different story if you turn professional. But others thought I was good enough. Liam Cashman used to always tell me I was wasting my time as an amateur, that I should have turned professional ages ago. John Queally was the same. It was nice that they thought I was good enough to go professional. I remember going up to Ted Walsh's house and asking him what he thought, and he gave me the last piece of confidence that I needed in order to turn professional.

I was a good amateur, I knew that, but I would have been a very ordinary professional if I had remained at the same level of performance, if I hadn't improved. It's a much higher standard of riding. You're going from the point-to-point fields, from competing against fellow amateurs, to taking on Ruby Walsh and Barry Geraghty and Paul Carberry and A.P. McCoy. It's like any sport, rugby, golf, tennis: an amateur taking on a professional.

I was going to have to improve, I knew that. I wasn't very good with my whip in my left hand, for starters. I could use it all right, and I could make it look like I could use it, but I knew I wasn't as effective with my whip in my left hand as I was with my whip in my right hand. I knew I needed to work on that. And on everything else. I was just going to have to be sharper and cleverer and stronger and faster.

I just thanked Ferdy, and we said good luck. That was it. There were no arrangements, no plan about when I would move to England or how that would happen, or what I needed to do in the meantime. I didn't put much thought into it. I never put much thought into anything in those days. Not really. I kind of thought that, any time I did put a lot of thought into something, I got it wrong. Same when I was riding in a race, I was better doing what felt natural, doing what I was doing by instinct, instead of having lots of time to think about what to do.

I rode at Boulta that Sunday. I had a fall off a horse in the five-year-olds' maiden and I broke my nose. My last ride in a point-to-point, I fell and broke my nose.

I didn't know it was my last ride though. Not really. As I say, I didn't put much thought into these things. I had never had any great longing to turn professional. I was just tipping away, living my best life, riding lots of good horses for good people, in demand, doing well, having the craic. I did know though, in the back of my mind, that if I was ever going to turn professional, I'd have to be going into a setup that had a hundred horses or more for me to ride. Martin Pipe had lots of horses. Philip Hobbs probably had 200. Ferdy Murphy had 150 or so. It would have to be to go to a trainer like that. There weren't many of those types of trainers around, but Ferdy was definitely one of them.

I called a few lads, just to ask them what they thought. I'm not sure why I called them really. My mind was made up. I was going.

The minute Ferdy said it to me in the Silver Springs, the horses are there for you, they're all yours to ride, I was on my way. It was probably out of courtesy that I called them. One or two said, are you mad? But most of them said, you'd be mad not to.

The following week, I was up at the sales in Fairyhouse. I loved going to the sales. I've always loved going to the sales. You go to the sales, and everybody is there together, at the same level. You go to the races, you're on one side of the rail. At the sales, they're all there, jockeys in their civvies, trainers, owners, John Magnier there in jeans and a jumper. David Nicholson, Jenny Pitman, all the top British trainers. I have always felt very comfortable at the sales.

My phone rang. Ferdy.

'You need to be in here tomorrow morning,' he said. 'Truckers Tavern's owner Ray Scholey is coming in to watch him work, and I need you to be on him.'

I didn't have anything sorted. I didn't have a flight booked, I didn't have a bag packed. I didn't even have a passport! I took out whatever gear I had in the back of my car, put it into a bag and got a taxi to Dunshaughlin village. I got two passport photos taken there, and I went to the Garda station in the village to get them stamped, then I went to the airport.

I went up to the Ryanair desk in the airport, I gave them my photos, stamped by the Gardaí in Dunshaughlin, and I showed them the article in the *Racing Post* about me turning professional.

'That's me,' I told the girl. 'I have to go there now. I'm starting a new job tomorrow. I need to get on a flight this afternoon.'

So I arrived at Ferdy's in the clothes I was wearing and a small bag on my back. Ferdy's son Paul was great to me then. He was an absolute gent, he looked after me so well. Not only did I stay with him, but I remember him taking me to an outlet store to buy some clothes.

I was straight into it from the start, no honeymoon period, flat out from the moment I got there. It was a serious outfit though. Fantastic.

All these horses, good horses, all for me to ride. Horse after horse, keep them coming, working and schooling, hurdles and fences, up the gallop on one of them, up to the top and back around again.

Next.

Everyone at Ferdy's was so nice to me. All the lads and all the girls. And the facilities were top class. Horses everywhere, lorries, cars, tractors, tack rooms, the best of everything. A cook there in the morning to make the breakfast.

The first mistake I made was thinking I was going to be a bit of a jockey. I thought maybe I'd be in the yard two mornings a week, have a sit on one or two, ride a couple of bits of work, do some schooling, go racing in the afternoon. But no. I didn't realise how hard it was going to be. Ferdy used to use the main gallops in Middleham, so you'd have to ride to the gallops, down through the village, turn right, around a couple of S-bends and up to the gallop. It was a long way to the gallop, it was hard work riding out there, and I was wasting at the time, trying to keep my weight down, trying to be as light as I could be. I wouldn't have been much craic now.

Ferdy would always be telling me too, don't worry about your weight, don't be wasting, ride what you can ride, but I wanted to ride everything obviously, I was afraid someone would get in and start taking rides from me. In order to ride everything though, I needed to be as light as I could be, far lighter than my natural weight.

Start at six o'clock in the morning, every morning. Work, work, work. Go all day long. I'd say Ferdy never slept, he was on the go all the time and he wanted you to be there, going along with him. I was happy to do that though, I enjoyed it, I enjoyed working with Ferdy and being with Ferdy, and I enjoyed riding good horses.

Truckers Tavern was a good horse, he was a pure tank of a horse and he was a bit ignorant. He wasn't brilliant to jump, he'd prefer to be bulling his way through a fence than to be jumping out over it. And he always had to lead the string, we'd be up there in front of everything else. The gallop was a U-shape, up the High Moor, they used to call it. Down and around, swoop around the bend, then back up the straight and back home again. It was hard work for the horses too, they'd be wrecked tired coming home.

And they were plagued by this grouse. The grouse used to get up from the grass and go in front of the horses, fly along beside the horses, then cut in in front of them. It was all like a game to the grouse, flying in and about among the horses, low to the ground, just above the horses' knees, weaving around the moving slalom course. Horses would be stopping and spooking, one horse would stop and another horse would run into the back of him. Carnage. Riders dropped and horses running loose all over the place.

The trainers had meetings and everything about this grouse, what they were going to do about it. There was a bad accident waiting to happen. A horse or a rider was going to get seriously injured or worse, everyone was agreed. There was a suggestion that they should just shoot the grouse, but they decided they couldn't do that, the rules wouldn't allow it, it wasn't the season or something. They came up with no solution, so the grouse was left to its own devices, left alone to continue to terrorise us all with impunity.

Until one morning, shortly after that meeting, I'm cantering along on Truckers Tavern on the gallop, up the High Moor, up there in front of all the other horses, the usual, and he's fast asleep underneath me. We're just loping along, I could have fallen asleep myself on his back. Next thing, the grouse gets up, and we hear the shouts from behind us.

'Aye aye, watch your back! Hold your neck strap!'

All that kind of thing.

So the grouse comes up alongside us. I'm not even sure if your man notices it, he's still asleep underneath me, just loping along. Even so, I'm paying attention, you never knew what he'd do.

I see the grouse flying along beside us, just out of reach, just above the ground. Then, suddenly, it cuts across in front of us, low to the ground, very close to Truckers Tavern's knees. I'm bracing myself for what might happen, I'm alert, I'm ready for anything when, suddenly, thump! No more grouse. Sweet as a nut, your man had timed his stride so that his near fore came down on top of the grouse. Feathers everywhere. He hardly broke stride.

Grouse problem solved, and Truckers Tavern was a bit of a hero.

It was cold up there though. Fuck, it was cold. And the snow. Two feet of snow. I'm not saying two feet now and meaning a foot and a half. It was two full feet of snow. And still we rode out in it. Up the moor, across the moor, across the grass, just a blanket of white. You wouldn't have a clue where you were going. We'd put down markers, but still it was difficult to tell where you were. Ferdy said the ground was safe, that it wouldn't be frozen because of the snow, it was only the snow lying on top of it. We worked anyway. We always worked.

Ferdy had warned me, one of the only pieces of advice he gave me in the Silver Springs when I had met him first was, buy thermals. Be sure to get good thermals and be sure to wear them when you ride out. Sure I didn't have time to buy thermals as it turned out. Or gloves. Or a toothbrush. I did well to have a pair of boxer shorts with me.

It was a steep learning curve, but I learned lots and I learned quickly. Ferdy was brilliant at teaching me. It was all new to me, not only riding in Britain, but also riding as a professional, riding in races on the track. I was used to point-to-points and bumpers and the odd handicap chase or handicap hurdle on the track, but I didn't really know about handicap ratings or bands or British form or two-mile pace versus three-mile pace. And I didn't know the subtleties of the tracks, the different tracks, soft ground at Haydock versus good ground at Cartmel. Where you could make ground and where you needed to sit still. It was all new to me. I knew how to ride, and that was it, and I knew how to ride over three miles, in point-to-points. Riding over two miles over hurdles was new. Different pace, things happened more quickly.

I had to ride for the first few weeks under my Irish amateur licence. They wouldn't give me a professional's licence in Britain because of my broken nose, for some reason. I didn't care. I just wanted to ride. I rode my first winner for Ferdy at Sedgefield on 12 November 2002, Inn Antique in a Class D novices' hurdle. Inn Antique had been with Paul Nicholls, he had won a novices' chase and a novices' hurdle for Paul, and he was having his first run for Ferdy that day. He won easily, I just had to steer him around, but it was good to get my first winner on the board.

The lads in the weigh room at the races wouldn't give you much leeway though. I remember going to Hereford shortly after I got there and riding a horse for Ferdy in a maiden hurdle. I went to the front at the third last flight and I ended up getting beaten. That was far enough from the winning line at Hereford, it was far enough out, I had probably gone on too early, I probably should have waited a little longer but, at the time, sharp track, given the information that I had at the time, I thought it was the right thing to do.

When you get beaten, you can always look back on the race and say, if I had done this or if I hadn't done that, I might have won.

But I didn't get much sympathy from the lads in the weigh room. Look at this guy now, the new young fellow over from Ireland, thinks he's cock-a-hoop, coming over to ride all Ferdy Murphy's horses. This amateur. I was watching a replay of the race in the weigh room, a couple of jockeys were gathered around the screen watching it. As I went for home on the replay, I remember Jimmy McCarthy laughing out loud, and shouting so I could hear:

'Did they move the winning post?'

I thought I had to adapt to the way British races were run. They always went faster from the start in Britain than they did in Ireland,

and they always went for home earlier. They went nearly flat out the whole way. I'm not sure why that was, maybe it was because the ground was usually better in Britain than it was in Ireland but, mainly, it was just the culture of the way racing was run. I thought I needed to be up there prominent with them but, actually, that was completely at odds with how I usually rode. I was always a patient rider, even when I was starting off in point-to-points. I always liked to get horses settled, let them get into their rhythm, take my time on them, have them finishing off their races. And that used to get me into trouble. People would think I wasn't trying on a horse, but I promise, I tried my best on every single horse I ever rode in my life.

Sometimes I got it wrong of course. I got it wrong lots. And when you get it wrong riding patiently like that, people can get upset. It can look bad. Strangely, if you go too early and get caught, you don't get much grief. But if you leave it too late and don't get there, you can get hauled over the coals. It makes no sense. The quickest way to get a horse beat is to ask him for his effort too early.

Some people loved the way I rode though. That's why I loved riding for people like Pat Fahy, John Kiely, Charles Byrnes, Arthur Moore. Take your time, allow him to get into his rhythm. That's why I loved riding at Cheltenham. They always went fast at Cheltenham and you could take your time, ride your race.

A horse will often go through a flat patch, about three-quarters of the way through a race. You can feel him tiring underneath you, your instinct might be to ask him for his effort then, keep him in the race. But if you don't ask him for his effort then, allow him go through his flat spot, then ask him for his effort on the far side of that flat spot, after he has got his second wind, then you can get your horse to finish off his race. I got lots of horses to finish in the places by doing that, second or third or fourth, allowing others go for home while I sat, allowed my horse to fill himself up again before asking him for his effort. Then he'd be finishing off his race, enjoying the experience more, picking up some prize money, sometimes all the prize money.

We got going early with Ferdy. I managed to win on some of those good horses, Inn Antique and Tribal Venture and Coole Spirit and Historg and Luzcadou. I won a good handicap chase at Cheltenham on New Year's Day on Ballinclay King. I rode The Quads for the first time in the Cross-Country Chase at Cheltenham's December meeting in 2002, and we won. I got a kick out of that. It wasn't the festival, but still, to ride a winner at Cheltenham was special, my first winner at Cheltenham, and I loved riding over the cross-country fences.

The Quads had actually been with Arthur Moore in Ireland before he joined Ferdy. He won a few good handicap hurdles for Arthur and he won a listed chase at Leopardstown, and he finished second to Bob Treacy in the Thyestes Chase in 1999. He was a small little horse and he wasn't a great jumper, but he was obviously well suited to the cross-country track at Cheltenham. I actually got a fall off him at Kelso that year, 2003, between Cheltenham and Aintree, he unseated me at the first fence in a handicap chase there and I broke my shoulder. I had to get an injection in my shoulder before I went out to ride Ballinclay King in the Grand National that year, my first ride in the Grand National.

Truckers Tavern was an important horse for Ferdy that season. He was a really good novice chaser the previous season, he had come over to Leopardstown for the Grade 1 Dr P.J. Moriarty Chase the previous February, when he had finished second to Harbour Pilot, then he had gone on to Cheltenham and finished fourth behind Moscow Flyer in the Arkle. The distance of the Arkle, two miles, was always going to be too short for him though, he was always a staying chaser in the making. From the time I met him in the Silver Springs, Ferdy was telling me that Truckers Tavern was a Gold Cup horse.

He always gave me a lovely feel at home. He wasn't a very fast horse, he was a stayer in the making, but he still felt like a good horse. I didn't have to wait long before I rode him in a race, we went to Kelso in Scotland in early December and finished third in a handicap chase. It was a lovely run though, he made a mistake at the second last fence, but he kept on well. We knew he would improve a lot for the run.

We fancied him to run well next time, in the Silver Cup at Ascot just before Christmas. We couldn't see him getting beaten actually, but it's jumps racing, and he was beaten. He went down to the first fence, got it all wrong and came down. That was fairly gutting.

He went down to Yogi Breisner's after that. Yogi was always brilliant when it came to sorting out a horse's jumping, or a jockey's riding over a jump. I had learned lots when I went to him after I won that scholarship to go to him and to Nicky Henderson's when I tied the novice riders' championship with Simon McGonagle. He was great for me, and he was great for Truckers Tavern because, when I rode him next time in the Peter Marsh Chase at Haydock in January, his jumping was much better.

We fancied Truckers Tavern going to Haydock too, as long as he jumped, and he did. It was a good old battle between us and Russ Garrity on Hussard Collonges, who had won the Sun Alliance Chase at Cheltenham the previous March, but Truckers Tavern was brave, he forged ahead on the run-in and we went away to win by over two and a half lengths.

That was massive for me, a big win on a good horse, in a high-profile race, a Peter Marsh Chase, my first big win as a professional, my first big winner for Ferdy. And Truckers Tavern was a big horse, a high-profile horse. It was important that I could prove I was able to ride good horses in good races.

He proved that day that he was, as Ferdy had always maintained, a potential Gold Cup horse.

We went to Newbury after that for the Aon Chase in February, and he finished third behind Valley Henry. We weren't too disappointed by that, Ferdy had let him down a little after the Peter Marsh, so he could build him up again for Cheltenham. The Newbury run was a run that would bring him forward again with a view to having him at concert pitch for the Gold Cup.

Everything went well during the lead-up to the Gold Cup. His work was really good, his final piece of work was great, and we went to Cheltenham thinking we had a real chance of winning. He was a 33/1 shot, but we thought we had a much better chance than that.

To be a part of it though, that was massive for me. The Cheltenham Festival. To be walking out into the parade ring at Cheltenham, I felt like I had arrived. Best Mate was just behind me, they applauded him as he came out and, I'll never forget it, I got a shiver down my spine. To be standing in Cheltenham's parade ring before the Gold Cup then, waiting to be legged up.

Best Mate was not the triple Gold Cup hero that he became, but he was still the previous year's winner, the warm favourite, he was the one we all had to beat. Beef Or Salmon was over from Ireland, Michael Hourigan's horse. He was second favourite behind Best Mate. He had become the horse I thought he might become when I rode him in the Land Rover Bumper. He was after winning the Ericsson Chase and the Hennessy Gold Cup, the two big staying chases in Ireland, Grade 1 races, and he was still a novice. Harbour Pilot was there, Valley Henry was there.

I was there though, and that was the stuff of dreams. I was 23, and riding a horse in the Gold Cup. Ferdy was brilliant with me beforehand, he took all the pressure off me.

'This is just another race,' he said to me in the parade ring. 'This is just like a point-to-point at Dromahane. You know how to ride in a point-to-point at Dromahane, right?'

I nodded.

'Ride this one as if you are riding at Dromahane.'

So that's what I did. I settled Truckers Tavern at the back of the field, got him travelling, got him jumping. Beef Or Salmon fell at the third fence, the first fence down the back straight, just to our outside, but that didn't faze Truckers Tavern. We were well back in the field, nearly last, and I had to give him a bit of a squeeze going past the stands with a circuit to run, but I knew he would keep going.

I was just behind Jim Culloty on Best Mate on the run down the back straight. He was travelling really well. Others were coming under a ride around me, we were making ground and I knew we were still going okay. We moved into fifth place on the run to the fourth last fence, we moved into fourth on the run down the hill.

We got in tight to the third last fence, the last fence before the home turn, and that took a bit out of him. I could see Best Mate still travelling up ahead, but Chives and Valley Henry were in front of me, and I thought I could beat them. Chives had been up there with the leaders for a long time, and Valley Henry wasn't the strongest stayer.

The three of them were well ahead of me rounding the home turn, but Truckers Tavern wasn't weakening. By the time we got to the second last fence, Best Mate had gone clear, but I had closed on the other two. We got past Chives before we got to the final fence, and we passed Valley Henry in the air over it. Then Truckers Tavern kept on all the way up the hill to the winning line. We were well behind Best Mate, but we had a nice break on the rest of them. Second in the Gold Cup. Runner-up in the Cheltenham Gold Cup. Magic.

Chapter 8

Ferdy was adamant that I needed to take my breaks. Work hard all day, every day, Monday to Saturday, then no racing in Britain on Sunday, take a break.

Re-charge.

I did that for a few weeks. Flat out for six days, then rest. I tried to do the Sunday English thing: go to the pub in the afternoon, Sunday lunch. Nah. It wasn't for me.

As I said, I had no interest in drinking. And I had no interest in resting. I wanted to be doing, I just wanted to be riding.

'You need your rest,' Ferdy would tell me. 'You won't last if you don't take your rest.'

I couldn't see it. I was young and full of energy and full of drive, and I couldn't see the need to be sitting in a pub on a Sunday afternoon. All I could see was racing going on in Ireland, races being contested and races being won by horses I could have been riding.

I didn't plan to go back to Ireland every Sunday, it just kind of evolved like that, like a lot of things in my life in those days.

I asked Andrew 'Frostie' Kelly if he would act as my agent. I obviously didn't have an agent when I was an amateur but, now that I was turning professional, it made sense that I had someone booking rides for me in Ireland, even though I was based in England. It made sense to me at the time anyway!

I only ever had two agents in my career, and they were both brilliant. When Frostie retired, I asked Kevin O'Ryan if he would do the job for me, and he was happy to. Kevin was great too, he is mainly a flat agent, but he was happy to take me on. He took Jack Kennedy on later too. We were the only two National Hunt jockeys he had on his books.

I started out riding for the trainers I used to ride for in point-to-points, when they had runners on track on Sunday. I just asked Frostie to keep an eye out for me. Frostie was brilliant. He would ring me:

'There are two horses there at Mallow on Sunday that you could ride. Will I put you down for them?'

I'd go back for them, and then there'd be two more at Limerick the following Sunday, three more at Navan the Sunday after that. A couple of them would win, and then you'd be in fellows' minds, and they'd be on to Frostie again, wanting you riding for them.

So I started going back to Ireland on Sundays more and more. I would get a flight back on Saturday evening, ride on the Sunday in Ireland, and go back to Britain on the Sunday evening or the Monday morning. I'd ring Frostie on the Thursday or on the Friday: what's there on Sunday?

I wanted to ride in every race when I was there. I'd have three rides at Mallow, and I'd be on to Frostie: why am I not riding in the beginners' chase? Paul Murphy, Ferdy's son, was great to me then too. Paul and his girlfriend. I'd get back to the house after racing on Saturday at six o'clock say, my flight from Leeds/Bradford would be at nine, and they'd go out of their way to get me there on time.

I rode for lots of good trainers on those Sundays, Noel Meade and Willie Mullins and Robert Tyner and Edward O'Grady and Paddy Mullins. I remember going back during the week one week, shortly after I had arrived in Ferdy's, to ride a horse for Paddy Mullins in the Clonmel Oil Chase in November 2002, Cregg House. Paddy Mullins was an unbelievable trainer, he was a genius with horses, quiet, understated. I remember his instructions to me that day: the longer you can convince him he's not in a race, the better you will do.

Cregg House ran a cracking race, we finished third behind Beef Or Salmon and Sackville.

Over two years later, when he was trained by Shane Donohoe, I ended up riding Cregg House in the Topham Chase at Aintree, over the big Grand National fences. He was a 10-year-old then, but he retained lots of ability.

I didn't get the ride until late. The Topham was on Friday, I was after riding out in Edward O'Grady's on the Thursday morning, the 2005 Aintree Grand National meeting was starting that afternoon. I only had one ride at the meeting, Arctic Copper for Noel Meade in the Grand National itself on Saturday, and I was so looking forward to it, my third ride in the National after Ballinclay King and Takagi. But I was set to finish up in O'Grady's and go home to watch Aintree on television when Shane Donohoe called to ask me if I would ride Cregg House on the following day. He said he'd give me a great spin. He had a light weight, he knew I might struggle to do the weight, but he said he didn't mind if I put up a pound or two overweight.

I remember, it was a bit of a scramble, getting flights organised and getting myself to the airport, but I got it sorted all right, I got a flight out that evening and I was in Aintree on Friday morning.

Shane was right, Cregg House gave me some spin. I got down to 10st 5lb to ride him, I put up just 1lb overweight. He was a 50/1 shot, but he really took to the big fences, and we ended up winning the race, staying on up the run-in to get the better of a horse named Haut De Gamme, who was trained by Ferdy!

It's stranger than fiction sometimes this game. I obviously wasn't still riding for Ferdy then, I was back in Ireland, but Ferdy was the first man over to me in the winner's enclosure at Aintree to congratulate me. That was a measure of the man Ferdy was.

That was a memorable Aintree for me. Arctic Copper was a 200/1 shot in the Grand National on the Saturday. He had very little chance. Paul Carberry had actually got off him to ride a horse for Paul Nolan, who had a chance, Colonel Rayburn. I didn't care, I was just delighted to be riding in the Grand National.

My instructions were simple: just get him to complete. Whatever you do, just get him around.

I lined up towards the inside and we set off in mid-division. He made a bit of a mistake at the third fence, the big ditch, but apart from that, his jumping over the big fences was very good. He was struggling to go the pace though, he started to drift back in the field over Becher's first time, and over Foinavon and around over the Canal Turn.

There were about 25 horses in front of us, and there weren't many behind us when we jumped The Chair and the water jump and raced away from the stands with a circuit to go, but we were still travelling okay. We lost more ground on the field over the five fences that take you back up to Becher's. That was the year the two loose horses carried A.P. McCoy and Clan Royal out at Becher's Brook but we were so far behind them it didn't really affect us. In fact, the loose horses had turned around and were having another go at jumping Becher's Brook when we got to the fence. Arctic Copper maintained his concentration and got over the fence all right.

The leaders were getting further and further away from us as we raced up the side of the track, back towards the grandstands. Paul Carberry pulled up Colonel Rayburn at the fourth last or fifth last fence, and I shouted over to him: 'I've got further than you!'

I was miles behind, but Arctic Copper was still plodding away. Tom Greenall pulled Glenelly Gale up at the third last fence, but I kept going. I was thinking of Noel's instructions, and also of the fact that I hadn't completed the Grand National course before, and Arctic Copper seemed happy to go along with it, in his own time, at his own pace.

Up ahead, Hedgehunter and Ruby Walsh were going for home, but I couldn't see them. Ruby could have been showered and changed and on his way to the airport by the time I got to the winning line. I just kept Arctic Copper going, over the second last, over the last, and up to the winning line. We got there all right, and we weren't last, we were 19th of 21 finishers. We were about a half a minute behind the winner though. I just about got to the pull-up in time to shake hands with Ruby before he started to head back in to the winner's enclosure.

There isn't a 19th-place-finisher enclosure, I just went back to where all the other beaten horses were unsaddling but, when I got there, the reception I got from the owners, it was as if I had won the thing! Arctic Copper was owned by the Grand Alliance Racing Club, it was a club that was made up largely of a number of senators and TDs and government ministers from Ireland, from all different parties, hence the name, Grand Alliance. Lots of them had backed him to finish the race, which explained the riding instructions that Noel gave me, and the enthusiasm of the celebrations!

That was my third ride in the Grand National: Ballinclay King in 2003, Takagi in 2004, Arctic Copper in 2005. It was my first completion, but I wasn't really getting any closer to winning the race.

I rode Joes Edge in the race in 2006 for Ferdy. I wasn't with Ferdy by then, Keith Mercer was Ferdy's first rider at the time, but he was riding Ferdy's other horse in the race, Haut De Gamme, and Ferdy asked me if I would ride Joes Edge. Fair play to Ferdy,

I was delighted to ride Joes Edge, I was delighted to have a ride in the Grand National again. We finished seventh, we were a distance behind the winner Numbersixvalverde, Martin Brassil's horse, and Slippers Madden, but at least I completed again. And you never knew where these things were going to lead. This one led to a good place all right, because the next time I rode Joes Edge, I was riding him in the William Hill Chase at the 2007 Cheltenham Festival the following March, and we got up on the line to win by a short head.

I rode Livingstonebramble for Willie Mullins in the Grand National in 2007, he was the third best of three horses that Willie Mullins had in the race, after Hedgehunter and Homer Wells, and he unseated me at Becher's first time.

In 2008, I rode Chelsea Harbour in the Grand National. Chelsea Harbour was trained by Tom Mullins and owned by Paul Duffin. Tom was always a good trainer, son of Paddy and Maureen, brother of Willie and Tony. Nearly everything he ran would win at some point. They'd improve as they would gain experience and, in time, they would find their level and they would win races.

I used to ride all of Paul Duffin's horses when I could at the time. Paul was always a good fellow, and he was very good to me. He had some good horses through the years, Made In Taipan, Oscar Dan Dan. My dad owned a horse in partnership with Paul later on, Tavern Times, who I won a few races on, including a Grade 3 hurdle at Tipperary in October 2011.

Chelsea Harbour wasn't a bad horse, I had won the Grand National Trial at Punchestown that February on him, but he wasn't a great jumper. He was a little barrel of a horse who would bull his way through fences instead of jumping out over them. I remember, Robbie (Puppy) Power, who had won the Grand National the previous year on Silver Birch for Gordon Elliott, was riding a horse for Charlie Mann in the 2008 race, Nadover. I was sitting beside him in the weigh room. Puppy had ridden Chelsea Harbour a couple times before that, he had ridden him in the Thyestes Chase and in the Paddy Power Chase, when he fell at the first fence.

'What are you riding him for?' he said to me.

I just looked at him blankly.

'Are you fucking mad?' he said. 'You're going to get killed!'

'How am I?' I asked him.

'Sure he has no chance of getting around,' he said.

I just thought, let's see.

'I'll tell you what,' said Puppy. 'I'll give you a hundred euro for every fence you jump.'

'Fair enough,' I said. 'Fair play to you.'

We got around. Chelsea Harbour jumped to his left throughout, but he was safe and we got around. We actually led the field from the Canal Turn final time over the line of fences across the side of the track to the fourth last fence, when he started to tire. But we completed, we finished ninth, only 10 or 11 lengths behind Puppy on Nadover.

Puppy saw me as we pulled up, and he burst out laughing.

'You didn't complete, did you?!'

'I did,' I said.

'Oh no!'

He was a year too early. Chelsea Harbour fell at the third fence in the Grand National the following year.

He started counting his fingers and thinking. He looked at me.

'Here, how many fences are there in the Grand National again?' he asked.

'Thirty,' I said.

* * *

Lots of people were very good to me during my time flitting between Britain and Ireland. Jennifer Walsh, Ted's daughter, Ruby's sister, was exceptional. She used to pick me up from the airport on a Saturday evening, and I'd often stay in her house before going racing with her on the Sunday. Timmy Murphy was very friendly with Jennifer too at the time, he was just starting to rebuild his career after his time in prison (Timmy was a lovely rider and Beef Or Salmon was a key horse for him in getting his career back on track), he was staying with Jennifer at the time, and I got very friendly with Timmy. He'd be going down to Michael Hourigan's or he'd be going racing and we'd travel together.

I remember one day in Killarney, going back to my car with Timmy after racing. I was after getting a fall and I was a bit sore, and I was wasting and I was tired and I went to get my car keys, and I couldn't find them. Everything just seemed to get on top of me, and I burst into tears! And Timmy was like, ah here, I'm after spending three months in Wormwood Scrubs, living with real-life criminals, so you can fuck off now with your tears just because you can't find your car keys.

Then I ducked under the railing to go out to the car park, and there they were, my car keys, on the ground.

Or Brendan O'Rourke would pick me up. Or, depending on where racing was on Sunday, I could stay with Paul Carberry.

One day, I was on my way back to ride at Punchestown when my flight was delayed. It was going to be very tight whether or not I would make it for my first ride, and I didn't have a lift organised from the airport to the racecourse. The usual. I got chatting to the man who was sitting beside me on the plane though, a lovely man, and he said he'd bring me to Punchestown, which he did. Dropped me outside the gate. Turns out, he was the father of Paul McGinley, the golfer. I ended up riding a winner for him a few years later.

I was riding winners in Britain all right in the early part of the 2002/03 season, three in November, five in December 2002, nine in January. I had no winners in Britain in February 2003. I had three winners in Britain in March, and I had two in Ireland. I had two winners in Britain in April, and two in Ireland. Same in May and June, two in Britain and two in Ireland in May, three in Britain and three in Ireland in June.

Ferdy was quiet during the summer, so I was able to come back to Ireland, base myself in Ireland, and then go back to ride for Ferdy in Britain whenever he wanted me during summer. I rode good winners for lots of different trainers in Ireland during that time, George Stewart, Seamus Neville, Mark Loughnane, David Kiely, Lucy Normile and, of course, Pat Doyle.

The autumn rolled around, the new season started in Britain, and I went back to Ferdy. I have to say, it was tough going back. I was thinking, I'd want to be riding a lot of winners now here if I'm going to stay here. I did ride a good few winners that autumn, I rode 11 winners in Britain in November 2003, my best month since I went over there. But I was always coming back home to ride on Sundays, and I loved that. I loved coming back to Ireland when I could.

It was driving Ferdy mad.

'You need your rest,' he would say to me continually. 'You're not going to last if you never take a break.'

I didn't think about it too much at the time but, looking back, I suppose I never really settled in England. I never bought a car in England. About two months after I started with Ferdy, I came back to Ireland and got my old car and I drove that back over.

I was all the while looking back across the Irish Sea. I never really cut my ties in Ireland. I probably didn't want to. I had such good relationships with so many people, so many good people looking out for me, so many good trainers who wanted me to ride their horses. I rode winners for Edward O'Grady and Mick O'Brien. I was very lucky, the horses I rode, the people I rode for.

I was a bit of a nomad in Ireland, but I loved that. Going wherever I needed to go in order to ride, staying with whoever would have me, Mark Grant or Ken Whelan or Paul Carberry, on the couch or on a spare bed. And I had money to stay in a hotel if I needed to.

It wasn't sustainable though. I know that now, and I kind of knew it at the time. I remember, one Sunday in Februay 2004, I was coming back to Ireland to ride, and Ferdy had had enough. He couldn't put up with it any longer.

'If you go off to Ireland now,' he said, 'you needn't bother coming back.'

So I did, and I didn't.

I didn't even consider not going. I had four or five rides booked, I couldn't be letting those trainers down. And anyway, whether I knew it fully then or not, Ireland was where I wanted to be.

I remember when I left, my overriding feeling was one of relief. I knew I was doing the right thing for me, I knew by then deep down that I wanted to be back in Ireland, but to actually make the move, to actually go to Ferdy and tell him I was leaving, to make the decision myself, that would have been difficult. I was never very good at planning. Much better for me that it was taken out of my hands, that the decision was made for me.

I didn't tell Ferdy. I didn't call him to tell him I wasn't going back. I just didn't go back. I figured, he had told me not to come back if I went to Ireland, and I had gone to Ireland, so he knew I wasn't going back. I probably should have called him just to confirm, but I figured he would know. I went back about two months later to collect my car and the stuff I had left over there, but I didn't see Ferdy then. I didn't see him again until I saw him at the sales a few months after that.

He was a great man though, Ferdy. He was only 70 when he died in 2019, far too young.

There was another huge reason why I wanted to be in Ireland at that time. My daughter Jaimee was born that year. I wasn't told I was the father until the day that she was born. That wasn't ideal. Of course, I dropped everything as soon as I was told, I went straight to the hospital. I'm not sure her mother was too happy to see me there. We weren't in a relationship at the time. To be honest, we were never really in a relationship.

I wanted to be around for Jaimee as much as I could though. I was a really proud, happy father. And my parents were brilliant with her.

I remember the day I told Mam and Dad that they were grandparents. I was nervous about telling them, I didn't know how I was going to tell them. I could have just sat them down and told them, that probably would have been a normal thing to do, but I couldn't imagine that, I couldn't imagine how they would react, I thought it would have been very awkward, so I decided I would go about it a different way.

There was this old tree on the farm at home that I had been wanting to knock down for ages. Dad didn't want it taken down, but it needed to come down. So I figured I would knock the tree, then tell my parents I had knocked the tree, then tell them about Jaimee. I don't know, I think I thought Dad couldn't kill me for chopping the tree down if, in the same breath, I told him he was going to be a grandfather.

So that went well . . .

They were thrilled to learn about Jaimee though, after the initial surprise. They were made up. Mam loved being called Granny. She was brilliant with Jaimee, she'd go to see her as often as she could.

I saw Jaimee as often as I could too, but it wasn't easy. It wasn't like I had a nine-to-five job and I could see her every second evening and on weekends. Weekends were always busy for me, I was riding and I was travelling. I'd take her at weekends when I was able. Sometimes I'd pick her up and bring her home, then I'd go racing, leave her with Mam and Dad, or my sisters, then I'd come back home from the races and I'd have to drop her back again.

Jaimee loved Mam's stew. She was a fussy eater, but she'd eat Mam's stew like it was made of honey. And Mam was always there, she was always there with Jaimee as much as she was able to be, and she always made it as easy as she could for me to spend time with her.

But I didn't get to spend as much time with Jaimee as I wanted to when she was small. I was there for the big days of course, Christmas and birthdays and Communions and Confirmations, all that, but I would have loved to have been around more, just for normal life. My family were brilliant, Mam and Dad, and my sisters used to pick her up and drop her back if I was away racing.

It was tough though. I see it now with our crew at home with Edelle, Lily and Liam and Finn and Tess, I'm never away from them. They'd rarely have a day without me. That's the difference. I know it was tough on Jaimee. I probably could have tried harder, but it wasn't easy, I was trying to ride as much as I could, trying to re-establish myself in Ireland, trying to build and maintain contacts with trainers and with horses, and that all took time. I didn't have as much time to spend with Jaimee as I would have liked. Maybe I didn't make as much time as I should have made.

She's brilliant though, Jaimee. She's a young adult now, she's Tess's godmother, and I try to get her involved in our family as much as I can, as much as she can.

* * *

I didn't fall out with Ferdy. I always got on with Ferdy, he was a great man and it was a massive opportunity that he gave me. And the people at Ferdy's were top-notch, nothing but nice to me. And, as I said, when I won the Topham Trophy on Cregg House at

Aintree in 2005, when I beat Ferdy's horse into second place, he was the first person over to congratulate me.

I learned the value too of not cutting your ties with people, of building bridges instead of burning them as you go. A few years later, in 2007, when Ferdy needed a rider for Joes Edge in the William Hill Chase at the Cheltenham Festival in March, he asked me to ride him. Graham Lee was riding Ferdy's other horse in the race, New Alco, who was one of the favourites.

Like Cregg House at Aintree, Joes Edge was a big outsider, he hadn't run since he had been well beaten in the Becher Chase at Aintree the previous November. I was delighted to ride him though, I just switched him off out the back, allowed him to creep and creep, and he stayed on strongly up the hill to get up and beat Juveigneur and Mick Fitzgerald by a short head! He was just my second winner at the Cheltenham Festival.

Ferdy also supplied me with my third, Naiad Du Misselot in the Coral Cup the following year. That was another lesson in the value of keeping doors open, which wouldn't have been a strength of mine when I was younger. I learned the value of not slamming a door shut behind you, locking it and throwing away the key.

I stayed in Paul Carberry's for a few weeks after I came back to Ireland. Paul was brilliant, he'd never judge you, he was just doing what he was doing, doing what he wanted to do, and he was happy for you to do the same. Or not. He didn't really care. Paul was always Paul, doing his own thing. If you chose to tag along, that was fine, and if you chose to not tag along, that was fine too.

I started going into Mick O'Brien two or three days a week, and that was brilliant. Mick was an exceptional trainer. He was a very good rider too, until a fall in America left him paralysed from the waist down. That didn't stop him though, he trained from his wheelchair. He trained top-class horses back in the day, like Chorelli and Tacroy and Bright Highway. He won the Mackeson Gold Cup at

Cheltenham and the Hennessy Gold Cup at Newbury with Bright Highway. That was in 1980, and there was no Irish-trained winner of the Hennessy after that until Willie Mullins won it with Total Recall in 2017, 37 years later.

Mick's daughter Ann-Marie was there too, and his son-in-law Denis Cullen. Mick had lots of horses for Sean Mulryan at the time. I learned so much there. The first time I ever came across earplugs for horses was in Mick O'Brien's.

I rode lots of good winners for Mick, lots of good horses, Bennie's Pride and Stashedaway and Wotsitooya. I won a listed chase at Galway on Wotsitooya and I won the Pat Taaffe Chase at Punchestown on him, and I should have won a Munster National on him. I went outside a by-passed fence instead of inside it, when you couldn't see the flagman, and we were disqualified.

Mick could give you a bollocking too now when he wanted to, and I got plenty of them. If you didn't go fast enough in a piece of work, or when you were schooling, you'd see the wheelchair rocking from side to side and you'd know he wasn't happy! Or if he thought you gave a horse a bad ride in a race, he could make you feel very small in the parade ring afterwards.

The bollockings never bothered me though. Not really. Mick was Mick and, in fairness to him, my time keeping wasn't brilliant. It would all be forgotten about a minute later though. He was similar to Liam Burke like that. Liam used to say he'd throw me out the front door and a few minutes later I'd arrive in the back.

My time keeping got me in trouble a few times with plenty of different people, including with Edward O'Grady. Edward was consistently the top Irish trainer at the Cheltenham Festival through the 1980s and 1990s. He trained Golden Cygnet, who is generally recognised as one of the best hurdlers ever, and he trained Drumlargan and Staplestown and Mr Donovan, they were all before my time, but I knew Mucklemeg and Time For A Run and Ventana Canyon.

I started going into Edward's to ride out before I ever went to England. Philip Fenton said it to me one day, why don't you come in, so I started riding out there. Ned Kelly was one of Edward's best horses then, he was unbeaten as a novice hurdler, and he won the Irish Champion Hurdle in January 2002 under Norman Williamson. I remember riding Ned Kelly out at Ballynonty the day after he had won the Irish Champion Hurdle.

I rode a few winners for Edward in Ireland when I was with Ferdy, and I started going in there more and more when I moved back. He never really said it to me, but I became his number one rider in a short space of time. He'd let you know in riddles, if you give me a hundred per cent, I'll give you a hundred per cent. That type of thing. I didn't give a fuck about any of that, I just wanted to ride the horses and sure, why would I give it any less than a hundred per cent? The big thing was, at breakfast time, after riding a couple of lots, if you were going into the house for breakfast, you were on the team. If you were having breakfast in your car, that wasn't good.

I rode Takagi to win the Bobbyjo Chase at Fairyhouse in February 2004, and I rode him in the Aintree Grand National six weeks later, when I got a bad fall off him at The Chair.

I also rode Back In Front for Edward to finish second behind Harchibald in the Morgiana Hurdle at Punchestown in November 2004, and I rode him to win the Bula Hurdle at Cheltenham's December meeting the following month. As an impressive Bula Hurdle winner, and the Supreme Novices' Hurdle winner from the previous season, that made him an automatic contender for the Champion Hurdle back at Cheltenham in March.

There were good horses at Edward's then. Sacundai and Takagi and Pizarro. Ned Kelly was coming back after a setback that kept him off the track for almost two years to go novice chasing. I rode him to win his beginners' chase at Fairyhouse in February 2005. There were a lot of high-profile horses there, and that was new to me. Edward O'Grady was high-profile. I was used to tipping around in point-to-points or for point-to-point trainers. There was attention on every horse of Edward's that you rode, there was a focus on them. There was an aura about them, a bit like the aura that is around the Willie Mullins horses now, and that was new to me.

I wasn't used to it. I was coming from point-to-points, or from Ferdy's, where you'd be going to Sedgefield or Carlisle or Wetherby or Hereford. At Edward's, you'd be going to Punchestown or Fairyhouse or Leopardstown. You couldn't come back in and say, hey lads, this is a lovely horse, he'll win a beginners' chase at Thurles. You've run at Punchestown, you're not looking to win at Thurles, you're looking to win at Punchestown and then go on and win at Leopardstown.

Every ride mattered, every day, and that was new. There was none of this, you can follow away and let things happen and, if they don't happen, so be it. There will be another day. If he runs well in defeat and learns from it, progresses from it, then that's good. He'll have his day. With Edward's horses, it was different. At Edward's, today was the day. Every day.

I never really felt at ease there. I wasn't able for the job, not really. I wasn't experienced enough for it. I wasn't good enough for it.

My timekeeping, and my attitude towards it, wouldn't have endeared me to Edward either. If I had to be somewhere at seven o'clock, I'd always aim for seven o'clock, on the dot, and usually I'd make it. The problem with that though, was that I wasn't leaving any leeway for anything unforeseen.

I was due to ride work for Edward one morning at half past eight, but I got a bit delayed along the way, so I was running late. I was coming up to Horse and Jockey, and I thought it would be a good idea to call him to tell him I was going to be about three minutes late. I shouldn't have bothered, I should have just cracked on and arrived three minutes late. Anyway, when I called Edward, he said, ah no, don't bother. We've already worked that horse. It's done.

That was annoying. It was unlikely that the horse had already worked. Edward was just trying to teach me a lesson I'd say. So I pulled into the Horse and Jockey Hotel, had a bit of breakfast and headed home again.

I got beaten on Sky's The Limit in the Grade 3 juveniles' hurdle at Punchestown in January 2005. Sky's The Limit was a very good horse, he went on to win the Coral Cup at Cheltenham as a five-year-old, and he won two Grade 1 races as a novice chaser, and he was well fancied for that juveniles' hurdle at Punchestown. The owners weren't happy with the ride I gave him, and I don't think the trainer was too happy either, but I had broken my hand the previous day, and I was struggling. A horse had jammed on with me on my way down to the start the previous day, and I had smashed my hand into his withers. I had spent the previous evening in Cashel hospital getting an X-ray: two broken bones in my hand.

I should have stood myself down, but I had good rides booked at Punchestown that day, a horse for John Queally in the beginners' chase, and one for Tony Martin in the two-mile handicap chase, as well as Sky's The Limit in the Grade 3 juveniles' hurdle. There was no way I wasn't going to ride. I shouldn't have ridden though, I wasn't a huge help to any horse I rode that day.

Maybe that had an impact on what followed.

Back In Front was on track for the Champion Hurdle two months later. Now, it was a hell of a Champion Hurdle that year, 2005. We were right in the middle of that golden era of Irish two-mile hurdlers, Brave Inca and Hardy Eustace and Harchibald and Macs Joy. I thought Back In Front was going to have to improve if he was going to win a Champion Hurdle, but he was a big contender, he was the Bula Hurdle winner and he was among the favourites.

I was driving home from the races one evening during the lead-up to Cheltenham, and Dad called me.

'You're not riding that horse?' he said, half-question, half-statement.

'What horse?'

'The Champion Hurdle horse,' he said.

'Back In Front?' I asked.

'Yeah, Back In Front. You're not riding him in the Champion Hurdle.'

It was more statement than question this time.

'Well it's fucking news to me if I'm not!'

There was silence for a second or two.

'Yeah, they just said it there on the news,' said my dad, half apologetically. 'Ruby Walsh is riding him in the Champion Hurdle.'

I changed direction. Instead of driving home, I headed for Edward O'Grady's. I couldn't believe it. It was a dark winter's night, it was about six o'clock in the evening when I arrived. I remember sitting in my car trying to pluck up the courage to go and knock on the door.

Edward answered.

'Edward, what the fuck?!'

'Ah I know,' he said. 'I'm sorry. Ruby Walsh rides.'

I didn't hear too much more. I think he said that the owners wanted Ruby Walsh, but I didn't really care what the reason was. It didn't really matter. I had just had a top ride in the Champion Hurdle pulled out from under me.

I thought it was bad form, first to jock me off, then to not tell me. I thought he could have called me, instead of me hearing from my dad, who had heard it on the RTÉ news.

I went into work the following morning of course, as if nothing had happened. I did overhear Tommy Ryan though, talking to Edward.

'That's an awful thing that you're after doing to that chap,' he was saying. He didn't know I was there, he didn't know I could hear, but he was letting Edward know what he thought. Tommy Ryan was a quiet man now, a gentleman, a very good rider and a great man. Edward said I could ride Back In Front at Punchestown.

It was all immaterial in the end though. Back In Front was sent off as joint favourite for the Champion Hurdle that year, 7/2 joint favourite alongside Hardy Eustace. As it turned out, it was Hardy Eustace who won it, his second Champion Hurdle, back-to-back Champion Hurdles. He was some horse, tough as teak, and Dessie Hughes did some job with him. He battled back up the hill under Conor O'Dwyer to get home by a neck from Harchibald and Paul Carberry in one of the most famous renewals of the Champion Hurdle run in recent times.

Back In Front finished ninth.

I have to admit, I was delighted he didn't win it. It was strange, I had ridden Ned Kelly for Edward O'Grady in the previous race, the Arkle, and there I was, watching the Champion Hurdle on the television in the weigh room with Ruby Walsh riding Back In Front, the horse I had won the Bula Hurdle on, in that very place, the last time he had run.

I watched closely, how's he travelling, how's he travelling. On the inside, just behind Hardy Eustace, going well. As they started to come down the hill, Ruby's hands started to move, as Conor O'Dwyer still sat still on the leader. Conor had a little look over his shoulder and I thought, not too bad. Then Ruby started to get more aggressive on Back In Front on the run to the second last, and he was swamped in a sea of horses on the run to the home turn. Relief.

These things can have a big impact on a young jockey's career. If Back In Front had won the Champion Hurdle, it would have been, they were right to jock that lad off and let Ruby Walsh ride him. The other factor is, if I had ridden him in the Champion Hurdle, and he had run like he did (which he would have), then they could have blamed the jockey. They would have been wrong, of course, but it happens. That wouldn't have been good either. For Ruby Walsh, somebody who was as good and as successful as Ruby was even then, it didn't matter. He just got off Back In Front and said the horse wasn't good enough. That was correct, of course, and it was fine because Ruby Walsh had said it. If Davy Russell had got off him though, Davy Russell who had never ridden a Grade 1 winner at that point, and said that the horse wasn't good enough, people might have questioned it. Maybe the jockey wasn't good enough. Either way, it wasn't a bad end to the story for me.

Back In Front was getting ready for Punchestown, I was riding him in a piece of work about a week before the Punchestown Champion Hurdle, and he broke a blood vessel. He bled from the nose, the blood was pouring out of him now, I had never seen anything like it. It was as if you had opened a bottle of red wine and you were pouring it out onto the gallop. I pulled him up straight away, and that was the end of that. He didn't run at Punchestown, and that was pretty much the end of my time riding for Edward O'Grady.

Chapter 9

I knew very quickly that Golden Row was a good horse. December 1999, I was just asked to go to Sean O'Brien's to ride a horse in a piece of work. I didn't know anything about the horse, and I didn't know much about the man who trained him, a young trainer named Charles Byrnes.

This was a serious piece of work. You'd ride work in Pat Doyle's or in John Kiely's and you'd go fast all right, but this was on another level. I didn't have an awful lot to compare Golden Row with now, I wasn't that experienced at the time, I wouldn't have ridden an awful lot of high-class horses before that, but even so, this fellow gave me a great feel.

He gave me a great feel again when he made his racecourse debut on 3 January 2000 in a bumper at Mallow, I just settled him in, fourth or fifth, allowed him to settle into his racing rhythm. The leader went clear, a horse of Ronald Curran's named Steel Edge, but I was in no panic, I was in no rush, I felt like I had a lot of power underneath me, that I could go and catch the leader whenever I wanted, and that's exactly what I did. We hit the front just outside the furlong marker, and we went on to win easily.

I didn't ride Golden Row again. He went on to be a good hurdler, he won seven of his 14 hurdle races for Charles, including the Grade 3 For Auction Hurdle, then he joined Edward O'Grady and won four chases, including a Grade 3 chase at Galway. I was right about him being a good horse, but I never got to ride him again.

I didn't ride for Charles again as an amateur but, I didn't know it at the time obviously, that was the start of a relationship with him that would run for the entire of my professional career. There aren't many trainers in the country who are more astute than Charles, he is one of the sharpest trainers I know, and we had some great days together.

Laetitia was the first big winner I rode for Charles. She had made the headlines before I got to ride her. She finished second in a bumper at Mallow in April 2005 to another horse who was trained by Charles, Alpha Royale. Alpha Royale was ridden by my good friend Martin Ferris, Laetitia was ridden by an amateur rider, Michael Purcell. Alpha Royale won by a length, but the stewards on the day took a dim view of the ride that Laetitia got, they suspended the amateur rider for 50 days and they suspended the horse for 60 days. She actually got to run in another bumper at Kilbeggan 13 days later, because her owner had appealed against the ban, and she duly won.

She had had just one run over hurdles before I rode her in the Grade 3 intermediate hurdle at Down Royal's big Champion Chase meeting in November 2005, and she won nicely for me. I won a listed hurdle back at Mallow on her, and she went on to go down by just a neck to subsequent Grade 1 winner Offshore Account in the Grade 3 Hugh McMahon Chase at Limerick a couple years later.

She was one of a number of good horses that Charles had at the time. Alpha Royale was a good horse himself, and Powerstation and Cailin Alainn and Cloudy Bays. I rode lots of winners for Charles. He was a great man to ride for. He'd call me if he wanted me to ride a horse work or to school a horse, he'd have him ready for me, I'd hop up on him, work him away, school him away, done. I was freelance at the time, but Charles would usually be at the top of my list. When Charles wanted me, he wanted me and it was time to go.

Cailin Alainn was a really talented staying novice chaser of Charles's. I'd say she wasn't that easy to train, I'd say Charles did a great job with her. I won two Grade 1 novice chases on her in 2006, the Drinmore Chase at Fairyhouse in November and the Powers Whiskey Novice Chase at Leopardstown's Christmas Festival. She went to Cheltenham the following month for the Cotswold Chase, her first run in a chase in open company, outside of novice class, and we were still travelling well when we fell at the third last fence.

She was in some form that day, she was running some race, the winner was still behind us, but she just got the third last wrong. It's a tricky downhill fence, and she just got it all wrong, she hit the middle of the fence and had no chance of standing up. And when she fell, she bounced up off the ground and ran up the hill and crashed into a rail. She was fine, but I'm sure she was never the same mare afterwards. She had some talent, Cailin Alainn, she had some engine.

Exotic Dancer won the Cotswold Chase that year, and he went on to finish second to Kauto Star in the Cheltenham Gold Cup that March. Our Vic was second, he was top class, he won the Ryanair Chase the following year. It was a top-class race and Cailin Alainn was right in there with them at the time of her departure.

Cailin Alainn ran in the novices' race, the Sun Alliance Chase, at the Cheltenham Festival that year, Denman's year, where she fell early on. That was a shame, it would have been interesting to see how she would have fared against Denman, but she didn't give me the same feel in that race as she had done in the Cotswold Chase six weeks earlier.

I won good races on good horses for Charles through 2005 and 2006. I didn't ride all of Charles's horses during that time, but I quickly learned that, when he was going to the trouble of booking me, he thought his horse had a big chance and, when Charles thought that one of his horses had a big chance, he was rarely too far off the mark. Weapon's Amnesty and Solwhit would come later.

I always loved riding for Charles, and I always loved riding for Arthur Moore. Arthur was always a top-class trainer. Arthur is steeped in racing history, son of Joan and Dan Moore, who trained L'Escargot and Tied Cottage and many other top-class National Hunt horses. Arthur himself has won some of the best National Hunt races with horses like Weather The Storm and Feathered Gale and Native Upmanship and, of course, Klairon Davis.

As well as being a brilliant trainer, Arthur was always one of the best people I knew to read a race. If you were riding for Arthur, not only would he tell you how you should ride his horse, he would also tell you what all the other horses were going to do.

One of the first big rides I had for Arthur was on The Railway Man in the Dr P.J. Moriarty Chase at Leopardstown in February 2006. The Dr P.J. Moriarty Chase was always an important race, it had been won by some of the top staying novice chasers in Ireland, Cahervillahow and Merry Gale and Harcon and Dorans Pride and Florida Pearl, and Arthur had won it six years earlier with Native Upmanship.

I'm sure I wasn't Arthur's first choice for The Railway Man. Conor O'Dwyer was riding the favourite in the race, Ted Walsh's horse Southern Vic, and David Casey was riding a horse for Willie Mullins, Our Ben. They would have been in front of me in the line for a horse of Arthur's at the time for sure, and there may have been others. I'm sure I was third choice at best. But I was delighted to get the call to ride him. To ride a horse with any sort of chance in a Grade 1 race was massive for me given that I had never won a Grade 1 race at the time.

I actually happened to meet Arthur by chance on the way in the gate at Leopardstown that morning.

'You'll ride a winner for me today,' he said to me.

Now, the only ride I had for Arthur that day was The Railway Man, and I'm thinking, there must be some confusion here, somebody has mixed something up. He can't mean that I'm going to win on The Railway Man, a 16/1 shot in a Grade 1 race.

That was exactly what Arthur meant. And in the parade ring before the race, he hammered home the point, and he told me how.

'There's a strip of fresh ground down the inside,' he said quietly. 'They're after moving the wings of the fences this morning, so there is fresh ground on the inside. Everybody will be going wide looking for the best ground but, actually, the best ground is along the inside, on the shortest route. You go down the inside, you'll save ground and you'll go the shortest route.'

So I did what Arthur told me to do, and the race panned out exactly as Arthur said it would. I held The Railway Man up early on, we made our progress gradually, into fourth at the third last fence, into second at the second last. We moved to the front on the run to the last, and he kept on well up the run-in for me to get home in front of Father Matt and Our Ben.

That was brilliant for me, my first Grade 1 win. It was like I was breaking through the ceiling, proving I could ride a Grade 1 horse, that I could win a Grade 1 race. For other fellows too who'd be watching on, owners and trainers, fellows realising that, actually, you were able to ride.

And the bonus was that it was the start of a relationship with Arthur. I started going into Arthur to ride out one morning a week after that, which put me in line for rides on Arthur's horses.

I rode Mansony for Arthur in the Dan Moore Memorial Chase at Fairyhouse in April 2006. That was obviously a race that was close to Arthur's heart, named after his father, and he had Mansony primed. It was my first time to ride Mansony in a race, but I had ridden him at home, I knew him well. He was a really nice horse, he travelled well for me, I just let him bowl away handy, we moved to the front at the fourth last fence, travelling well, everything in order. Then wham, we got the third last fence wrong and came down. It was just one of those things.

I was gutted for Arthur, he had won the race two years earlier with Fadoudal Du Cochet, and he would have loved to have won it again. Mansony didn't run again that season, he didn't go to Punchestown. Arthur put him away and got him ready for the following season. He made his debut that season at Leopardstown's Christmas Festival in a valuable handicap chase, I rode him again and, this time, we got it all right. He kept on well to beat Our Ben, who must have been sick of the sight of Arthur Moore horses by then.

Mansony was a brilliant horse for me. I rode him in 19 races in total and we won six of them, finished second in two and finished third in six. Two of those wins were in Grade 1 races, the Champion Chase at the Punchestown Festival in April 2007 and the Paddy Power Dial-A-Bet Chase at Leopardstown's Christmas Festival in December that year. The day he won the Champion Chase at Punchestown, I broke the parade. He was just getting so wound up, he was in danger of throwing his race away in the parade, so I took it into my own hands and I let him off, down to the start on his own, and he relaxed. If I hadn't done that, he probably would have run his race before we started, he would have got too worked up, he probably would have had no chance of winning. The stewards didn't look on my actions too favourably though, they fined me €500.

I just hunted Mansony around out the back, let them at it up front. We didn't start to make ground towards the leaders until the third last fence but, when we started to make ground, I knew we were going to go close. We didn't hit the front until after we landed over the final fence, and we got up to win by just over a length from Justified and A.P. McCoy. I loved that ride, I got a big kick out of that win, just getting up late on to win by a length.

So the number of trainers I was riding for was increasing, and I was back to trying to juggle them all. It was different to my point-to-point days though, because racing was on different days, not just on a Sunday. So if there were two novice chasers with two different trainers, and if there was a novice chase at Limerick on a Tuesday and another novice chase at Thurles on a Thursday, you'd try to get them to split them up. It wasn't always easy, some trainers, when they were going, they were going, but I tried to keep everybody happy, Charles Byrnes and Mick O'Brien and Pat Doyle and Robert Tyner and John Kiely and Jimmy Mangan and Liam Burke and others.

Liam Burke asked me to go in early one morning, he told me he was working a horse in Paddy Condon's field, and he wanted me to ride him in this piece of work. We normally started in Liam's at half past seven, but he asked me to go in this day at half past six. I didn't care, I didn't think anything of it, I just said I'd be there.

This was a gorgeous horse. Beautiful mover, did everything easily, worked really well.

'His name is Thyne Again,' said Liam afterwards. 'He goes in a maiden hurdle at Gowran Park on Thursday.'

I didn't know what was going on, and I didn't really care. I just knew I had a nice ride in the maiden hurdle at Gowran Park on Thursday. A Good Thyne gelding, owned by the Simply The Best Syndicate, headed up by Jerry Nolan, who sadly passed away there in 2021.

Thyne Again had run just once before that, he had run a nice race in a novices' hurdle at Galway a couple of weeks earlier, ridden by Martin Ferris, staying on to take seventh place. Liam thought he had improved a lot since then, and I started to realise they were fancying him to go well at Gowran.

They were intending on backing him too, so they were trying to underplay him. They talked him down. And very few people knew about the piece of work in Paddy Condon's field, which is how they wanted it to be, which is why we worked him at half past six in the morning when nobody was around.

He was a big price for that maiden hurdle at Gowran, he was sent off at 14/1 and I think they backed him at bigger prices in the morning. I knew they'd backed him all right, I knew this was important.

Thyne Again felt good on the way down to the two-mile start at Gowran Park. He felt fresh and well and ready to go. You get down to the two-mile start at Gowran, and you show your horse the first hurdle, just so he knows he's going to be asked to jump it. But he was going too quickly as we approached the hurdle, I couldn't stop him, so he ended up jumping the hurdle!

I didn't say anything to the starter. I was afraid to say anything. I just got him back, lined up at the start. Because I didn't say anything to the starter, they held an enquiry and they fined me for jumping the show hurdle. That annoyed me. Another 500 quid, a lot of money.

That aside, the actual race went well. Thyne Again settled well for me and, when I asked him to pick up, he picked up well. We caught David Casey on a horse of Mouse Morris's, Mickataine, on the run-in, and we went on to win well.

Of course, Thyne Again should never have been a 14/1 shot for that maiden hurdle, he was such a good horse, and he proved it later. Liam Burke had had some good horses before Thyne Again, Magical Approach and Nolans Pride and Coolnahilla, and he would win the Galway Plate later with Sir Frederick and he would win the Thyestes Chase with My Murphy, but Thyne Again was his best horse ever, and he was an even better chaser than a hurdler. He missed the whole of the 2006/07 season, but I went on to win the Irish Arkle on him in January 2008, and the Nas Na Riogh Chase at Naas the following month.

It was desperate when Thyne Again died in early 2009. He was getting ready for Cheltenham that year, he was just doing a routine canter at Liam's and, afterwards, he pulled up, then collapsed and died. It was desperate for Liam and his team, to lose such a talented horse.

* * *

I knew Philip Rothwell from my time at Kildalton College. He was in my class, he was one of the lads I used to go to ride out with in Aidan O'Brien's.

I rode a couple of horses for Philip when he first took out his licence, just a couple during the 2003/04 and the 2004/05 seasons, a few more in the early part of the 2005/06 season. Then, the week before the 2006 Cheltenham Festival, Philip asked me if I would ride Native Jack for him in the Cross-Country Chase at Cheltenham.

I was made up. Native Jack had won a couple of chases for Arthur Moore, and he had won a point-to-point at Boulta and another point-to-point at Ballindenisk before he went back to the track and won the P.P. Hogan Chase over the banks course at Punchestown that February. Johnny Cullen had ridden him to victory there, he was Johnny Cullen's ride, but Johnny was injured in the lead-up to Cheltenham, so the ride was going. Right time, right place, fair play to Philip for asking me to ride him.

I always loved the cross-country course at Cheltenham. I loved the intricacies of it, the plotting your way around it. It brought you back to steeplechasing's roots, back to where it all began, over banks and hedges and rails, like when the first steeplechase was run in County Cork in 1752, between the church steeple in Buttevant and the church steeple in Doneraile, about 40 miles from my home in Youghal. That's where steeplechasing got its name, almost 300 years ago, when Edmund Blake and Cornelius O'Callaghan decided to have a race on their horses from one church steeple to the other.

There's a notion going around that there's no place for a cross-country chase at the Cheltenham Festival, but I completely disagree with that. It's a brilliant race, and it's what National Hunt racing is all about. From a rider's perspective, it gets you thinking, it gets you learning how to ride the race. You have to know the track, figure out where you're going to be on the track at different points of the race.

You have to know your horse, you have to know what he or she is capable of, what he or she is not capable of, and you have to ride your race accordingly. It's the same with kids on their ponies, they should be out hunting, they should be out eventing, showjumping. You learn so much more by doing that than just by gunning a horse as fast as you can around a track. I think there should be more cross-country races and cross-country courses than there are.

Punchestown's banks course is the same, it's a great test. It can be a bit tight, and if you get caught in traffic on the last bend, you can be in trouble. It's a downhill run from there to the winning line and it can be hard to make up ground. But it's a great course. They should have cross-country courses at other tracks as well though. Fairyhouse should have a cross-country course.

You had to think your way around Punchestown's banks course, just as you had to think your way around Cheltenham's cross-country course. Not that you didn't have to think your way around any course in any race, but there was much more to the cross-country course than there was to a normal park course.

I'd always want to be on the inside for a right-hand turn, then on the inside again for a left-hand turn. I'd pick my spot on the course where I wanted to change direction. So you jump off at the start, inside, inside, inside, then you have to switch. And I never minded being towards the outside for the Aintree fence, the fence that's like the Canal Turn at Aintree, where you turn to your left directly afterwards. There would be a clamour for the inside there, there'd be lots of traffic, but I never minded being outside, because you go right-handed shortly afterwards. I always wanted to be inside on the bends, you'd save more ground on the inside on the long sweeping bends than you would at a fence. And I never minded jumping the big bank in the middle because, if you did, when you landed, you were on the inside.

I had some memorable days on the cross-country course at Cheltenham. Winning on The Quads at the December meeting in 2002 was memorable, very early in my time with Ferdy. Native Jack was obviously memorable, my first Cheltenham Festival winner.

I had another memorable day at the cross-country course in November 2008 on Dix Villez, during my time with Gigginstown. I always walked the track before racing. Every track. John Kiely put that into my head, be sure to walk the track. The track setup might be different to what you're used to or how you imagined it. And John Kiely used to always say, walk the track after they have had a race or two on it. That was all doable when you were an amateur, when you only had one ride on the day, when you were riding only in the bumper, the last race. I couldn't always walk the track after they had had a race on it, but I always walked it before racing.

I remember walking the track at Navan one day. Now Navan is a big galloping track, you can take your time at Navan, you have to keep enough in reserve to get home. But this day, they had set the track up tight around the inside, almost on the golf course, to give the ground on the outside time to recover. It was a totally different track to ride with that setup. It was much sharper, you couldn't be as patient as you usually could be at Navan.

Or at Leopardstown, when they set up the track on the inside as opposed to the outside. Again, a very different type of track. You want to go out in a race knowing the track, knowing your horse, having an idea in your head of how you want to ride your race.

You'd be influenced too by what other riders were going to do. I always had a fair idea through the majority of my career what different riders were going to do. Like in bumpers, Philip Fenton was going to make the running, and you'd figure it out from there. Or when you were riding against Ruby Walsh, Barry Geraghty, Shay Barry, Johnny Cullen, you knew what they were going to do, so you could plan your race based on what they were going to do.

Towards the end of my career though, you couldn't do that. You didn't know what other lads were going to do, because they didn't know themselves! If Shay Barry said he was going to bounce out and make the running, you knew that Shay Barry was going to bounce out and make the running, and you could track him. Towards the end of my career though, someone would say they were going to make the running, so you'd line up beside him, sit in just behind him. Then he'd sit seventh, and you'd be completely out of position. And you only had yourself to blame, because you believed him when he told you he was going to make the running when, actually, he hadn't a clue what he was going to do.

I was a bit late getting to Cheltenham on the day of Dix Villez's race, so I took a buggy to get to the different points on the track where there might be an advantage to be gained.

The rule was always that you had to be outside the C marker, C for chase, H for hurdles, and that you had to have the red flag to your right and the white flag to your left. Just as in point-to-points. That's why you sometimes hear lads saying 'between the flags' when they're talking about point-to-points. There were little hedges around the cross-country course that seemed to mark out the course, but they were only there as a guide.

The stewards used to say to us every time, before we went out in a cross-country race at Cheltenham, that the little hedges were only there as a guide, that if you got pushed out the wrong side of a hedge, you could still continue, you could still be in the race.

This was always in my head, because there was a section of the course where the hedges guided you far wider than you needed to go if you were following the markers. I drove down to that part in my buggy that day at the 2008 November meeting to check it out, and it was still like that. I thought, that would be some shortcut. I had been thinking about it for a while, I checked it out every time I rode at the track, but I had never done it, I had never cut the corner, and I couldn't check with the stewards or anybody because, of course, if I checked with them, they'd put up a marker straight away. I put it to the back of my mind and I went back to the weigh room and got changed.

The stewards had their usual chat with us before the cross-country race. At the end of the chat, as I was walking out the door, I thought that I would double check:

'The hedges are only guidelines, right?' I asked.

'Yes,' one of the stewards said. 'Just guidelines. If you get pushed out through a hedge, you can still continue, you are still in the race.'

And I was thinking, am I going to do this or not?

I still hadn't fully decided when we lined up and got racing. Dix Villez was trained by Paul Nolan and owned by Michael O'Leary's Gigginstown House Stud, and he travelled well for me, popping away, enjoying himself, enjoying the obstacles. He had never run over the course before, and you never know how they're going to take to it, you never know if they're going to enjoy jumping the different obstacles, but he was loving it. We kicked off handy, we moved to the front after the third fence and I just allowed him to settle into his rhythm. He made a mistake at the timber rail fence, and he made another mistake at the hedge, three fences later, but he still travelled well.

Then we came up to the corner. I still wasn't sure what I was going to do. It was there for me though, the space was there, the shortened route. Fuck it. I cut across the track, in between the little hedges that guided you around wider. It looked like I was going off the track, cutting the corner, but I knew I was staying on the right side of the markers.

It was in my head all right, but I didn't know I was going to do it until the moment I did it. I suppose it was like a lot of the things I did! I just saw the space, saw the opportunity, went for it.

I didn't get ahead of the others, it just saved me a few lengths and I slotted in and joined the field. None of the other riders said anything to me at the time as I joined them again. I don't know what they were thinking. What's Russell at? But Dix Villez seemed to love that. Whatever it was about that manoeuvre, he stuck his chest out afterwards, he seemed to get stronger through the race for it.

I'm not sure how many lengths it saved us, but we won by three lengths, and it must have saved us more than that. You never know though, races are races, you don't run them on paper, you can't say that we saved 10 lengths and we only won by three so we would have been beaten by seven. It's more nuanced than that. He might have won anyway, even without cutting the corner. He might have had enough in reserve. We'll never know for sure.

I heard the boos as I was pulling up. Obviously there were people in the crowd, punters in the stands, who thought I had taken the wrong course and who thought we would be disqualified. I didn't think I had, I didn't think we would be.

John Thomas McNamara had finished second on Garde Champetre.

'I don't know what they're booing at,' he said as we pulled up. 'You've done nothing wrong.'

That gave me the reassurance I needed. I might have been a bit worried on the way back in, but once John Thomas said I was safe, I knew I was safe. And the only reason he knew it was fine was because he must have thought of doing it himself. He obviously saw it too, he just didn't do it. I did it for the divilment as much as anything. I'm not sure it made the difference between winning and losing, but it was great craic to do it.

Paul Nolan, Dix Villez's trainer, came running down the track to meet me, his phone in his hand, going mental.

'What were you thinking?!'

He shows me his phone: Michael O'Leary.

'He's going crazy!'

I try to calm Paul down.

'Paul,' I say quietly. 'Don't worry. I've done nothing wrong. We won't lose the race.'

Paul looks up at me, him on the ground, me on the horse.

'Really?' he says. 'You think so?'

'I do.'

Paul puts his phone back to his ear.

'Michael!' he says. 'Michael!'

Brief pause as Michael O'Leary responds.

'No, no, no,' says Paul. 'He says he's done nothing wrong. He says there's no way he'll lose the race.'

Another pause as Michael replies again. Paul smiles and puts the phone into his pocket.

'He says you're a fucking genius!'

I didn't cut any corners on Native Jack. This was 2006, the 2006 Cheltenham Festival. There had only been one running of the Cross-Country Chase at the Cheltenham Festival before that, the previous year, which had been won, unsurprisingly, by John Thomas McNamara on the 12-year-old Spot Thedifference. Spot Thedifference was a big price for the race in 2006, he was 13 then obviously, but he was still dynamite over the cross-country fences, trained by the master cross-country trainer Enda Bolger. I regarded him as one of my main dangers and, of course, you always had to fear John Thomas.

I got some spin off Native Jack though. Philip Rothwell had him in some form. I switched him off out the back early on, got him settled, got him jumping. He loved the course, he really took to the obstacles, which wasn't surprising given how well he had gone at Punchestown. They're different tracks, the cross-country tracks at Cheltenham and at Punchestown. Just because you go well around one, it doesn't follow that you're going to go well around the other, but even so, if you show an aptitude for one, if a horse shows that he likes jumping varied obstacles, then it is not a negative for the other.

Native Jack and I made our ground gradually, and we moved up in behind the leaders on the run to the home turn. I tracked John Thomas into the home straight, there were four in a line in front of me, but a lovely gap developed just outside Spot Thedifference as Never Compromise moved a little to his right. I asked Native Jack to pick up, and he did, moved into the gap and moved up alongside Spot Thedifference on the run to the final obstacle.

Spot Thedifference jumped the last better than we jumped it, he stole about a half a length on us, but I knew Native Jack had plenty left. I asked him for all he had, up the hill at Cheltenham. We ate into John Thomas's lead, we got up alongside him halfway up the run-in, and we went on. I just kept kicking and pushing all the way up the hill, in front at Cheltenham, at the Cheltenham Festival, and we hit the line.

That was some feeling, my first winner at the Cheltenham Festival. It meant everything. It wasn't the Gold Cup or the Champion Hurdle or the Champion Chase, it was the Cross-Country Chase, but to me, and to Philip Rothwell, it was everything.

It was a hugely important milestone for me. It meant that I joined that select band of jockeys, Cheltenham Festival-winning jockeys. I had proved I could do it, that I could win on the big stage. I had proved it to others as well as to myself, it got my name out there, in the minds of owners and trainers if and when they needed a jockey for a big horse or a big race.

As I said before, Cheltenham had always been this magical place for me, the Cheltenham Festival, far removed from my reality. When Dad was going over there when I was a kid, I never thought I could one day go there, not to mind ride there, not to mind ride a winner there.

I obviously didn't know it at the time, but it was the start of my run of winners at the Cheltenham Festival. Between that year, 2006, and 2018, 12 years later, I rode at least one winner at every Cheltenham Festival. Thirteen Cheltenham Festivals in a row. I rode 25 Cheltenham winners in total in my career, and I was very grateful for all of that. It was always brilliant to walk out of Cheltenham on the Friday evening with a winner on the board.

When I retired in 2023, I was joint fourth in the all-time list of Cheltenham Festival-winning jockeys, behind Ruby Walsh, Barry Geraghty and A.P. McCoy, and level with Pat Taaffe. If you had told me, when I was jumping poles at home on Thunder, that I would ride as many Cheltenham Festival winners as Pat Taaffe had ridden, I would have told you that you were dreaming. It was dreamland for me, and there I was, living the dream.

Chapter 10

People ask me what was the best ride I ever gave a horse. Tiger Roll is a popular guess. Lord Windermere also. The Storyteller is another who makes the shortlist, winning the Brown Advisory and Merriebelle Stable Plate Handicap Chase at Cheltenham in 2018.

Actually, for me, it was Strontium.

Tallow, February 2001. Strontium was a small handy horse who was trained by John Gleeson and who barely got three miles. I had ridden him to win at Dromahane six weeks earlier, and John asked me if I would ride him again at Tallow.

There were only six horses in the race, but they flew from the start. I was happy to allow them at it up front, I just took my time in behind. I had walked the course earlier, and had noticed there was a strip of fresh ground along the inside, so I stayed along the inside, saving energy and racing on the best of the ground.

I got very far behind the leaders, but I wasn't that worried, I knew I was going at a good pace and that the leaders had to be going too fast. I knew John wouldn't have been worried either. That was the beauty about riding for lads like John Gleeson, they'd leave you off to do your own thing, to ride the race the way you wanted to ride it. They knew you'd be trying to do the right thing for the race and for the horse.

The problem was that, back then, the people would cross the track once the horses had gone past, so every time we came around to the winning post, I was so far behind the second last horse they wouldn't see me. The people would start to cross the track before I had got to them! They kept forgetting about me, they thought I had pulled up. We had a couple of near misses. My boot almost hit off one guy on the way past with a circuit to go.

I kept creeping and creeping. I didn't move a muscle. Miley's Choice pulled up, Strong Boost pulled up. Down the hill, we kept plugging, kept closing on the leaders, Private Peace and Nellie Gale. We caught them at the final fence, and we went on to win by three lengths.

* * *

Before there was ever such a thing as sports psychologists, I had Timmy Beecher and Peter Vaughan.

Timmy Beecher was a brilliant man to jump a horse and, as I mentioned before, he was a brilliant man to go to for advice. He lived just out the road from us at home, in Tallow, and everyone looked up to him. As a child, I looked up to Timmy too, I used to marvel at how good he was with horses. And he was always such a kind man, gentle, unassuming.

If anyone ever had a horse who was struggling with his jumping, they sent him to Timmy Beecher, and Timmy would figure out the difficulties he was having, and fix them. It is no surprise that Timmy's sons Paul and Tadhg are top-class showjumpers.

I would often give Timmy a ring when I started getting going in my career. I'd give him a ring on the way home from the races just to talk through things, and, if you were feeling down about something, he'd always make you feel better.

Like, I'd be after eight or nine or 10 rides in a row, and every single one of those horses had made a mistake at an obstacle, and I'd be on to Timmy, Jesus Timmy, I can't get a horse to jump for me. You'd be trying too hard, or trying to jump the fences for the horses instead of letting them jump themselves. And Timmy would just say something to you, something small that you were doing or not doing. And it would be the way he'd say it to you too, the confidence he would give you.

It was the same with Peter Vaughan. I went through a stage in my career when I would speak to Peter just about every single day. I'd call him on the way home from the races too, I'd be beating myself up because I'd got beaten on a horse that I thought I should have won on.

Now, if you look back on a race, on any race, in which you were beaten by a short enough margin, you can always point to something and say, if I had done that I might have won, or if I hadn't done that I might have won. If I had kicked on earlier, or if I had sat in for longer, or if I'd asked him for a big jump at the second last, or if I had allowed him to go in and pop the last. You can argue about the merits of jockeys or rides as much as you want, but the reality is that, the vast majority of the time, the best horse in the race on the day wins it.

I often didn't see that though, I'd be beating myself up on the way home about a race I had lost, convincing myself I should have won it. Then I'd ring Peter, and he'd just put it into perspective. Sure that horse was not good enough to win that race, he'd say. You did well to get him to run as well as he did. Or, yeah, you could have waited longer, but he wouldn't have won anyway.

I'd just be ringing him for someone to ring on the way home, I wasn't necessarily looking for vindication or consolation, but Peter was always good for that anyway. He knew me well, he knew everything about me. He knew what to say and how to say it and, after 10 or 15 minutes on the phone to him, I'd have forgiven myself.

I always rode by feel, and Timmy and Peter knew that. You couldn't go without the horse. Sometimes you'd be in the middle of a race, and you'd know you should be going, that it was time to move, but you'd know that the horse didn't have the energy, you'd know that, if you asked him for his effort there and then, you'd burst him, he would run out of energy very quickly.

So you'd be there waiting for him. Like driving a car, and you're trying to start it up, waiting to feel the power in the engine, waiting for the turbo to kick in. Come on, come on, come on! Sometimes you'd be waiting, and it wouldn't happen until it was too late. The race would be gone beyond you, and you might run on to be placed. Sometimes it wouldn't happen at all, you just wouldn't get that feeling of energy. But other times, the power would kick back in on time, and you could go then, finish off your race strongly, get up to win.

And because I rode a lot by feel, instructions that I'd get before a race would be pretty much irrelevant in most cases. There were exceptions though. I'm not sure how good a rider Arthur Moore was, and I don't know how good John Kiely was, I believe they were both good, but God they could read a race. They were brilliant, they'd know exactly what was going to happen in the race before it happened, and any instructions they gave you, you took them on board.

Some trainers though, they'd give you so many instructions, they'd turn a race into a maths equation.

I'd be listening to them, or I'd be hearing them, and I'd just be thinking, I'm not going to be able to do any of this. So I'd just ride my own race. Or they'd be talking, and I wouldn't be listening, I'd be looking up at the sky. And when I was riding for those trainers, I used to delay my arrival into the parade ring so they wouldn't have time to give me instructions.

'How're you, sorry, the bell has gone, I need to go.'

Sometimes they'd be giving you instructions when they were legging you up, they'd be shouting instructions after you as you were leaving the parade ring on the horse.

The trainers I enjoyed riding for most, trainers like Gordon Elliott, Charles Byrnes, they wouldn't give you any instructions. Like Gordon's instructions before 2018 Grand National: you know what you're doing. That was it, they were his instructions. Or Charles. He'd talk about everything else except the race. Plenty of rain around isn't there? He'd be after having the price of a small farm on a horse you were about to ride for him in a race, and he'd be talking about the weather.

He nearly wouldn't want to talk to me about the race, because he'd be afraid that he'd influence what I might have in my head. He'd know I'd have my plan, and that I'd adapt it through the race if and as I needed to. But if he said something, even something small, that could have an impact. Like, looks like there's not much pace in the race, or Willie's horse looks well. I always found that the last thing someone said to you before you left the paddock would be the thing that would stay with you most during the race.

We were nearly always thinking the same way though, Charles and me. We'd often think the same things, without saying them to each other. It was rare that we weren't on the same wavelength. Like at the 2010 Punchestown Festival, when we were taking on Hurricane Fly with Solwhit.

Solwhit was a fantastic racehorse, he won eight Grade 1 races, a Stayers' Hurdle and an Aintree Hurdle and an Irish Champion Hurdle and a Punchestown Champion Hurdle among them. I remember the day I first rode him, at Punchestown in April 2008. I was returning from injury after breaking my wrist at Fairyhouse, I probably wasn't really ready to come back, when Frostie called me.

'Charles has a horse going in the four-year-olds' hurdle on Wednesday,' he said. 'You have to ride him.'

I was feeling a bit sore and a bit sorry for myself, and I wasn't sure. I didn't know anything about Solwhit, he had won in France and he had finished down the field in a hurdle race at Fairyhouse the previous week under Slippers Madden. But I didn't know anything about him, I didn't know what colour he was.

'You have to ride him,' said Frostie again.

'Okay,' I said. 'Put me down.'

Solwhit won that race by four lengths, with way more than that in hand.

Hurricane Fly was a brilliant hurdler, but he was a pain in the arse in the end for Solwhit. We just couldn't beat him, he was so good. When I won the Punchestown Champion Hurdle on Solwhit in 2009, Hurricane Fly was still a novice, he had won the Champion Novice Hurdle three days earlier. We did beat him in the Morgiana Hurdle at Punchestown in November 2009, but that was it. We didn't beat him again.

Solwhit usually wouldn't do a whole lot when he got to the front. He loved to be ridden in behind, he loved to be passing horses, he'd give you everything. But when he got to the front, he figured he had done his job, he just wasn't as generous. You had to ask him for everything. So I usually rode Solwhit patiently, held up in behind, delivered late and passing horses.

This day though, Punchestown Champion Hurdle day at the 2010 Punchestown Festival, the way the race was setting up, it looked like there wasn't a lot of pace in the race, and I was thinking I might ride Solwhit a little further forward, try to catch Hurricane Fly out, try to outstay him. Solwhit was a strong stayer over two miles, he would win a Stayers' Hurdle over three miles later in his career, but he was never going to win a speed test against Hurricane Fly, a dual Champion Hurdle winner. Remarkably, Hurricane Fly ended his career as a 22-time Grade 1 winner over two miles.

They've changed it since, but it used to be the case that it would get quite congested at the bottom bend at Punchestown. Roadworks, we used to call it, where there could be a lot of congestion and you could get stuck in traffic. So I was thinking, if we got ahead of the traffic at that point and kicked, Hurricane Fly could get stuck in among horses, and we might gain an advantage that might be enough to see us home.

I had this in my head when I went into the parade ring before the Punchestown Champion Hurdle in April 2010. Hurricane Fly hadn't run since we beat him in the Morgiana Hurdle at Punchestown the previous November, and I was thinking we might have a race-fitness advantage over him. All this was swilling around in my head when I met with Charles in the parade ring.

'I don't know,' Charles started saying, quietly and deliberately. 'But, you know, should we have a try, should we try to slip your man?'

'Say no more Charles,' I said, delighted he was thinking along similar lines. 'I've been thinking about it for the last few days and I've been thinking the same.'

'Grand.'

And that was it. We both knew we were on the same page, and that gave me the confidence from Charles, which was always a big help in riding the race I wanted to ride. And it all panned out exactly as Charles and I thought it might, except for the end result. I started off in a prominent position, and I moved to the front at the third last flight. I kicked at the second last, and we wheeled around the home turn. I didn't know where Hurricane Fly and Paul Townend were, but I was hoping they were stuck in traffic somewhere behind me, and that was exactly where they were.

I knew we had a nice break on the field when we straightened up for home and faced up to the final flight. I didn't look, but I could tell by the noise. I went for everything then on the run to the last, stretch Hurricane Fly, test his stamina and his race fitness, see if he can catch us.

We got to the final flight and I could hear him, I could see him out of the corner of my eye, Hurricane Fly's nose, Paul Townend's blue sleeve. He drew level with me, but he didn't get past. Not initially. Solwhit battled back bravely for me, he gave his all. But then, about three strides from the winning line, he could give no more and Hurricane Fly surged forward. When we hit the winning line, we were about a neck behind him.

It was a disappointing end to the story, but I knew Solwhit had given his all, and I knew I had given him the best ride I could possibly have given him. Hurricane Fly was just too good.

I loved Solwhit. I adored that horse. He was so brave, he was so genuine, he'd do anything for you. I was riding him in that schooling hurdle at Tipperary in November 2014 when he fell and broke his shoulder. It was just one of those things, he stepped at the hurdle and came down.

That was the saddest of days. I couldn't ride any more that day, I was too upset. He was a special horse. I took a lock of his hair.

That was the day of Lily's christening. I'll never forget it. It should have been a day of celebration but I just couldn't get into it after what had happened to poor Solwhit. I remember the day too, the weather, the rain, the wind, and my mood. And Edelle's family and my family all there, but I just couldn't pick myself up.

I still have that lock of Solwhit's hair at home.

* * *

The Punchestown Festival is different to the Cheltenham Festival. It's important of course, it's very important, and there's serious prize money to be won, and the races are hugely competitive, the Grade 1s as well as the handicaps, but Punchestown is a little more

On my way to school, with my briefcase and my shiny red shoes!

The fact that I was missing my two front teeth didn't stop me smiling

I'm looking very happy with myself, as Thunder and I are the centre of attention

First Holy Communion, with the family and the priest

Whitebarn Vixen was a right good pony, and she was able to do everything, from racing to showjumping

On my way to my first point-to-point victory on Spanish Castle at Tallow

I had some great days on Solwhit, a special horse for me

Me and Lord Windermere, neck and neck with David Casey and On My Own, on our way to victory in the 2014 Cheltenham Gold Cup

Some feeling: Tiger Roll just holds on in the 2018 Grand National

A kiss on the head from Michael O'Leary after Tiger Roll's second Grand National win in 2019

It's all about the glamour!

Winning the Grand Steeple-Chase de Paris in 2019 on Carriacou

It's great craic, Hurling for Cancer Research Day, with over €1.5 million raised for cancer research since 2011

Strutting my stuff on the stage in *Dancing With The Stars*!

Neither Edelle nor I knew where a chance encounter at the 2012 Galway Races would lead!

After winning on Liberty Dance at Thurles in December 2022 – my last winner, or so I thought! – with Edelle, Jaimee, Lily, Liam, Finn and Tess relaxed. There isn't the intensity at Punchestown that there is at Cheltenham. I don't know what it is, maybe it's because you're at home, because you can drive home every evening, there's not the same intensity of scrutiny.

Galway is different again. Again important, again great prize money to be won, especially in the Galway Hurdle and the Galway Plate, but there's a holiday atmosphere around Galway, there's a holiday crowd there and, again, it doesn't have the intensity that Cheltenham or even Punchestown has.

I always loved Galway though. When we were kids, we'd always go to Galway. We'd all go, Mam and Dad and all of us. Dad would go racing for the day and Mam would usually stick around and look after us, but sometimes Mam would go racing too and bring us. It was the only time really that Mam would go racing, it was the only meeting she would go to.

It wasn't easy for me to get a good ride in the Galway Hurdle because, back then, you usually wanted a horse who had a low weight for the Galway Hurdle. No Galway Hurdle winner between 2000 and 2005 carried more than 10st 7lb, and 10st 7lb was close to my lowest weight even then. Three winners carried 9st 9lb or less, and I would have had to have cut off a limb to do that type of weight.

I got my chance though in 2007. Brendan O'Rourke was very good to me then, he was one of the many people who used to pick me up from the airport and bring me racing when I was coming home from Ferdy's. His wife's family owned a horse who was on track for the Galway Hurdle that year, Farmer Brown, who raced in the colours of Plantation Stud.

Farmer Brown was trained by Pat Hughes, another really astute trainer, a target trainer. Brendan asked me about a month before the Galway Hurdle if I could commit to riding him in the Galway Hurdle. So I rode him in hurdle races at Sligo and at Killarney in

May, and he won both races. He ran well in a maiden on the flat at Leopardstown then in July. He finished second to a progressive young horse of Dermot Weld's and, if he hadn't been hampered late in the race, he might have won. It didn't really matter that much, the Galway Hurdle was the plan, and Pat had him spot on for it.

Actually, Pat couldn't see him getting beaten, and they backed him accordingly. A public gamble developed that saw him sent off the 9/2 favourite, which was a really short price for a horse in a Galway Hurdle with 20 runners, one and a half times around Galway's tight 10-furlong circuit, up and down hills, and all that can go wrong in a Galway Hurdle.

It nearly all went wrong very early actually. Farmer Brown stepped at the first hurdle, he stood way off it and landed on top of it. I have no idea how he stood up, but he did. He remained in the race. It wasn't ideal now, we lost ground and we lost energy and momentum, we had to take our medicine, but he was such a good horse, he was so well handicapped, he had so much in hand, that he was able to make his ground easily on the run down the hill. We led on the home turn, and he stayed on well over the last and up the hill to win comfortably.

We got some reception when we came back in. It felt like everyone on the course had backed him. It was a great training performance by Pat Hughes, to have the horse as well as he was on the day. I was delighted for Brendan and his family, to win a big prize like that, and for me, just my second ride in the race, a Galway Hurdle in the bag.

Chapter 11

Eddie O'Leary rang me one day in September 2007. He just asked if I could meet his brother Michael the following Wednesday morning in the Radisson Hotel at Dublin Airport.

That suited me fine. I was riding at Downpatrick that day and the airport was on the way.

I knew Eddie O'Leary a little bit. I would have met him at the sales, he would have been operating at the sales I was at under his Lynn Lodge Stud banner. I didn't know Michael at all. I knew he was a businessman and I knew he was the man behind Gigginstown House Stud, who owned the Gold Cup winner War Of Attrition, but I'm not even certain I knew for sure that he was the Ryanair man. I didn't read the business pages.

Gigginstown House Stud were making a mark in Irish National Hunt racing though. They were buying good horses and they were winning good races. Only J.P. McManus had had more winners than Gigginstown House Stud as an owner in Irish National Hunt racing in each of the previous three seasons.

Michael got into racehorse ownership, first with David Wachman, with Tuco. Strange coincidence, I had actually ridden Tuco to victory in his only point-to-point, at Tallow in February 2001, and I had finished third to him on Beef Or Salmon in the 2001 Land Rover Bumper.

Michael had horses with lots of trainers after that, Michael Hourigan and Paul Nolan and Charlie Swan and, of course, Mouse Morris. Famously, Mouse had trained War Of Attrition for Gigginstown to win the Cheltenham Gold Cup in 2006. War Of Attrition was their first real flagship horse, and his Gold Cup win was probably a catalyst for Michael O'Leary wanting to invest more deeply in National Hunt racing.

I had actually ridden for Gigginstown a couple of times before September 2007. I had ridden Hear The Echo for them and for Mouse to win the Grade 2 Paddy Fitzpatrick Memorial Chase at Leopardstown the previous February. I'm sure that Conor O'Dwyer, who won the Gold Cup on War Of Attrition, would have had first choice there, Conor rode One Cool Cookie in the race, but One Cool Cookie underperformed and Hear The Echo ran out a good winner. Hear The Echo actually won the Irish Grand National the following year with Paddy Flood on board, carrying 10 stone, way too light for me. I rode Cailin Alainn in the race for Charles.

I had a bit of an inkling all right that Michael might offer me the job as Gigginstown's first rider, but I'm not sure how they landed on me at the time. Conor was riding lots of their horses, but they didn't really have an obvious first rider as such. There was talk that they were looking to get a jockey to ride all their horses.

Obviously there was the Pat Doyle connection, and that was in my favour. I had a strong connection with Pat, and Pat was training a lot of the young horses for Gigginstown, getting them going, starting them off in point-to-points. Pat never said anything to me about it, I'm sure that he was very deliberate in not saying anything to me, but maybe that was how I first came to Michael's attention. I still don't know whether he did or didn't, but I'm sure Pat would have put in a strong word for me.

Either way, I don't think I was the first choice. I think they approached one or two others before they approached me. I'd say it was a bit like the lad in the night club, during the slow set, going around asking different girls to dance.

'Will you dance with me?'

'No.'

'Will your friend dance with me?'

I didn't think about it too deeply before that meeting with Michael though, I didn't figure out how I was going to react if Michael did offer me the job, what I was going to say. I didn't think about whether or not I wanted the job, I didn't look into how big or small a job it would be, I didn't ask anyone for advice, I didn't call Timmy Beecher, I didn't call Peter Vaughan, I didn't call my dad.

I didn't stop to think about the potential downsides of taking the job, what I would be getting into, what I would be giving up. Of course, I should have thought about it. I should have thought about what the job would entail, what commitments I needed from Michael, under what conditions I would or wouldn't take the job. But that was just me. Like when I was offered the job with Ferdy, I didn't tend to give these big decisions too much thought. I just went along with whatever was happening, went in whatever direction I was being taken. It was a bit like how I rode, I rode by feel. I never had too rigid a plan going into a race. I always preferred to see how the race developed and ride from there.

The discussion between Michael and me in the Radisson that morning didn't last too long. Michael said they were going to be getting more and more into this, that they were serious about it, that they were going to be buying plenty of young horses and giving it a real go. That they wanted their own rider who would commit to riding all the Gigginstown horses, insofar as was possible or reasonable. And that all their horses would be there for me to ride.

We had a cup of tea, and he offered me the job. That was it. I had a lot on my mind, I was thinking about my rides at Downpatrick that afternoon. I was actually riding a horse for Gigginstown in the beginners' chase there, Tully Hill, trained by Paul Nolan. (He didn't count, he didn't handle the fast ground.)

I was hearing all that Michael was saying, but I was thinking about all I would be giving up. Riding for Arthur Moore, riding for Robert Tyner, riding for Charles Byrnes, riding Solwhit. I kept thinking about Solwhit, that somebody else might get to ride Solwhit.

And then I'd be married to Gigginstown, committed to them. Michael said I'd be free to ride other horses if I wanted to, and Gigginstown didn't really have a horse at the time who would be competing with Solwhit, but I was thinking they could have a high-class hurdler soon and, anyway, that never worked. You're either riding for someone or you're not.

And, in my experience, it had never suited me to be tied down, I always liked to be free to make my own decisions, to juggle my own horses and try to fit them in. Be my own boss. Any time I had been tied down in the past, I was thinking, Ferdy Murphy, Edward O'Grady, it never ended well.

I stood up and shook Michael's hand. Sorry Michael, thanks for the offer, but no. Michael shook my hand, no problem, and off I went.

I got into my car and drove out of the Radisson Hotel car park. I drove down the road, out of the airport, around the first roundabout, all that Michael had said going around in my head, all the young Gigginstown horses, potentially top-class horses. Then I thought about Solwhit. Gigginstown becoming a powerhouse owner, second in the country behind J.P. McManus. And Solwhit.

I got to the second roundabout, the one where I'd usually turn right and go down the M50 to get to the M7 to get back down the road. Today though I was turning left, onto the M1 and on the way to Downpatrick.

Fuck. What have I done?

I grabbed my phone and started scrolling through the numbers to try to find Michael's. I didn't have him saved as a contact, but he had called me before our meeting so I had a few numbers in my Recent Calls list that had no names on them. One of them had to be his. I took a guess. I clicked on one of them and the phone rang.

'Hello?'

'Hello, Michael?'

'Davy.'

'I don't know what I was thinking,' I said. 'I'd be crazy to turn down your offer. I'd love to take the job, if it's still available?'

I held my breath.

'That's great,' said Michael.

Exhale.

'But I want to ride Solwhit.'

'We don't care,' Michael said. 'If we have some yoke in a race who's not good enough, and you can ride something better, no problem. We want you to be champion jockey.'

This is brilliant, I was thinking. And I had nearly blown it, I had nearly left it all behind.

And it *was* brilliant. Michael was right, they had all the established horses, but they had lots of new young horses coming through too. War Of Attrition was injured at the time, he didn't return until the 2008/09 season. The first time I rode him in a race, he won a Grade 3 chase at Punchestown in October 2008, his first run back after more than 650 days on the sidelines. Mouse did brilliantly to get him back. But there were still lots of talented horses there, Mossbank and Siegemaster and One Cool Cookie.

It was some job for me to fall into. I didn't really realise it before I started, but, really, it was a phenomenal job to land on my lap.

It was so enjoyable, riding for Gigginstown at the height of it, riding good horses, lots of good horses. Going to the races with four or five or six rides, nearly all of them well fancied, all of them going there with big chances, one or two or three favourites. And Michael and Eddie were brilliant to me, they were brilliant to deal with. I had their full backing, a hundred per cent, I was their man and that was all there was to it.

They never questioned a ride I gave any horse. They never doubted what I was doing. Not in the beginning. As time went on, they started to get stronger on this idea that I had to ride every horse prominently. That wasn't my way. To me, every horse had to be ridden the way every horse had to be ridden. Each one was different. Some of them had to be ridden prominently, I thought, but some of them needed to be dropped in. There were a whole lot of different reasons why a horse would need to be dropped in and ridden patiently.

And I didn't do instructions easily anyway. As I said, I was at my best, I was at my most comfortable, when trainers left the riding up to me, when I had completely free rein to ride the horse whatever way I wanted to ride the horse. Like with Gordon Elliott and Charles Byrnes. No instructions. You know what you're doing, nice weather we're having.

I was never very good at figuring out instructions. I rode by feel, not by a list of commands, not by a manual. If I was trying to ride to instructions, if I had to colour by number, I couldn't ride by instinct, and I always thought that my instinct was my main strength as a jockey.

This was the best job in the world though in my eyes, the Gigginstown job, and we had great success from the start. We were winning with good horses and we were winning with ordinary horses. Gigginstown had lots of horses spread out among lots of different trainers, and I tried to get around them all. Michael Hourigan and Noel Meade and Philip Rothwell and Paul Nolan and Mouse Morris and Shane Donohoe and Dessie Hughes and Arthur Moore and Charlie Swan. Charles Byrnes and Jim Gorman and Tom Taaffe and Ted Walsh and Colm Murphy and Pat Doyle and Henry de Bromhead and Gordon Elliott and Willie Mullins. They had some number of horses and they had some number of trainers training them.

I couldn't get around all the trainers obviously, it just wasn't possible. There just weren't enough days in the week. I'd try to ride a lot of the horses in schooling bumpers or in schooling hurdles, where a lot of different trainers would bring their horses along and I could ride different horses for different trainers. It made it busy though, there could be eight schooling hurdles on any given day and I'd be riding a Gigginstown horse in six or seven of them. I loved it though, all these horses, and all the ability and all the potential they had.

I always got into Willie Mullins's though. Every week, one day a week. Part of the programme was that I had to go into Willie's one day a week. You were a bit of an outsider going into a yard, any yard. You weren't one of the lads, you weren't part of the team, you weren't in there early in the morning, every morning, but the trainers and the lads were generally very good to me, they made me feel very welcome. And Michael gave me the confidence to do that anyway. They're your horses, he'd say to me. They're yours to ride, so go in and ride them.

It was the same at the sales. I remember going to the Derby Sale in Fairyhouse the year after I had taken the job and seeing Eddie O'Leary there, buying these well-bred store horses. Unbroken and untried and well-bred three-year-olds who could be Gold Cup winners in waiting. He's paying 80 or 90 or a hundred grand for these horses, and I'm thinking, that's mine to ride, that's mine to ride, that's mine to ride. I was like a spoilt child: Daddy's going to buy you 15 new ponies.

Back then, Pat Doyle would train the young Gigginstown horses, get them going, run them in point-to-points, before they'd move to other trainers and start racing under Rules. And that was good for me, because I was in Pat Doyle's lots, once or maybe twice a week, and I'd get to sit on these horses as youngsters. That meant that, if I couldn't get to Paul Nolan's or to Dessie Hughes' or to Philip Rothwell's to ride the young horses after they had joined their new trainers, I would still know them, so I wouldn't be at a disadvantage when it came to riding them in races. I would have ridden them or schooled every single one of them at least 20 times before they went to their new trainers, so I knew every one of them well.

Michael was true to his word too, he let me off to ride other horses, no problem. He even let me off to ride a different horse even in the same race as a Gigginstown horse, if that horse obviously had a better chance of winning. I was able to ride Forpadydeplasterer for Tom Cooper, for example, to win the Grade 1 Deloitte Hurdle at Leopardstown in February 2008 despite the fact that Gigginstown had Panzer Chief in the race.

I had two winners at the Cheltenham Festival in March 2008, and neither was for Gigginstown.

That was a strange Cheltenham Festival, it was the Cheltenham Festival of the high winds, when racing was abandoned on the Wednesday and they ended up fulfilling the programme by running 10 races on the Thursday and nine races on the Friday. I rode my two winners that year on the Friday, Naiad De Misselot for Ferdy in the Coral Cup, which should have been run on the Wednesday, and Tiger Cry for Arthur Moore and Chris Jones in the Grand Annual.

Arthur wasn't sure until the last minute whether he was going to let Tiger Cry run on the ground. It was as soft as he would have liked it. But the horse was in tremendous form, he had thrived even after he had arrived in Cheltenham, so Arthur decided to allow him to run, and he won well.

Tiger Cry was owned by Chris Jones, he carried the same colours as the colours that were carried by Klairon Davis, who was owned by Chris's dad, also Chris, when he won all those big races back in the 1990s, the Arkle and Champion Chase and the BMW Chase. It was great to wear those colours, to win at the Cheltenham Festival in those colours. And Chris was brilliant to me later in my career too, after I lost the job with Gigginstown. He was one of my biggest supporters during those difficult times.

* * *

Cheltenham Festival winners were important for Gigginstown House Stud. They were only interested in the big days, winning the big races, and Cheltenham was obviously as big as it got. They didn't have a Cheltenham Festival winner in 2007 or in 2008, so it was a big deal when Weapon's Amnesty arrived there in 2009, three years after War Of Attrition had won the Gold Cup. Weapon's Amnesty was running in the Albert Bartlett Hurdle three years after the previous (and first) Gigginstown Cheltenham Festival winner, and he was expected to go well.

Weapon's Amnesty was a really talented horse. He had his issues, but Charles Byrnes was superb in managing his career. He was a tall horse, by Presenting, a narrow horse, and he had to go left-handed. He was beaten at Leopardstown on his final run before the 2009 Cheltenham Festival, but that was over two and a half miles, and we expected him to improve for the step up to three miles in the Albert Bartlett Hurdle.

I actually had Weapon's Amnesty's half-brother. Robert Widger and I bought him at the Goffs Land Rover Sale in June 2008. This was before Weapon's Amnesty even ran on the track. He had been beaten in two point-to-points before that, but we liked his half-brother, we thought he was value at €18,000.

We actually sold him the following December at the Brightwells breeze-up sale, ironically on the day I rode Weapon's Amnesty to win his maiden hurdle at Gowran Park. Philip Rothwell bought him for €15,000, €3,000 less than we paid for him. That wasn't very astute business there by Robert Widger and me! And Weapon's Amnesty won the Grade 3 Dorans Pride Hurdle at Limerick's Christmas meeting a few weeks later. If we had waited a little while, we probably would have got a whole lot more for his half-brother. He was named Current Resession (spelt like that, really) and he won his bumper all right, but he obviously wasn't nearly as good as Weapon's Amnesty.

I loved riding Weapon's Amnesty, because you could ride him cold, out the back. He could be keen enough, so it was important that you got him settled early on, and he loved passing horses. I rode him in behind the leaders in the 2009 Albert Bartlett Hurdle and delivered him to hit the front at the final flight. He idled a little on the run-in, that was his way, but he stayed on well enough in the end to get home by a half a length.

That was fantastic, my fifth Cheltenham Festival winner. It was Gigginstown's second, their first after War Of Attrition's Gold Cup, and that obviously meant a lot to Michael and Eddie. And the following year, when Weapon's Amnesty went back to Cheltenham and won the RSA Chase, he was their third and my sixth.

Weapon's Amnesty was injured after that, which was a real shame. Charles gave him every chance, nursed him back, tried to get him right again and, actually, he did make it back to the track, for the Christmas Hurdle at Leopardstown in 2012, almost three years after he had won the RSA Chase. I rode him there, I just rode him to look after him, get him to run well if I could, but he never travelled, he just wasn't the same horse, and he was retired after that.

It was a real shame, because Weapon's Amnesty could have gone right to the top as a staying chaser, he could have been a Gold Cup horse. He was a top-class staying novice, as a hurdler and a chaser, he is one of just three horses to win the Albert Bartlett Hurdle and the RSA Chase, and one of the others is Bobs Worth, who won the Gold Cup.

* * *

During the lead-up to the 2011 Festival, with First Lieutenant on track for the Neptune Hurdle, I was chatting to his trainer Mouse Morris.

'How many Cheltenham Festival winners have you ridden?' he asked.

I had to think about it for a second. Weapon's Amnesty's two, Native Jack, Naiad De Misselot, Tiger Cry. Five. And Joes Edge. Six.

'Six,' I said.

'Yeah, well this fellow will be your seventh.'

I loved First Lieutenant. I knew him from very early, another Presenting horse, he was bred by Mary O'Connor just out the road from us in Tallow. And I knew his dam well, a Fourstars Allstar mare, Fourstargale, I actually rode her in a bumper at Punchestown back in the day. John Thomas usually rode her though, he won a couple of bumpers on her at Limerick.

My soft spot for First Lieutenant later in his career cost me a few big winners. Gigginstown had three runners in the Grade 1 Drinmore Chase at Fairyhouse in November 2011, I rode First Lieutenant, and Ruby Walsh won the race on one of the other Gigginstown horses, Bog Warrior. I could have ridden him. First Lieutenant broke a blood vessel in the race.

Gigginstown had three runners again in the Grade 1 Fort Leney Chase at Leopardstown that Christmas, I chose to ride First Lieutenant, and we finished second behind Brian O'Connell and Last Instalment. I could have ridden him too.

I remember First Lieutenant at the sales, at the Derby Sale in 2008, he was offset in one knee. Eddie gave a lot of money for him,

€255,000, everybody said it was madness to give so much money for a horse with an offset knee. But it just shows you, the judge that Eddie O'Leary is, all that First Lieutenant went on to achieve, we know now with the benefit of hindsight that he was one of the cheapest horses at that sale.

I got beaten on First Lieutenant the first time I rode him in a race, in a novices' hurdle at Fairyhouse in November 2010. The ground was awful that day, on the inside track at Fairyhouse, he kept stumbling, he didn't handle the ground, and he was lame when he got home. I don't think they used the inside track at Fairyhouse for a while after that.

He was an odds-on shot that day, we thought he would win and I'm sure a lot of punters backed him. I know one who did anyway, the fellow who jumped in over the rail and tried to have a go at me, shouting at me, cursing and blinding, while at the same time telling me how bad a rider I was. I tried to catch a hold of him but I couldn't. It's probably just as well for both of us that I didn't.

It was a different story at Leopardstown that Christmas in the Future Champions' Novice Hurdle, different day, different ground, different scenario. Zaidpour was the odds-on shot, First Lieutenant was a big price, but he always travelled well for me and he stayed on well to hold off Zaidpour's challenge.

He had guts as well as class, First Lieutenant, and he showed them again at Cheltenham the following March in the Neptune Hurdle. Plenty of people said that Oscars Well would have won if he hadn't made that mistake at the final flight, but I'm not sure we wouldn't have won anyway. It was a bad mistake that Oscars Well made, he lost his hind legs and he lost lots of momentum, but First Lieutenant finished off his race strongly, he galloped up the hill to get up and beat Rock On Ruby by a short head, and he might have beaten Oscars Well too even if that horse had jumped the final flight well. That was a strong race too, Rock On Ruby won the Champion Hurdle the following year.

Mouse was right though, Mouse is often right, he did provide me with my seventh Cheltenham Festival winner. And my eighth came about two hours later, when I won the Coral Cup on Carlito Brigante, who was trained by Gordon Elliott.

I knew Gordon well. I knew him from our point-to-point days when we were both amateur riders. I knew him from sharing lifts with him if we were going up to a meeting in the north, there'd be a load of us in the car, Norman Geraghty and Simon McGonagle and, maybe if we were lucky and he consented to join us, John Thomas McNamara!

Gordon would usually arrange it so that I'd end up driving. We'd be meeting in Slane, and it was a fair old drive for me from Youghal to Slane, about three and a half hours, and I was still only about two-thirds of the way to the north when I got to Slane, which was just down the road for Gordon. So I'd get to Slane early, I'd be having a snooze in the car and, next thing I'd know, Gordon would be sitting in the passenger seat beside me.

Let's go.

Gordon was a very good amateur rider, he was brave, he rode short, he was stylish, but he always struggled with his weight, so it wasn't surprising when he went down the training route. He started his training operation from scratch and he built it up. He won ordinary races with ordinary horses, and he kicked on. He went wherever he needed to go, he went to places where he thought he could win races, he started taking his horses across to Britain in 2006 and 2007, to Perth, to Newton Abbot, to run in races he thought they could win, and they did. Then he won the Aintree Grand National in 2007 with Silver Birch. It is still astonishing that Gordon hadn't trained a winner in Ireland before he won the Grand National, the most famous horse race in the world.

I wasn't really riding for Gordon at the time. I was riding for Gigginstown obviously, and I ended up riding for Gordon when he had runners for them. He wasn't one of the trainers I used to go to and ride out with regularly though. Not once a week anyway, maybe once a month on average. Like, if there was a race meeting at Fairyhouse or at Navan, I might go up the night before, stay with Gordon that night and ride out in the morning before racing.

Gordon was very relaxed about it. If I could come in, I could come in, whatever suited. He was always very easy like that. No pressure. He had his own riders anyway.

Gordon started off training the young horses for Gigginstown but, as time went on, he began to train more and more for them. Michael and Eddie reduced the number of trainers they had horses with too, which was good for me, it meant I didn't have to try to get around as many yards. But, when they did, Gordon was always very much part of the team.

The first genuinely good horse Gordon had for Gigginstown was Tharawaat, a well-bred horse by Alhaarth who had run a few times on the flat for Barry Hills and Sheikh Hamdan Al Maktoum. I rode Tharawaat to win his maiden hurdle at Navan in early November 2008, and to win the Grade 3 juveniles' hurdle at the Hatton's Grace Hurdle meeting back at Fairyhouse later that month. He was a good juvenile hurdler, he ran in the Triumph Hurdle at Cheltenham that season, but he was sent off at a big price and he finished down the field behind Zaynar.

Carlito Brigante was sent off as favourite for the Triumph Hurdle the following year, 2010, after winning his first two races for Gordon but, while he ran well for me for a long way, ultimately he came under pressure and we could only finish fourth.

We thought he would go well in the Coral Cup in 2011 though. He had been beaten in a two-horse race on his previous run, but that was on soft ground over two miles. We thought the better ground at Cheltenham would suit him, and that the step back up in trip to two miles and five furlongs would be in his favour. Also, importantly, Gordon had him in some form. It was his first run in a handicap hurdle too, he had been competing in graded hurdles and in conditions hurdles, and we thought he would appreciate the move into handicap company.

That was a big day for Gordon, he had his first Cheltenham Festival winner earlier in the day when Derek O'Connor rode Chicago Grey to victory in the National Hunt Chase, the big staying novices' chase for amateur riders. It was a lot, to hope you could have the first Cheltenham Festival winner of your career and the second Cheltenham Festival winner of your career on the same day but, to be honest, there was never a point in the race where I thought Carlito Brigante wouldn't win.

After we had jumped two hurdles, I thought we would win. It was a strange and rare feeling. He travelled so well for me, he bounced off the ground and did everything I wanted him to do in the race. I just let him move into the lead on the run to the final flight, and he cleared away up the run-in. Our nearest pursuer, For Non Stop, fell at the last, but it didn't matter, he wouldn't have got close to us.

Carlito Brigante was my eighth Cheltenham Festival winner, and the 2011 Cheltenham Festival was my sixth Cheltenham Festival in a row with at least one winner.

Chapter 12

On the Sunday before the 2012 Galway Festival, I was out pucking a ball around at home when I went up to catch the ball and felt this shooting pain in my back. I thought I was after pulling a muscle, so I stopped playing and went inside to rest. The pain was still there after a while though, it wasn't getting any better, so I thought I'd better go and get it seen to, the day before the Galway Festival, I wanted to be okay. I went to Cork University Hospital, got an X-ray and got the diagnosis: spontaneous pneumothorax, a punctured lung.

They took me in straight away and they were able to draw the air out of it and fix me up. All I was concerned about was whether I would be able to ride at Galway, and I was. I had a few decent rides early in the week, Discoteca in the opening four-year-olds' hurdle on the Monday, Maxim Gorky in the handicap hurdle. I had Rebel Fitz in the Galway Hurdle later in the week, and I didn't want to miss that. I was fine though, all was good with my lung, I didn't think about it again.

Those two rides on the first evening were both for Gigginstown. I finished fourth on Discoteca for Gordon in the opening four-year-olds' novices' hurdle, and I finished second on Maxim Gorky for Noel Meade in the second race, the handicap hurdle.

Monday evening, the first evening of the Galway Festival, was always a mixed card, two hurdle races followed by five other races, flat races and amateur riders' races and a bumper, and I wasn't eligible to ride in any of those. It was the same on Tuesday, only two National Hunt races that I was eligible to ride in, and I didn't have a ride in either. So I had a free day on Tuesday, I figured it would be okay to extend my curfew a little on Monday evening.

We had great craic that evening in Galway city. There was a good crew of us out now, and we met up with some of the Limerick hurlers. Limerick had just been knocked out of the championship, they had been beaten in the quarter-final of the All-Ireland by Kilkenny the previous day, so they were on an evening out in Galway, they were letting their hair down a bit. Niall Moran and Donal O'Grady and Gavin O'Mahony and Brian Geary. Brian was retiring from inter-county hurling, so the lads had to mark it.

I didn't know Edelle O'Meara then but, in a parallel universe, as I was on my way to Galway on the Monday morning, she was coming home from a four-week spell in America. She had literally arrived in the door of her family home in Portumna as her parents were on the way out the door to go to the races. Her parents asked her to go with them, she said no, she was wrecked, just in the door from America. But it's your father's birthday, we'll go to the races, then we'll go for something to eat in town for your father's birthday. So she went along.

Just shows you, sliding doors moments. You never know how life would have worked out if she hadn't.

So, while Edelle was in town with her parents, she met a friend of hers, and she went on down the town with her, to Shop Street and onto The Quays. I was staying in a hotel in Claregalway so, after our night out, having the craic, I was getting into my car, my silver Toyota Avensis, completely sober, but it was late, about two in the morning. All the lads were clambering into my car, party back in Davy's hotel, they were saying. Next thing these two girls arrive along and one of them starts talking to one of the lads. Turns out, Edelle's friend Marie knows one of the lads. So I do the only thing a gentleman could have done in that situation, I started chatting to Edelle. The fact that she was drop-dead gorgeous wasn't a factor, honestly.

The two girls joined in the craic at the 'party', such as it was. It was fairly mild now as parties go, there were as many cups of tea in the residents' bar as there were pints of Guinness. I was kind of the host and I was kind of the DJ, but I still managed to spend most of the night talking to Edelle. As well as being gorgeous, she was sound, just a really cool person. So I said to her friend Marie that I would love to take Edelle out to dinner the following night.

I spoke to Edelle the following day, she was happy to go out for dinner with me, so I asked her to choose the restaurant. This was Galway Races week now, it would have been difficult enough to get a table, so Edelle suggested a place in Bearna, about 10 miles from the city. I was thinking, grand, there's a good chance we won't meet anybody we know out in Bearna.

Actually, there isn't. As we walk into the restaurant, the first person I see is Ken Whelan, the former jockey who is now a jockey's agent. He's there having dinner with his wife. How's it going, this is Edelle, all that. Then we're sitting down, just about to order and next thing, in walks my dad! He just comes straight over to us, this is Edelle, all that again. Then Jerry says he's going to get Phyllis, and off he goes.

Edelle looks at me.

'Who's Phyllis?'

'My mother.'

So our first date, Edelle and me, trying to have a quiet meal together, trying to get to know each other, and we are joined for dinner by my mam and dad. They thought we had been together for ages and that I just hadn't bothered telling them, but no, this was a first date all right. Edelle was brilliant though, we had a great night.

Lucky she had picked the restaurant.

Edelle is a secondary school teacher, she has a Master's in Biomedical Science and she teaches Maths and Chemistry. She wasn't really sure she wanted to be a teacher but, the year her mother was undergoing chemotherapy, she took a year out. The school across the road from her home were looking for a Chemistry teacher at the time, so she just went in to help out, and she discovered that she loved teaching Chemistry to kids.

She is also a national pole vault champion. She was always big into athletics, she would go to the athletics club every week as a kid. She was a sprinter and she was a high jumper, she was a gymnast as well, but she's 5ft 4in, she couldn't get beyond 160cm in the high jump, so one day her trainer suggested she try the pole vault, so she did. She was a natural. She competed at a high level, she won a couple of national pole vault titles. She was very good. She used to go up to Belfast to train with her national coach, Jim Alexander, drive from Portumna to Antrim every week. Unfortunately, she got deep vein thrombosis in her upper body, brought on by her pole vaulting, and eventually she had to retire.

I didn't mention to Edelle at dinner that I was a jockey. It just didn't come up, and I didn't see the need or the point. I think she thought I was a hurler, or a farmer, or a fireman, or maybe all three. Anyway, she went home and told her dad she had been out to dinner with this guy, Davy Russell.

Her dad was suddenly interested. The jockey?

Edelle's late father was into racing. He had a betting shop in Portumna and he used to go racing around the western tracks, Galway and Ballinrobe and Sligo and Roscommon. Edelle would go with him sometimes when she was smaller, and she used to work in the betting shop on Saturdays, but she was never really into racing.

No, he's not a jockey. I think he's a fireman.

I won the Galway Hurdle on the Thursday. I rode Rebel Fitz to victory for Mick Winters, we just held on from the fast-finishing Cause Of Causes. I knew Rebel Fitz well, and it was brilliant to win the Galway Hurdle on him, for Mick Winters and Brian Sweetnam, a second Galway Hurdle for me. I had ridden Rebel Fitz to win three times as a novice hurdler the previous season and, on his final run before Galway, we had won the Grade 3 Grimes Hurdle at Tipperary. And, as with Farmer Brown in the 2007 Galway Hurdle, he was well fancied by connections and he was well backed by the public.

I rode him patiently, well back early on, and I took my time on him. We must have had about 12 horses in front of us jumping the second last flight, but I knew he had plenty of energy left and, when I took him towards the outside on the run to the final flight, he gave plenty. We hit the front at the last and he stayed on well up the hill.

Cause Of Causes gave me a bit of a fright I have to say, I was just punching the air at the winning line, the Galway Hurdle in the bag, when I saw Cause Of Causes' head and Davy Condon's arm on my left. People said I was celebrating too early, but I wasn't. I thought the race was over and I just stuck out my arm, like Johnny Murtagh used to do when he had won a big race on the flat. I thought we had held on all right, but I decided that, if we were beaten, I'd go all the way around the track to the far side, get to the road over there, and get off the horse and go into town. I definitely couldn't have gone back into the unsaddling enclosure if we had been beaten.

I met Edelle that night again, she came along to join the celebrations in town after Rebel Fitz's win. That was another good night. There was a fundraiser the following Friday night, a barn dance of all things, in Portumna in which Edelle was involved, she asked me if I could go along to it. I had no rides at Galway on the Friday, again there were only two National Hunt races and I didn't have a ride in either, so that was fine. But Mick Winters and Rebel Fitz's owner Brian Sweetnam, brother of the international showjumper Shane Sweetnam, were having a bit of a gig in Kanturk for Rebel Fitz's win, so of course I had to go to that. So I went to Kanturk first, then I headed up the road and got to Portumna for the end of the barn dance.

Edelle's mother, God rest her, was terminally ill then, she passed away a few weeks later, but she was in great form that night and it was lovely to meet her. Her dad passed away in 2023, but he followed my career really closely from the day I met Edelle. He'd be onto me, asking me about different horses. Or he'd be onto Edelle, how's Davy doing, what did he think of this or what did he think of that? Edelle idolised her dad, and she really cherished that connection she had with him through racing in his later years.

That day, Galway Hurdle day, before Edelle left her house to go into town, her dad was watching the *Six One* news on RTÉ when the sports news came on: Rebel Fitz won the Galway Hurdle. He called Edelle into the sitting room. Is that your man Davy Russell?

So, not a fireman after all.

* * *

Sir Des Champs won nicely at Navan in January 2011. I kept him a little wide, I kept him on the better ground, but it didn't matter, he had lots in hand. That was his first run for Gigginstown, his first run in Ireland, his first run for Willie Mullins. But he wasn't a novice, he had won a hurdle race in France the previous year, so he wasn't eligible for any of the novice hurdles at Cheltenham that year. He ran instead in the Martin Pipe Conditional Jockeys' Handicap Hurdle, but I obviously couldn't ride him in that as I wasn't a conditional jockey. Emmet Mullins rode him, and he won. It didn't look likely at the top of the hill, it appeared that he was struggling to go the pace, but his stamina kicked in then, they usually go fast in that race, and he stayed on well to get up on the line.

That was Sir Des Champs all over. He was obviously a talented horse, but he was slow. And it was almost as if he'd get bored halfway through a race. You'd be travelling away and travelling away grand there, and next thing, he'd just down tools and you'd have to drive him along. It was as if he decided he had done enough, that it was just too easy, so you'd have to drive him along. A set of cheekpieces might have helped him, he wore cheekpieces when he won that hurdle race in France, but he only ever wore cheekpieces once when he was with Willie, in the Bet365 Gold Cup at Sandown in April 2016, when he was pulled up.

He had a great novice chasing season the following year, 2011/12, he ran five times and he won five times. I couldn't ride him when he won the Grade 2 Greenmount Park Novice Chase at Limerick at Christmas, I was busy at Leopardstown riding a double. Emmet Mullins rode him again that day, but I rode him in his other four races, including the Grade 1 Growise Champion Novice Chase at the Punchestown Festival and the Grade 2 Jewson Chase at the Cheltenham Festival.

He was brilliant that day. I'd say that was his best performance that year and one of the best of his career. It was over two and a half miles, a distance that was short of his best, but he did everything, he travelled, he jumped, he showed pace and he showed his class, and we won easily. He was my Cheltenham Festival winner that year, continuing my run of Cheltenham Festival winners.

I wanted to be champion jockey too, and I was getting closer. I finished fourth in the championship in 2004/05 with 48 winners, and third in 2005/06 with 75 winners. Then I finished second, then second again, then second again. I just couldn't beat Ruby Walsh. In the 2007/08 Irish National Hunt season, I rode 125 winners. It would have been enough to have won every championship since I had turned professional but, that season, Ruby Walsh rode 131, more winners than any jockey had ridden in an Irish National Hunt season since Charlie Swan set the record of 147 in 1995/96.

I was second again to Ruby in 2008/09 and again in 2009/10. Ruby missed a lot of the 2010/11 season through injury, but his understudy at Willie Mullins's, Paul Townend, beat me, 80 to 75.

That was frustrating. You'd think, when you'd have Ruby beaten, you'd go and win the championship. But then Paul came along, he was only a young fellow at the time, but he rode all those horses for Willie Mullins that Ruby would have ridden, and he was brilliant on them. I remember Paul pony racing, he was special, he was always a special rider. He was a lovely rider as a kid, and he's a lovely rider now as a man. And he's a lovely fellow. He deserves his position now as Willie Mullins's first jockey, he took over from Ruby when he retired, and he has been champion jockey six times to date.

That was his first championship, the 2010/11 championship, when he beat me by five, and I was starting to think that it just wasn't going to happen for me.

But it did happen for me the following season, I was champion jockey in 2011/12, and that was brilliant. Finally. It was one of the main things I wanted to achieve in my career. To be champion, to ride more winners than anybody else in a season. Winning all those big races, the Grand National, the Gold Cup, of course they were all brilliant, but to be champion was on a different level. Whatever sport you're in, whatever discipline you compete in, everybody's ultimate objective is to win, to be the best, to be the champion in that discipline. If I had got to the end of my career without being champion jockey, that would have been a major regret.

* * *

I was Gigginstown's jockey, but I wasn't every trainer's jockey. Some of the trainers weren't happy with the way I was riding their horses, and some of them might have been happy enough but, if results weren't going well with the Gigginstown horses, those trainers needed a reason why. It couldn't have been the trainer and, if it wasn't the trainer, then it was probably the jockey.

I remember riding a Gigginstown horse at Leopardstown one day, at the Christmas Festival in 2008. He was a really nicely bred horse, an Aga Khan-bred horse who had won a maiden on the flat over 10 furlongs for John Oxx. He had a lovely profile as a potential National Hunt horse, and the trainer told me that he was a Triumph Hurdle horse.

It was a messy race, there was carnage at the second flight where two horses ran out, it was all over the place, and the horse didn't run well. We finished sixth, that was as good as he was. But the trainer started giving me grief when I came back in, in front of Michael and Eddie. Usually I'd take it on the chin and walk away, but I couldn't on this occasion. I gave it back to him. Triumph Hurdle? Are you joking? This fellow wouldn't win a donkey derby.

The horse ran 10 times after that, and he lost 10 times.

But there was lots of that, trainers blaming me when things didn't go well. More quietly, more subtly, in Michael and Eddie's ear, not as blatantly as that, not in the unsaddling area after a race.

Charles Byrnes wouldn't have done it, I was Charles's jockey. Pat Doyle wouldn't have done it, Gordon Elliott wouldn't have done it. Gordon would call a spade a spade, and he was getting the results. Dessie Hughes was solid. Good trainers. It was the trainers who weren't getting the results who needed to give a reason why they weren't.

I would touch base with Eddie or Michael every day. Every day on my way home after racing, I'd text them or call them. I always preferred it when Michael was at the races though. It meant that he could see at first hand what was happening and, if things didn't go to plan, you got all the explanations and all the giving out done there and then at the races. If Michael wasn't at the races, you could be in for a long phone call on the way home.

I tried to ride the horses the way Eddie and Michael wanted them ridden, up with the pace, handy away, out of trouble. I really did. I always had the best of intentions, but I struggled with it. Like, you'd start off handy, but they'd be going fast up front and you wouldn't be able to lie up easily. After two fences, you're fourth, and you're bursting your horse just to get him to lie up handily. You're trying to be handy and you're trying to be handy, but he's struggling to go the pace, he's on his head for the whole race. Then, all of a sudden, the race is over and you've finished fifth.

Given free rein in a situation like that, I'd let him drop in a little bit. If they were going faster than he could go, I'd give him a chance, drop him back in the field, allow him to find his position and his rhythm, fill him up, give him a bit of confidence, then try to get him to make ground. I always wanted to set off, get horses relaxed, let them settle in whatever position was comfortable for them, then spend the rest of the race improving that position. Get him to finish off his race well, enjoy the experience.

I could see it from Michael and Eddie's point of view. They were spending big money on good horses, and they wanted them ridden a certain way. They thought that was the way that would maximise their chances of winning. They wanted it kept simple, ride the race simply and the best horse will win and, often, Gigginstown would have the best horse. I'm not saying they were wrong either, it's a fairly strong argument. And I'm not saying I was right. I'm just saying I struggled with the concept, that the simplicity of it all, the one-size-fits-all approach, was difficult for me to grasp. I always thought race-riding was more nuanced than that, I thought that different horses and different situations called for different courses of action.

DAVY RUSSELL

I just wasn't able to do it, not every time. I hate to see horses running keenly. I think it's such a waste of energy. I always wanted to get a horse switched off and comfortable, travelling easily and relaxed. Some of them could do that in a prominent position, but others needed to be switched off in behind horses, covered up in among horses, conserving energy, passing horses. Lord Windermere was one of them.

Chapter 13

The first time I rode Lord Windermere, I ended up on the floor.

Jim Culloty called me one day in February 2013 to ask if I would be free to ride him in the RSA Chase at Cheltenham the following month.

Jim is obviously best known as Best Mate's jockey. When Best Mate won the Cheltenham Gold Cup in 2004, he became the first horse since Arkle to win three Gold Cups in a row, and Jim Culloty rode him to victory in all three. Actually, Best Mate won 14 times in his career, and Jim rode him to 13 of those victories.

Jim also rode other top-class horses for Best Mate's trainer Henrietta Knight, Lord Noelie and Edredon Bleu and Folly Pleasant and Impek among them, and he won the Grand National in 2002 on Bindaree for Nigel Twiston-Davies, thereby becoming one of a small band of jockeys who have won the Gold Cup and the Grand National, and he did it in the same year. He had recently started training and was just getting going.

It was unusual for Gigginstown not to have a high-class staying novice chaser in any given year, a horse who would be good enough to run in the RSA Chase, but they didn't that year, so I was delighted to get Jim's call. I went down to his place, Mount Corbitt House in Churchtown in Cork, and I had a sit on Lord Windermere, cantered down over a couple of schooling fences and landed at the back of the last. As soon as we landed, Lord Windermere stopped and whipped around, but my momentum carried me forward, over his shoulder, out the side and onto the ground.

Lord Windermere just stood there looking down at me: welcome to Mount Corbitt.

It was an open RSA Chase that year, 2013, there was no Denman or Weapon's Amnesty in the race, no Bobs Worth, and we were going into it with a chance. I settled Lord Windermere towards the back of the field early on and along the inside, got him relaxed and jumping. I stayed on the inside on the run down the hill and over the third last. We were travelling well, I knew I had plenty of horse underneath me but I wanted to continue to conserve energy, it's a long way from the final bend to the winning line at Cheltenham, up the hill. Lord Windermere had never raced over three miles before in his life, and I didn't want to ask him for his effort until I had to.

It all got a bit tight on the run around the home turn, and he actually stumbled a little before we straightened up. He recovered his equilibrium fairly quickly though, and I moved him to the outside as we turned for home. We had about four lengths to find on the leader Boston Bob when we landed over the second last fence, but we had momentum up, and I knew he had plenty of energy left.

Lyreen Legend and Paul Carberry were between me and Paul Townend on Boston Bob but, out of the corner of my eye, I could still see Boston Bob crumple on landing over the final fence and hit the floor. That left me with just Lyreen Legend to beat, and we got the better of him halfway up the run-in before going on to win by over a length.

That was brilliant, another Cheltenham Festival winner, an RSA Chase win. It was my first time to ride Lord Windermere in a race, and he had been great. It was great for Jim too, his first big win, his first Grade 1 win as a trainer, and for the horse's owner, Dr Ronan Lambe, an absolute gentleman.

I had no ride in the next race, the Champion Chase, I just watched on the television in the weigh room and marvelled, as everybody did, at Sprinter Sacre. He was such an impressive winner, one of the best two-mile chasers ever. Then I went out in the next race, the Coral Cup, on Un Beau Matin, and we fell at the final flight. We were beaten at the time, we would have finished sixth or seventh or eighth, but it was a hard-enough fall, I felt quite sore afterwards around my ribs. I didn't think too much about it though, I just went back to my hotel and rested.

The following day, the Thursday morning, I'm out on the gallops, I'm riding Sir Des Champs out, just letting him stretch his legs in the morning, the day before I'm going to ride him in the Gold Cup. He's in great form now, he has a right chance in the Gold Cup.

So I'm walking back up the hill with him, I'm leading him up, and he's marching back up the hill, full of energy. I feel a bit short of breath as I'm walking up the hill with him and, when I get to the top of the hill, I feel this pain in my back. A little like the pain I felt when I stretched for the ball back at home when I was pucking around before the Galway Festival seven and a half months earlier.

I get to the opening in the car park outside the stable, I still have a hold of Sir Des Champs' reins, but the pain is getting worse, I know I'm in trouble. I can see Fiona Mullins, Emmet's sister, over by the archway, but I don't have a stable pass to get into the stable yard, so I call to her and she comes over and takes the horse.

'Are you okay?'

I'm just standing there, the pain getting worse, trying to figure out what to do. My car is about 65 yards away, the security hut is about 45 yards away, and I'm thinking, I won't make it to my car, so I head for the security hut. It was the luck of God that I did, because the security guard called a paramedic straight away, who came along immediately, figured out it was my punctured lung, my spontaneous pneumothorax, and rushed me to Cheltenham General Hospital.

You learn lots with these things, you learn lots about the medical side of it, and the thing I learned about a punctured lung is, it's not the actual puncture that causes the pain. It's that, when the lung deflates, the air gets between your lung and your chest, so the lung can't inflate again. That's what causes the pain.

I also learned that soldiers carry a tub of talcum powder with them in their pack so that, if they get shot, they squirt the talcum powder into the wound! So, when their lung pushes back out again, it sticks to the wall of their chest and can reinflate.

They were brilliant at Cheltenham General Hospital, they had me fixed in no time, lung drained and blown back up again and I'm bouncing and ready to go again on the same day. I rode a horse for Tom Taaffe and Fitri Hay in the first race on the Thursday, the Jewson Chase, Argocat, and all was fine. Then I went out in the next race, the Pertemps Final, on Stonemaster for Gigginstown, trained by Dessie Hughes, and my lung went again. I knew I was in trouble again, I couldn't draw a breath.

We finished the race anyway, we pulled up, and I remember I was there on Stonemaster, walking down the chute to come back into the unsaddling enclosure, I couldn't hold the horse, I could hardly breathe. A.P. McCoy had finished fourth on Shutthefrontdoor, he was just in front of me, and I remember asking him if he could hold my horse, because I couldn't. He mustn't have heard me or understood me, because he looked at me as if I had two heads, then headed off down the chute away from me!

I got back in though, and I got to see the doctor. We're in trouble again here lads. So that was the end of the 2013 Cheltenham Festival for me. They took me to hospital, put in the pipes and kept me there for a few days.

It was gutting to miss the rest of Thursday and all of Friday at Cheltenham of course. I was due to ride First Lieutenant in the third race on Thursday, the Ryanair Chase, the race after the Pertemps Final, but I obviously couldn't do that. Bryan Cooper took over on him and rode him to finish second to Cue Card.

That was a dreadful day, that Thursday at Cheltenham. That was the day John Thomas McNamara had that sickening fall at the first fence in the Kim Muir Chase, which resulted in him fracturing his C3 and C4 vertebrae. That was a terrible day. John Thomas was one of the most gifted and one of the most successful amateur riders ever, we had some great times together, there was great rivalry between us, but there was also great camaraderie, and I was so sad when I heard of his accident. He was paralysed from the neck down, and it was desperately sad when he passed away three years later.

* * *

A.P. McCoy rode Sir Des Champs in the Gold Cup on the Friday, and he ran well to finish second behind Bobs Worth.

Solwhit won the Stayers' Hurdle on the Thursday. I was delighted for Charles but I was gutted for me, even though I wouldn't have been riding him anyway. I was set to ride Bog Warrior for Gigginstown, I had to ride for Gigginstown even though I knew Bog Warrior would struggle on the goodish ground, I knew Solwhit had a far better chance of winning the race. (Bog Warrior was well named.) If Bog Warrior hadn't run, I would have ridden Solwhit obviously, but Bog Warrior ran all right, they were always intent on running him even though he had very little chance on the ground. Paul Carberry rode Solwhit, and he gave him a super ride. I was happy for Paul and I was delighted for Charles and for Solwhit's owners, the Top Of The Hill Syndicate. I was just sad for me.

I figured I'd be back to ride Solwhit in the Liverpool Hurdle at the following month.

I needed surgery to fix the problem, I knew that. After all the assessments, they said I could have keyhole surgery, which had a 96% success rate, or I could have open surgery, which had a 98% success rate. Obviously, the open surgery had a slightly higher success rate, but the difference was marginal, and the actual surgery was far more invasive. Open surgery would have put me on the sidelines for weeks. With keyhole surgery though, I could be back within days, and, with a 96% success rate, the odds were good.

For me, it was no-brainer. Keyhole surgery, I'd take my chances, 96% versus 98%, and I'd be back for Aintree to ride Solwhit in the Liverpool Hurdle and First Lieutenant in the Betfred Bowl and something in the Grand National. The problem was that the British Horseracing Authority (BHA) wouldn't accept keyhole surgery, they said I had to have open surgery if they were going to give me a licence to ride again in Britain. That was the stipulation.

I went over to London on the Thursday before Aintree with all my paperwork, to get clearance so I could ride at Aintree. But no, the BHA's doctor Michael Turner wasn't having it, he said the risk was too great. He wouldn't let me ride there unless I had open surgery. But, if I had had open surgery, I wouldn't have been back in time for Aintree.

I was fuming. It made no sense. I wasn't going to be allowed to ride in Britain again unless and until I had open surgery. The keyhole surgery, with its 96% success rate, was not good enough.

Compare that to how the Chief Medical Officer for the Turf Club in Ireland, Dr Adrian McGoldrick, dealt with my situation. I showed Dr McGoldrick all the tests, all the results, same as I did in London, and he said, work away. You'll be fine, you'll be good, we'll keep an eye on you.

DAVY RUSSELL

That was Adrian McGoldrick for you, always working with you, always looking out for the jockeys, always with their best interests at heart. He was a brilliant Chief Medical Officer. Safety was paramount, of course, but he applied a whole lot of common sense, and that was refreshing. I needed to be back riding if I was going to try to be champion jockey, so I was so grateful to Dr McGoldrick that he applied some common sense to the situation.

I was back riding at Mallow on 21 March, one week to the day after I'd had my incident at Cheltenham. Nine days later, I was ruled out of Aintree.

That was a difficult Aintree. Bryan Cooper deputised for me on First Lieutenant, and he won the Betfred Bowl. I always felt that was the start of the end of my time with Gigginstown. I always felt that win just loosened the bonds of our relationship a bit, and strengthened Bryan's relationship with Michael and Eddie.

That was a big winner for Bryan, who'd had three winners at the Cheltenham Festival the previous month. He was a young rider on the up, he was riding plenty of winners and he was riding lots for Gigginstown. He was more or less riding all the Gigginstown horses I couldn't ride, and First Lieutenant at Aintree, in a Grade 1 race, in a Betfred Bowl, that was his first big win for Gigginstown, his first Grade 1 win for Gigginstown.

It wasn't easy, riding at Thurles on the first day of the Aintree Grand National meeting. And it wasn't easy, riding at Navan on Grand National day, watching the Grand National on a television screen from the weigh room at Navan, watching on the same screen from Navan as Solwhit won the Liverpool Hurdle under Paul Carberry.

Dr McGoldrick put my open surgery off until after the Punchestown Festival, I was able to ride away until the end of the season, and that was good. I was a couple of days in the Mater Private hospital under Professor Lars Nolke, who was superb. Johnny Harrington was actually in the ward across the way, and he came across to see me often. Johnny was a brilliant man, a gentleman, Jessie's husband and a fantastic operator within the racing and bloodstock industries, known and respected by so many people.

I won the championship again that year too, my second championship, back-to-back championships. I beat Ruby Walsh by two winners, 103 to 101. That was brilliant. I rode a winner at Downpatrick on the Wednesday before the Grand National meeting started, and I rode a winner at Navan on Grand National day. If I had been involved at Aintree, if I had been allowed to go, if the BHA had given me a licence, I might not have ridden either one of those winners and, consequently, I might not have been champion National Hunt jockey in Ireland in 2012/13.

Chapter 14

I didn't have a great Christmas festival for Gigginstown in 2013. I finished seventh on Wrath Of Titans in the four-year-olds' maiden hurdle on the first day, I finished third on Savello in the two-mile handicap chase and I finished second on Trifolium in the Grade 1 two-mile novices' chase. Analifet was a long odds-on shot for the Grade 2 juvenile hurdle on the opening day, she was fully expected to win, but she went wrong and I pulled her up after the third flight. She came home with a pelvic injury.

The next three days weren't any better either. The Game Changer was sixth, Maxim Gorky was seventh, Akorakor was third, Empire Of Dirt was 12th, Rule The World was second, Si C'Etait Vrai was second, First Lieutenant was second, Rockdown was third, Urticaire was fifth, Bright New Dawn was fifth, Panther Claw was lapped.

I didn't have one winner for Gigginstown that Christmas, and all those chances.

I did win the maiden hurdle on the second day on Double Irish for Gordon, but he wasn't a Gigginstown horse. And I won two handicap hurdles for Charles Byrnes on Sea Light, but he wasn't a Gigginstown horse either, and those wins might actually have counted against me in the context of Gigginstown. Sea Light carried 10st 10lb in both races, so at least I didn't have to get down to a very light weight for him. I got down to 10st 8lb to ride Analifet, the filly who suffered the pelvic injury, a Gigginstown filly trained by Willie Mullins in the Grade 2 Knight Frank Hurdle. She was an odds-on shot, and I was never going to not ride her. In the end, I felt her go wrong after the third flight, and I pulled her up, but I think the fact I got down to 10st 8lb to ride her didn't help me with Michael.

He didn't want me going under 10st 9lb.

Michael was always on at me about me riding light. He didn't want me getting down too low. He always said that, when I was riding light, I wasn't at my best. That I struggled to even talk so, if I couldn't talk, how was I able to ride? He didn't want me wasting away to get down to 10 stone nothing to ride an ordinary horse in an ordinary handicap, when they had Grade 1 horses in Grade 1 races, and they needed me in the full of my powers for them.

Christmas was always a tricky enough time for the Gigginstown horses, I thought. They were usually busy enough in the autumn and in the run-up to Christmas. The Christmas festivals were like the last part of the early part of the season, they'd run into Christmas, and I often felt that some of them were just about in need of a break by then. Then they'd have their break after Christmas, one run or no runs before Cheltenham, and then onto Aintree or Fairyhouse or Punchestown. Some of them got away with it at Christmas, but some of them didn't, some of them had gone beyond their peak at that point and were ready for their mid-season break.

There had been rumours going around about me and Gigginstown at the Punchestown Festival apparently the previous April, in 2013. I hadn't heard them, and I hadn't heard anything about them until Michael said it to me shortly afterwards.

'About those rumours that were going around about your job at Punchestown,' he said.

'What rumours?' I asked.

I was genuine. I hadn't heard any rumours. I didn't know there were rumours.

'Well, there's nothing to them,' Michael said. 'Your position is secure.'

It was a strange one, knowing that your position was insecure and then knowing that your position was secure all in the space of about 20 seconds. Although, you know, when a Premier League chairman expresses the board's full confidence in the manager, the end of the road is often not too far away.

I don't know for sure what the reason was or what the reasons were for the ending of my tenure as Gigginstown's first jockey, but it was probably a combination of a number of things. There was the weight issue for sure, me riding light because I wanted to be available for as many rides as possible, because I didn't want to miss out on a ride, because I didn't want to miss out on a winner. Although I was getting better at that. I wasn't getting down to a ridiculously low weight for anything. I thought Michael was right, that I was in better form, that I was a better rider, when I was riding at 10st 9lb or 10st 10lb or above as opposed to 10st 6lb or 10st 7lb.

There was also the way Michael and Eddie wanted their horses ridden, I'm sure. There was the fact that I didn't ride all of them handy away, up with the pace, out of trouble, one size fits all.

It was an issue. I knew it was an issue. I could have just ridden every horse up with the pace, I could have just followed the instructions, but that wasn't my way. I didn't believe that that was the best way to ride every horse. There were horses who liked to be ridden handily for sure, there were horses who were uncomplicated and, for them, in general, the right way to ride them was probably up with the pace. Keep it simple. But there were other horses who, for different reasons, in my opinion, were better off being dropped in, and when I was riding those horses, I dropped them in.

I always rode a horse to get him to do as well as he could do in a race. Lots of horses, I dropped in and I got them to finish second or third or fourth, and sometimes first, whereas, if I had ridden them more aggressively, they would have finished fifth or sixth or seventh. But Michael and Eddie didn't want that. They wanted me to win, to ride every horse handily, so that it would win if it was good enough. A horse finishing third that would have finished sixth if it had been ridden differently was no good to them. It still didn't win.

I probably should have just ridden every horse handily and, if the horse didn't win or didn't run well or had a bad experience, it wouldn't have been my fault. I would have ridden to instructions. I would have saved myself a lot of heartache.

Things had changed between the time I started riding and New Year's Eve 2013. Perceptions had definitely changed. I felt there was this notion gaining traction that, if you weren't up with the pace, you weren't giving your horse the best chance.

I found it difficult riding to instructions anyway, I found it difficult when it wasn't left up to me to ride the horse the way I thought best, and to have the freedom to change things, to make decisions, as things changed either before or during a race. When I started riding for Gigginstown, I was the man, I could ride how I wanted. Towards the end though, I was being given instructions and often, if I didn't think they were the right instructions, I wouldn't ride to them. I didn't think about it too deeply at the time but, in hindsight, I should have realised this was bound to cause friction.

There was my character as well I'd say. I wasn't a great communicator. I used to get cross with myself, and that would impact others. Everybody would be there wanting to enjoy the day, and I'd make an issue about something, a horse that didn't win or a horse I didn't ride the way I wanted to ride. It was probably rooted in my own insecurity. People talk about imposter syndrome, and I'm sure I had a bit of that. I always felt I had to work hard at it.

All my life, as a young rider, as an amateur, people would be telling me how good a rider I was. We couldn't do without you. Fellows taking their horses out of races and putting their horses in races so I could ride them. I fed off that. Now suddenly, you're riding the Gigginstown horses, and they *can* do without you. It's not the rider, it's the horse. That fed my insecurities.

And there was the fact that Bryan Cooper was available.

Bryan was a really nice rider. Son of Tom Cooper, who had trained Forpadydeplasterer to win the Arkle and Total Enjoyment to win the Champion Bumper at Cheltenham, Bryan had been going great guns with Dessie Hughes and Tony Martin. He had ridden three winners at the 2013 Cheltenham Festival, Benefficient, Our Conor and Ted Veale, and he was coming in for the Gigginstown horses that I couldn't ride. He had that big win in the Betfred Bowl at Aintree in April 2013 on First Lieutenant when I was ruled out with my punctured lung, and he had ridden Toner D'Oudairies to victory in the Daily Star Chase at Punchestown in October 2013 when I had chosen to ride First Lieutenant instead.

Maybe Michael and Eddie wanted to secure Bryan for the future in case somebody else snapped him up.

I saw Michael at the races at Punchestown on New Year's Eve 2013. I remember, I was a little surprised to see him there, he wouldn't normally be at Punchestown on New Year's Eve, but I was happy to see him. As I said before, the post-mortem with Michael was always easier when he was there, at the races, when he had been there to see the race live, and talking to him in the unsaddling area afterwards, instead of calling him in the car on the way home and telling him what had happened.

I won the first race, the beginners' chase, on Rogue Angel for Gigginstown and for Mouse Morris, the horse who would go on to win the Irish Grand National in 2016. I was riding Un Beau Matin in the third race, the two-and-a-half-mile hurdle, and I was riding

Halling's Treasure in the three-year-olds' maiden hurdle. I had no ride in the second race, so after the first Michael said to me, come on, we'll go for a cup of tea.

I had no idea what was coming. Honestly. I didn't have a clue. I knew he wanted to talk to me about something, but it could have been anything.

We were just standing there, each of us with a cup of tea in hand, and Michael started talking about my weight, he said I had messed about with it at Christmas, that I had been warned, two or three or four times, that he wasn't putting up with it any more. It's the end of the year, he said, so we'll just leave it at that now.

It took me a few seconds to realise what he was saying and, when I did, it hit me like a juggernaut. A kick in the stomach. I could feel a physical ache. I was thinking, it's not the end of the year at all. Sure, the calendar turns tomorrow, but we're right in the middle of the National Hunt season.

It was a punch in the solar plexus and it knocked the wind out of me. The job I had, one of the best jobs in racing, gone. All those top-class horses – they're your horses, go and ride them – whisked away from me and given to someone else to ride.

Also, and I hadn't really thought about it before it ended, but it was always going to be the case that, when it did end, there would be a gaping hole. The problem with riding for Gigginstown was that you were all-in on Gigginstown. It was all-consuming, to the point where you didn't have the time nor the availability to ride many other horses, to begin or maintain relationships with other horses and owners and trainers. I tried to maintain my relationships with the trainers who had been good to me from the beginning, Charles Byrnes and Robert Tyner and Pat Doyle and Pat Fahy and others, but it wasn't easy, I just wasn't that available for outside rides. So take Gigginstown away suddenly, and you are left bare. Horses you can ride are thin on the ground at that point. You have to start building up your contacts and your arsenal again.

'Is there anything I can do to change your mind?' I asked.

I knew there wasn't.

'There isn't,' Michael said.

There was no point in arguing, so I didn't. Like, there's no point in arguing with the referee. Fellows do it, but it's a complete waste of time. The decision was made, and there was nothing I could say that was going to change that.

Then he patted me on the back.

'Now, go and prove me wrong.'

That annoyed me. I didn't need to prove anything. I was the rider I was. Michael knew the rider I was when he asked me to ride for him, and he knew the rider I was when he dropped me. It also annoyed me that he asked me to speak to the media, to tell them about the split. I said I wouldn't. No way. This is your doing, I said, not mine. I didn't want this, so I'm not going to be the one who is going to break it to the media.

I made five phone calls on my way home that evening. I phoned Edelle and I phoned my dad. They were both great. Sure you're better off without them, my dad said. You're still the rider you've always been. I phoned Frostie Kelly, my agent. You're going to have to do a little bit of work now Frostie. It won't be as easy as putting my name down beside all the Gigginstown horses and sitting back. You're going to have to graft now.

At least we were able to laugh about it a bit.

I phoned Jim Culloty to tell him I was available to ride Lord Windermere in the Gold Cup. Jim had been looking for me to commit to riding Lord Windermere in the Gold Cup for a while but, of course, I couldn't commit. Not until I knew what Gigginstown's Gold Cup plans were, not while I was their first rider, and there was talk of Last Instalment going for the Gold Cup. But, now that

I wasn't going to be riding a Gigginstown horse in the Gold Cup, I could commit to Lord Windermere all right. Jim said it was the best news he'd had in ages.

It felt nice to be wanted.

My fifth phone call was to Peter Vaughan, and Peter was brilliant, as he always was when I was feeling down about a horse or a race. He just listened to me, helped me see the positives. And there were positives. There was an easing of the pressure for starters, and there was the fact that I would be more available to ride for the trainers I used to ride for. Charles Byrnes, Robert Tyner, Arthur Moore. Pat Fahy wanted to use me more, Henry de Bromhead seemed to like my riding style. They were all consolation prizes though, those positives didn't even come close to out-weighing the negatives.

The days of going racing with three or four or five well-fancied Gigginstown horses were over and, with the loss of the job, I thought, my chance of ever winning the Cheltenham Gold Cup was gone. Gigginstown were buying lots of potential Gold Cup horses, that was the type of horse they bought, a big, strapping National Hunt horse, a potentially high-class staying steeplechaser. My best chance of winning the Gold Cup rested with riding for them. And even with the Gigginstown job, it was never going to be easy to win the Gold Cup. Without the job, it was going to be nearly impossible.

I was fairly down when I got home that evening. Edelle was brilliant, she tried to help me see the positives too. We were supposed to be going out that night with friends for New Year's Eve celebrations, but I didn't feel up to it. At about 10 o'clock, I just said goodnight and went to bed.

* * *

Tramore on New Year's Day, I was still Gigginstown's first jockey. I went there as Gigginstown's first jockey. The declarations had already been made for Tramore on New Year's Day before my cup of tea with Michael at Punchestown on New Year's Eve.

Edelle came with me in the car to Tramore, and it was no harm that she did, there were lots of media people around on the day and it was good to have her around. The news had broken and the media were wanting quotes from me. I didn't say too much, just that the situation was as they had it, that I wouldn't be Gigginstown's first jockey after that day.

I tried to be positive though. I kept thinking of the lyrics of a song, 'Closing Time', by Semisonic: *Every new beginning comes from some other beginning's end.*

I finished second on Roi Du Mee in the listed chase at Tramore, my last ride for Gigginstown as their first jockey, and I won the last race on That's The Dream for Robert Tyner. That was kind of ironic, on my last day as Gigginstown's jockey, I rode a winner for Robert Tyner, back to where it all began for me. It was back to the future in a sense, a sign of the future as well as the past. Every new beginning comes from some other beginning's end.

Speaking of which, Bryan Cooper went to Fairyhouse and won the opening maiden hurdle for Gigginstown on Lieutenant Colonel.

There was a listed chase at Thurles the following Monday when the change came into focus. I rode Make A Track for Charlie Swan, and I wore the white Gigginstown cap, the second colours. Charlie would always have been batting for me. I rode lots of winners for Charlie, and Charlie was a brilliant jockey, he was champion jockey in Ireland nine times in a row and, in 1995/96, he rode 147 winners, more winners than anyone else has ever ridden in an Irish National Hunt season before or since. Charlie could understand the way I rode.

Bryan Cooper wore the first cap, the maroon cap with the white star, on Toner D'Oudairies for Gordon, but Make A Track was sent off at a shorter price. Toner D'Oudairies won the race as it turned out, with me and Make A Track finishing second after we had been slightly hampered when Willie Mullins's horse Rupert Lamb fell at the fourth last fence.

I got quite down about it all for a little while. As well as losing the job, as well as losing all those good horses that were all yours a day earlier, there was also the dent that your confidence took. Here's somebody telling you they don't want you to ride their horses anymore, that you're not good enough to ride their horses, that somebody else is better. No matter who you are or what walk of life you're in, if you are told that you're not good enough to do something anymore, something you had been doing for the previous six years, it wouldn't be normal if your confidence didn't take a bit of a hit.

So I was about to go from riding in and around a hundred winners every season, to riding 70 winners, 50 winners, 30 winners. That's what I was facing into. That steady stream, the reliable flow of winners from Gigginstown House, the high-class horses, the youngsters with all the potential, reduced to a trickle and then to a halt. Riding for Gigginstown, you'd go out on a horse and you'd be disappointed if you didn't go close, on every Gigginstown horse in every race. Then, with the Gigginstown horses out of the equation, you start scraping around for rides, any rides, all rides. Frostie calling trainers with horses he thinks you can ride and he thinks have a chance. You go out in a maiden hurdle and you finish 15th and you're thinking, what the fuck is going on?

I thought about retiring then. It crossed my mind. I was 35. National Hunt jockeys usually finished in their late 30s or early 40s. Could I do it all again? Start again, scavenging around for rides, trying to happen upon the big horse, the big win? Would people want to put me up? He's not good enough for Gigginstown, why is he good enough for us?

But deep down, I knew I couldn't retire. Not like that, not on the back of losing the job. I couldn't let that be the thing that retired me.

There was a part of me that was in absolute despair. It was such a backward step, losing the job, losing the horses, losing the profile, and how public it was, how everybody knew that Gigginstown thought I wasn't good enough for the job.

'Now prove me wrong.'

Fuck sake.

If you don't have a big job, I was thinking, you're just another jockey. Just one among lots and lots of jockeys who will usually win a race if they are on the best horse. I don't like using the term, but you're just a journeyman jockey. Was I just a journeyman jockey?

And I concluded that I couldn't be champion jockey again if I wasn't riding for Gigginstown. Sure, the championship is about the number of winners you ride in a season, it's about quantity, not quality. It's about riding winners at Thurles and Tramore and Sligo and Downpatrick. A winner in a division of a 80–95 handicap hurdle at Clonmel counts the same in the championship as the winner of the Irish Gold Cup at Leopardstown. But, if you're not riding at Leopardstown and Punchestown and Fairyhouse, you're not going to get the good rides at Thurles and Tramore and Wexford. I figured I wouldn't win the championship again after I lost the Gigginstown job. Thankfully, that was another thing I was wrong about.

There was another part of me though that enjoyed the post-Gigginstown days. I enjoyed going back to the start, going back to my roots in National Hunt racing, where it all began, with Robert Tyner and John Kiely and Charles Byrnes. It had been all very easy in a sense, looking at the entries, picking out the Gigginstown horses: he should win, he should win, she should run well, he only has one to beat. It was more intricate looking at the entries and trying to pick out the horses who had chances who you could ride. Of course, it wasn't as easy, there was more graft to it but, in a sense, there was more satisfaction too when you got it right.

My attitude to it alternated all the time, depending on the day of the week or the hour of the day or the minute of the hour. Sometimes I was energised by the challenge, other times I despaired.

I got great support from lots of different owners and trainers then, that was brilliant, I really appreciated all of it, and I actually went to the 2014 Cheltenham Festival with an okay book of rides. I had Lord Windermere in the Gold Cup for starters. He had only done moderately well since he had won the RSA Chase the previous year. He was well beaten in the Hennessy Gold Cup at Newbury and in the Lexus Chase, Dougie Costello rode him in both races. Then I rode him in the Irish Gold Cup at Leopardstown in February, and he was well beaten again. That was strange, me on Lord Windermere, with Gigginstown having the 1–3 in the race, Brian O'Connell winning the race on Last Instalment and Bryan Cooper finishing third on First Lieutenant.

Lord Windermere wasn't until later in the week at Cheltenham, he was in the Gold Cup on the Friday, the final day of the festival. On the first day, the Tuesday, I had Western Boy for Pat Fahy in the Supreme Novices' Hurdle, Ted Veale for Tony Martin in the Arkle, and Vintage Star for Sue Smith in what is now the Ultima Handicap Chase. They all ran well, but none of them reached the places.

My big ride for the week though, outside of Lord Windermere, was Morning Assembly for Pat Fahy and Clipper Logistics, who was set to run in the RSA Chase on the Wednesday. I had ridden Morning Assembly to win his maiden hurdle at Naas in January 2013, but I hadn't ridden him in any of his novice chases earlier that season. His three runs before Cheltenham that season were all before New Year's Eve, and my commitments to Gigginstown wouldn't allow me. I actually rode a Gigginstown horse against him in two of those three races.

But Pat was on to me very soon after I lost the Gigginstown job to know if I could ride his horse in the RSA Chase. He and

Steve Parkin of Clipper Logistics, and Joe Foley of Ballyhane Stud, who was involved as well, were always big supporters of mine, and Morning Assembly was a really talented horse. He was a lovely ride to have going into Cheltenham.

I knew that my Cheltenham Festival winning run was in danger going into the week, but I thought, if I was going to keep my run going, if I was going to make it nine Cheltenham Festivals in a row with at least one winner, Morning Assembly was probably going to be the horse who would provide me with that winner.

Alas, it wasn't to be. He ran great, I had him well back in the field and along the inside early on and, when we made ground on the run down the hill, over the fourth last and the third last, I thought we had a big chance. But I had to ride him along on the run around the home turn, and we just couldn't get any closer to the leaders. He kept on well up the hill to take third place, but O'Faolains Boy and Smad Place were just too far in front of us.

I had a ride for Jenny Candlish in the Coral Cup, who didn't count, and I rode Special Tiara for Henry de Bromhead in the Champion Chase, who ran okay up to a point.

I didn't have a ride in the Fred Winter Hurdle, but I watched on the television as the field went to the second last flight. The Gigginstown horse Clarcam went to the front under Bryan Cooper at the second last flight, and he appeared to be travelling well, but he just clipped the top of the flight and came down. You winced as he came down, you feared for Bryan, he was in front of a fairly well-stacked field, there were lots of horses and lots of hooves coming after him. The camera moved on, it followed the runners but, in the back of my mind, I was hoping Bryan would be okay.

He wasn't. The news gradually came out that he had suffered a fairly bad leg injury, probably broken, and that he was going to miss the rest of the meeting and a lot more besides.

It goes without saying, you never hope someone will get injured, you never wish ill on a fellow jockey. You are all rivals, but you are all colleagues as well. It's a strange dynamic. Once you leave the weigh room, you are all in competition with each other. But you all share the weigh room, like players on the same team share the dressing room. And there is a massive camaraderie there, probably accentuated by the constant threat of injury or worse.

Two ambulances follow you around as you work.

Jockeys look out for each other and, if someone gets injured, you empathise deeply, you know it could have been you, and you recognise that it could be you next time.

That said, somebody has to ride the horses, somebody had to take up the rides that Bryan had for the rest of the week. The horses were still going to run, someone was going to ride them, and I was thinking it might as well be me as someone else. I phoned Gordon to tell him I was available to ride Tiger Roll in the Triumph Hurdle on Friday. Gordon said great, he'd have a chat with Eddie but, as far as he was concerned, there would be nobody else riding Tiger Roll only me.

I phoned Noel Meade to tell him I was available for Very Wood in the Albert Bartlett Hurdle, I phoned Tony Martin to tell him I didn't have a ride in the Grand Annual and that I would love to ride Savello. Tony was brilliant. He said he'd confirm later but that was great.

I always loved riding for Tony. He always wanted his horses ridden the way I wanted to ride them. Give them a chance, ride them where they're comfortable. If I was four lengths down jumping the last on a horse of Tony's he didn't care, and they'd still get up and win. I've heard him telling young riders, ride this like Russell or Carberry or Walsh.

You're my man, he said, and could I ride Benefficient in the Ryanair Chase on Thursday as well?

Frostie was also at work behind the scenes, and I got the ride on the Gigginstown horse Mozoltov for Willie Mullins in the first race on Thursday, the JLT Novices' Chase, but that was a waste of time, he was hampered by Oscar Whisky's fall at the first fence and we came down. Benefficient never travelled in the Ryanair Chase and I pulled him up. He came home lame.

News came through too on Friday's horses. Paul Carberry was going to ride Very Wood in the Albert Bartlett Hurdle, but I could ride Tiger Roll in the Triumph Hurdle and Savello in the Grand Annual. I readied myself on Thursday evening. Busy Friday ahead.

Chapter 15

After Tiger Roll won the Grand National in 2018, people asked me if I always knew he was going to be a superstar. I said that I didn't.

In March 2014, Tiger Roll was just another promising horse, a four-year-old who had won a juvenile hurdle at Market Rasen on his racecourse debut the previous November, who had been bought by Gigginstown afterwards. He had finished second in the Spring Juvenile Hurdle at Leopardstown on his first run for Gigginstown and for Gordon. The only connection between Tiger Roll and the Grand National then was that, when he won that race on his racecourse debut at Market Rasen, he was trained by Nigel Hawke, and Nigel Hawke is the man who rode Seagram to victory in the 1991 Grand National.

To me back then, Tiger Roll was another ride at Cheltenham, a ride in the Triumph Hurdle, a chance of another Cheltenham Festival winner. It was only a small chance though, he was a 10/1 shot, he had ground to make up on Guitar Pete on their running in the Spring Juvenile Hurdle at Leopardstown for starters. I think Gordon was looking at running him in the Fred Winter Hurdle at Cheltenham instead but, in order to run in the Fred Winter Hurdle, he would have had to have had another run between the Spring

Hurdle and Cheltenham, so they decided to just allow him to run in the Triumph Hurdle.

We were forced wide at the start, we were wider than I wanted to be jumping the first flight, but Tiger Roll jumped it well and we started to settle down. It's a short run from the start to the first flight over two miles on the New Course at Cheltenham, but it's a long run from the first flight to the second, onto the main track and up in front of the stands. Then jump the second flight and off into the country for a complete circuit of the track.

Ruby Walsh was in front on one of the Willie Mullins horses, Abbyssial. I was trying to get Tiger Roll settled, trying to get him tucked in a little behind the leaders, but he was keen enough, still wide. Only Barry Geraghty on Royal Irish Hussar was wider than we were on the run between the first two flights. Barry came across in front of me on the approach to the second flight, so at least I had a bit of cover.

There was carnage at the second flight though. Abbyssial dived at the flight and came down. A few horses in behind were hampered, and Adriana Des Mottes, the other Willie Mullins horse in the race, was brought down. I was wide, we weren't impacted at all, but that incident changed the race a lot for me, it thinned the field out, and it meant I was able to slot in just behind the leaders, only three horses wide as we raced around the bend that took us away from the stands.

After that, the race went like clockwork. Tiger Roll settled into his rhythm and jumped really well for a horse who was having only his third run ever. We travelled well down the hill, jumped the second last flight well, and we moved into a share of third place on the run around the home turn. On my inside, I saw that Daryl Jacob had lost his irons on Calipto, one of the favourites, so I was thinking I should have him beaten. David Bass and Paul Carberry were in front of me. It looked like Paul Carberry was travelling well on Guitar Pete, but I knew I had plenty of horse underneath me and, in reality, Carberry always gave the impression that he was travelling well!

I moved to the outside on the long run down to the last, but I didn't ask Tiger Roll for anything. He picked up on his own and we moved up on the outside of Guitar Pete as Carberry went for his whip. We moved to the front before we got to the final flight, I saw a long stride at the final flight and asked him up. Ping. He had the energy to make it. We landed in front and then he took off up the hill. He stuck his neck out, galloped all the way to the winning line.

That was as big a winner as I've ever ridden, Tiger Roll in the 2014 Triumph Hurdle. For all the reasons. Initially, I only had one ride on Gold Cup day, the last day of the 2014 Cheltenham Festival. Lord Windermere, a 20/1 shot in the Gold Cup itself. If I was going to ride a winner at the 2014 Cheltenham Festival, I was going to have to win the Gold Cup on a 20/1 shot.

Then, all of a sudden, wham. Things change, you have a ride in the Triumph Hurdle, you win the Triumph Hurdle, and suddenly you're gone from being an ordinary rider to being a good rider again. In the space of six minutes, on a ride you didn't have, on a horse you didn't know. And then you're walking on air again. And you're going into the Gold Cup with a winner in the bag and all the confidence that that brings.

Barry Geraghty shook my hand as we pulled up after the Triumph Hurdle, Brian Hughes, Noel Fehily, Mark Bolger. It's hard to describe, a winner at Cheltenham. Pat Healy was there to take the photographs. I did the angel wings again, for Martin Budds. Alice Plunkett interviewed me for Channel 4.

You come back into the winner's enclosure on a high, all celebrations, all well-dones. You're floating, you're full of confidence. It wasn't that I thought I had done anything wrong up to that point. All the horses I had ridden over the course of the first three days at

Cheltenham, I was happy that I had given them all good rides, I was sure in myself that I had given all of them the best possible chance they could have had of winning. I wouldn't have changed anything on any of the rides I had given any of the horses. They just weren't good enough.

But a winner changes everything. You've got the job done, you've achieved the objective. All the accolades. Brilliant ride. Everyone happy. It's a relief too, your name on the board. Another Cheltenham winner, another year with a Cheltenham winner.

You can become a different rider at Cheltenham after you've ridden a winner. You feel like you can do anything, you feel like you own the place. You ride a couple of losers, you can start to shrivel up a bit, doubts creep in, confidence starts to seep away. But ride a winner, and you are filled up again, replenished, rejuvenated, ready for anything.

I was ready for the Gold Cup, that's for sure. Lord Windermere's owner Dr Ronan Lambe was in the parade ring beforehand, and Jim. Dr Lambe didn't say much, just good luck, and Jim didn't give me any instructions really. Just follow away, he said. See how you go.

That's what I did, followed away. I didn't have any option really, Lord Windermere wasn't fast enough to be any closer to the leaders than he was. I was further behind the leaders than Jim wanted me to be, I found out later, but I was as close as I could have been, Lord Windermere was going as fast as I could make him go without bursting him.

We flew down to the first fence. Lord Windermere and I started off in the middle of them along the inside but, by the time we got to the first fence, we were nearly last. We flew onto the second fence too and, by the time we got there, we were last. Stone last. About three lengths behind the second last horse.

We swung around the bend, away from the stands, two complete circuits to go. Around the bend and into the back straight, and the race is starting to settle down a little bit, but we're still flying. Lord Windermere is going just about as fast as he is able to go, but we're still stone last.

We're going down the back straight and they're getting further away from me. The two-length gap to the second last horse has grown to three or four, but there's not a lot I can do about it. You wouldn't have chosen to be a detached last, but I knew they were going fast up front, and I knew there was a long way to go.

I gave him a little squeeze after we had jumped the water jump, just to remind him he was in a race, but I didn't want to ask him to go any faster than he wanted to go. I could have sat down and driven him, but that wouldn't have been the right thing to do. You would only have been doing that for the optics. If you ask a horse to go faster than he is able to go, if you try to push him out of his comfort zone too early in a race, he won't get home. Best to keep him in his rhythm, best to conserve energy, hope that they have gone too fast, hope that they will come back to you. It's how I rode for my entire career.

Lord Windermere was giving me enough of a feel that he was happy. Down the hill and into the home straight again, and we're still detached last, but he's okay. I'm thinking, this pace has to take its toll at some stage. Up past the stands and I have a look up at the big screen, the field is racing as one group, and then there's us, Lord Windermere and me, detached last, like an extra limb that nobody is that bothered about.

Away from the stands for the final time, one more circuit to go, and I can feel him getting tired, but he's still going okay, he's still comfortable at this pace. Down the back straight, over the first there, we move up alongside Knockara Beau and Jan Faltejsek and we jump past them over the water jump. As we do, I can feel my fellow growing, feel him getting stronger. It's amazing the effect something like that can have on a horse, just going up on the outside of another horse who is tiring and moving past him. He grows in confidence and suddenly he's travelling again. I'm sure that confidence is a thing with horses as much as it is for humans.

We move up in among horses, in between A.P. McCoy on Triolo D'Alene and Tom Scudamore on The Giant Bolster on the run to the ditch and we jump it well. Out of the corner of my eye I see Last Instalment making a mistake and unseating Brian O'Connell. We start to lose a bit of ground on the run to the fifth last fence and I give him a squeeze. I'm not really riding him along, just giving him a little squeeze. It's okay, still a long way to go, but we just don't want to lose touch again.

Up to the top of the hill and down over the fourth last and we're just on the coat-tails of the others. Houblon Des Obeaux jumps away to his right and he looks beaten. Down the hill and I stay on the inside, stay in touch. Triolo D'Alene and The Giant Bolster are a few lengths ahead of us now, and the leaders are another few lengths ahead of them, but still, no need to panic. Just stay in touch, I'm thinking. Every time I try to get closer, I can't, not without asking him to do more than he can do, so I sit and hope, cajole, creep. The leaders have gone fast, I'm thinking. They have to get tired at some stage.

We're racing to the home turn now, and there must be six or seven or eight horses in front of us. You don't count. You just know there are lots of them. We could have gone to the outside and tried to start to pass them, but that would be giving away ground, and still, there's that hill to climb, the famous Cheltenham hill, before we get anywhere near the winning post.

We turn for home and it's game on. I'm thinking I'll swing off the home turn, sling-shot-like, gather some momentum and come a little wide in order to try to deliver a challenge, but our path to the outside is blocked, so I stay towards the inside. I think we can still make up ground on the inside before we have to come out to go around anybody. I see a stride at the second last and he comes up for me. The leaders are within sight now. For the first time since we left the starting gate behind us, two circuits and about six minutes earlier, I can see the leaders.

I come off the inside and get into the clear. Two horses in front of me, Noel Fehily on Silviniaco Conti, Barry Geraghty on Bobs Worth. David Casey is to my right on On His Own, Paul Carberry to my left on Lyreen Legend, and now I drive, now I kick, ask Lord Windermere for everything he has. It's the Gold Cup, this isn't going to be easy, but we can't leave anything behind.

You pray you're going to meet the last fence on a stride. You're riding away and you're just hoping the stride is there. I see it, I show it to Lord Windermere, ask him to make it and he does, jumps the final fence in his stride and lands running, momentum up. Silviniaco Conti goes on and goes a bit to his left, about two lengths in front of us. I just keep concentrating on keeping my horse going, keeping his momentum up, ensuring that he continues to go forward.

We get past Noel Fehily halfway up the run-in and he moves back to his right. Lord Windermere sees this and moves to his right too. I keep my reins in my left hand and my whip in my right hand, trying to keep him straight, but he's moving to his right anyway. I can feel another horse coming at me on my right, I see On His Own's head, I see David Casey's beige arm. We drive on up the hill, I'm screaming now and driving and kicking and pushing. I drive to the line, I drive through the line. I don't stop driving until I'm certain that the winning line is behind us.

Did we win?

David Casey slaps me on the back, I slap David Casey on the back.

I think we've won, I think we've crossed the winning line first, but there's no confirmation, so there's no exhilaration, no celebration. People are congratulating me, but I'm not accepting the congratulations, because I'm not sure. I feel like a bit of a prick, not accepting the congratulations, but it's a photo finish, and everyone is saying there will be a stewards' enquiry. Everyone is saying that David and I came very close on the run up the hill.

They announce the result, first number eight, Lord Windermere. We've passed the winning post first all right, but still there is no elation. I'm shocked, it doesn't feel like the Gold Cup, it doesn't feel like I'm after winning the Gold Cup. It's like winning it in stages, first the photo finish, now the stewards' enquiry.

What should it feel like? I don't know, I've never won the Gold Cup before. Maybe it's because I haven't fully won it yet, maybe it's because the prospect of a stewards' enquiry looms and, sure enough, very quickly the claxon sounds: stewards' enquiry.

Throughout my career as a professional jockey, David Casey was always one of my good friends in the weigh room. We sat beside each other in weigh rooms all over Ireland and Britain for years. But we didn't say much to each other after the 2014 Gold Cup. In the stewards' room, we both argued our cases, I argued the case for Lord Windermere, why we should keep the race, that we didn't improve our position, that the best horse won the race. David argued his case, that we interfered with him, took him off a straight line, and that that had cost him the race.

I genuinely did think that Lord Windermere was the best horse in the race, I didn't think we should lose it. But you never know in stewards' enquiries, you never know what way the stewards are going to be thinking.

It was a weird feeling, first past the post in the Gold Cup and still you can't celebrate. Winner of the Gold Cup, for now, but knowing that it can be taken away from you.

They sent us out of the stewards' room so that they could deliberate, discuss the evidence, consider the evidence that David and I had presented. So we're waiting there, David and me, outside the stewards' room, not saying much, awaiting the verdict. I look out the window, I can see Jim Culloty and, all of a sudden, he starts lepping and jumping around the place!

What?!

They had announced the result over the Tannoy. We couldn't hear the Tannoy where we were, but they decided to announce the result before telling us. Result stands. First number eight, Lord Windermere.

It was all a bit surreal. The way it happened. A photo finish, not sure if you had won or not, then, yes, you've won it, but hold on, we have to see if you can keep it or not. And yes, you can keep it, but we're going to tell the world before we tell you.

And it's the Gold Cup, the Cheltenham Gold Cup. It's different to the Grand National. The Grand National is the most famous horse race in the world, the race that breaks through the boundaries of racing and breaks into mainstream sport, into mainstream news. To win the Grand National is remarkable, it's the first race that people want to talk to you about.

But the Grand National is a handicap. The better you are, the more weight you have to carry in the Grand National, the theory being that every horse should cross the winning line at the same time, that every horse has an equal chance of winning. It would be like in the Olympics, in a 1,500-metre race, the best runners giving everyone else a head start.

The Gold Cup is different, it's the purists' race, steeplechasing's Blue Riband. The best staying chasers compete in the Gold Cup and the best one wins it. All competing on a level playing field, all off equal weights. When you go to the National Hunt sales looking at young horses, you are trying to buy a horse who will potentially win the Gold Cup. That's the ultimate goal. And yet, only one horse can win it every year.

And only one rider. In 2014, I was that rider. Crazy.

I could have said anything then. People are putting cameras and microphones in your face and asking you questions. It had been a tough few months, losing the job, scrambling around for rides. When I lost the Gigginstown job, that was it, my chance of winning the Gold Cup gone. And yet, here I was, after winning the Gold Cup. That showed them. I could have said that then but, thankfully, I didn't. Like when Graham Bradley lost the ride on Alderbrook in the 1996 Champion Hurdle, because he was late going in to ride him work one morning, and he went and won the race on Collier Bay. I didn't say anything. Delighted to win the Gold Cup, I said. Unbelievable. Thanks to Jim and to Dr Lambe. Nothing about Gigginstown.

The race after the Gold Cup is the Foxhunter, for amateur riders, and the race after that is the Martin Pipe Hurdle, for conditional riders. I couldn't ride in either race obviously, so it gave me time to try to figure out what just happened, what winning the Gold Cup meant. It wasn't enough time, a few hours wasn't enough. A few days wasn't enough time, maybe even a few weeks. It took a while to sink in, and it definitely hadn't sunk in by the time I went out to ride Savello in the Grand Annual.

I was floating on air by then, and I knew that Savello would win. He was a 16/1 shot, he had no chance, but I still knew he would win. It's ridiculous, my sense had no base in logic. This was the Grand Annual, one of the most competitive two-mile handicap chases on the calendar, 23 runners and no hiding place. Savello hadn't won all season, he hadn't won in over a year but, the way I was feeling, I could have walked on water.

There was a delay at the start, Oscar Hill bolted and was eventually withdrawn, and that didn't help Savello, he lived on his wits a little bit. So down at the start, as we waited for Oscar Hill to be caught, as he ran around the cross-country track as happy as a clam, delaying everybody, I said to the lads, let's just stop and stand, let them relax. If we had continued to walk around, I thought Savello would get worked up and might lose his race before it started. So I wanted him to stand still, and he would only stand still if the other horses stood still as well.

And they did. You'd never see it, it doesn't happen, 23 horses before a race, primed for competition, and all of them just standing still. Eventually they caught Oscar Hill, he was withdrawn and the starter said go.

It was one of those races where everything went my way, everything went as I thought it would. I lined up on the inside, handy enough, and we settled just behind the leaders. They flew, the leader Next Sensation set a scorching pace, but I was happy that it was too fast, I was happy to allow him off, keep Savello travelling in his rhythm. And he did travel, he travelled everywhere for me, he jumped everything for me.

We had plenty of horses in front of us on the run around the home turn, we were only about sixth or seventh, but we were still travelling, and I was sure we would win. It's some feeling. You feel like you can do anything when you have that confidence. I kept him towards the inside, I didn't bother coming wide into the home straight, I knew that the gaps would develop in front of us. And they did.

The leader Next Sensation kicked again when he landed over the second last fence, he kicked into a lead of three or four lengths, but I knew we would catch him. He got in a bit tight to the final fence, and Claret Cloak came up on our outside and relegated us to third place for a few strides, but I knew that Savello had lots of energy left, I asked him for it and he gave it all. We went between horses on the run up the hill, Next Sensation to our left, Claret Cloak to our right, and he stretched out well to win by over a length.

I knew he would.

It put the seal on a truly remarkable day. Any day you have a Cheltenham Festival winner is a remarkable day. And the day you win the Gold Cup, that's just out of this world, a career-defining day, a life-defining day, and to have the bonus of a Triumph Hurdle and a Grand Annual as well, the first race and the last race, three Cheltenham Festival winners in one day. And you weren't going to be riding two of them at the start of the week.

We had the annual party in the weigh room after racing. It was nice to be there with all the lads as the Gold Cup winner. I had to be in Birmingham Airport for 10 o'clock to get my flight home, so I had plenty of time, I could relax and enjoy the craic.

I got to the airport just before 10, and it was all very quiet. Quieter than you would have thought it should have been on the last day of the Cheltenham Festival, when all the Irish would have been flying home. There was no queue at the desk when I went to check in, and then the realisation dawned on me: the flight was gone. Check-in time wasn't at 10 o'clock, my flight was at 10 o'clock.

All the other flights were gone too, there were no flights left, the airport was dead. All I wanted was to get home, back to Edelle and the lads, but it wasn't possible that night. There was nothing else I could do, so I booked a flight for early the following morning – I was riding at Limerick the following day, the day after winning the Gold Cup – and checked into the Novotel beside the airport. I must have got the last room in the hotel, because it was tiny, but it didn't matter. It might have been the broom cupboard, but I didn't care. I would have slept on a kitchen chair. I wasn't sad or lonely or annoyed though. I was tired all right, as the adrenaline that had fuelled the week started to run out. Mainly though, I just had this huge feeling of contentment.

What did you do on the night you won the Gold Cup? Where did you go? How did you celebrate? I went to the Novotel in Birmingham Airport, on my own, and I was asleep by 11 o'clock.

Chapter 16

I was fasting and I was wasting and I was trying to be as light as I could be. No Gigginstown job, no set job at all, I wanted to be in the position to ride whatever was available, within reason. I didn't want to rule myself out of the chance of riding a horse who had a good chance in a handicap just because I couldn't do 10st 6lb or 10st 7lb.

The downside of that though was that I wasn't in great form. I was constantly hungry and I was continually cranky. I wouldn't have been great company. Little things would annoy me easily. Like in a mares' hurdle at Kilbeggan in June 2014, I was riding a mare for Peter Fahey, Queen Alphabet. She was a decent mare, I had ridden her to finish fifth in the listed mares' bumper at the Aintree Grand National meeting two years earlier, and I had ridden her to win her maiden hurdle on her previous run at Kilbeggan. We thought she would win.

That was before I encountered Danny Mullins in the race. He was riding a horse for his mother Mags, a mare called Princess Leya, and he was just messing around in front of me. Patrick Mullins led on a mare for his dad Willie, Pink Hat, and I sat in second place behind him, just towards the outside, with Danny on my inside.

Patrick's mare was jumping to her left in front of me, so I just kept my mare straight and moved up on the inside. But when I did,

Danny rode his mare forward so that she was up alongside me. So I let him go on in front of me, and I moved up again on the inside but, when I did, Danny rode forward and kept me in. I was like, go on or sit back, make up your fucking mind, but don't be just riding your race to annoy my horse. Eventually Danny's mare tired and I was left to challenge Patrick, but Queen Alphabet couldn't get to Patrick's mare. She had used up so much energy messing around with Danny's mare, she had nothing left for the finish.

I was livid. I shouldn't have been, but it was a combination of everything. No Gigginstown job, worried, wasting, weakened, hungry. We pulled up after crossing the winning line, and we made our way towards the chute that takes you from the racecourse at Kilbeggan back to the parade ring. I waited for Danny.

'What the fuck was that?'

'What the fuck was what?' he asked.

'That!' I said, getting more annoyed. 'What were you at out there?'

'I was just riding my race,' Danny said.

Then I boxed him. Smack! Before I knew what I was doing, I had closed my fist and hit him, square on the side of the face.

It was wrong, I knew it was wrong as soon as I did it, but it had all got on top of me. When you're wasting, little things annoy you more than they should, and big things look like mountains. Smack. Then he started bleeding. I don't know where all the blood came from. I didn't know that one nose could hold so much blood. It streamed out of him, continually, a steady flow and no stopping it.

I've done it now, I thought. They'll take the licence off me now. You can't go around boxing people in the face when things don't go your way.

They called a stewards' enquiry, and they had me and Danny in.

'What went on there then?'

I said I was just making my way back down the chute and, the next thing I know, there's blood pouring out of Danny's nose.

'Danny?'

'Ah my horse's head came up sir and smacked me in the face. Then my nose started bleeding.'

Fair play to Danny. He could have hung me out to dry, and he would have been well within his rights to do so. I was absolutely, completely, 100 per cent in the wrong. Danny could have stuck the knife in and twisted it. Fair play to him. I always appreciated that.

I met Philip Reynolds the same day at Kilbeggan. I had never met Philip before, but I knew who he was, son of former Taoiseach Albert Reynolds. I knew his brother Abbie a bit, Abbie was always into his racing. But Philip came up to me that day and asked if I would wear a T-shirt for Darkness Into Light, to help raise awareness and bring hope to people who have been impacted by suicide. No problem, delighted to. After a photo shoot we got chatting, and Philip told me that he had a few horses, asked me if I would be interested in riding them for him.

Philip didn't have a lot of horses at the time, he had one or two with Willie Mullins and he had one or two with Charlie Swan and he had one or two with Eddie Harty and one or two with Noel Meade. But of course, I said I would ride his horses if I could. Mall Dini would come along shortly afterwards, and Presenting Percy shortly after that.

I met Chris Jones around the same time. Like Philip, Chris obviously liked the way I rode, and he asked if I would be interested in riding his horses. And so the door was opened to me to horses like Mala Beach and Zabana and Noble Endeavor and Mega Fortune. Philip Reynolds and Chris Jones were hugely important owners to me during that time, and I will always be grateful for the support they gave me in those days. I was delighted I was able to repay the faith they had in me.

More connections leading to more connections. Dr Ronan Lambe, Lord Windermere's owner, had horses with Dermot Weld as well as with Jim Culloty. He only had horses with two trainers, and he asked if I would ride the horses he had with Dermot Weld too.

I was out on my own now, cut loose, no big owner to back me. Survive or die. It was a harder graft, and you're dealing with your insecurities too. No job, not good enough for Gigginstown, trying to get rides, trying to get on good horses, trying to prove to everyone that you're still a good rider. And to yourself.

Dr Lambe was a quiet man, I never really got to speak to him much, but a lovely man, and he was so enthusiastic about his racing. I have Dr Lambe to thank for my connection with Dermot Weld.

I started going into Dermot's once a week, schooling, riding work, whatever he wanted me to do. That was brilliant. He made you feel like a king, he made you feel like Pat Smullen. You'd arrive on the Curragh and your horses would be tacked up, ready to go. You'd get up on one, ride him work, get off him, and the next one would be ready to go.

He's some trainer, Dermot Weld. He was a true groundbreaker. He was the first person to take a horse from the Northern Hemisphere and win the Melbourne Cup, a race they said a horse from the Northern Hemisphere could never win. He was the first European trainer to win a leg of the American Triple Crown. And all the big races, on the flat as well as over jumps, the Derby, the Oaks, the Guineas, all five Irish Classics. And king of Galway for about a hundred years in a row.

Windsor Park was always a classy horse. He had won two bumpers and he had won two races on the flat before I rode him in a race for the first time to win his maiden hurdle at Leopardstown's Christmas Festival in 2014.

He'd scare you though schooling. I used to love riding him in races, but I hated schooling him. All he wanted was to go as fast as he could, flat out over his hurdles, when you wanted to take him back, teach him. And he'd step at his hurdles, he'd grab at them and he'd just about get there. He'd give you the heebie jeebies. But he had class now. He was a right one.

I remember people saying I gave him a bad ride at Leopardstown in February 2015, when we finished second behind Nichols Canyon in the Deloitte Hurdle. But I just wanted to get his jumping right, because I knew how good he was. I didn't want to force him, I knew that, if I forced him, he'd start to step at his hurdles. It took him a while to warm up in the race too, so we were delighted with how well he stayed on to take second place.

He had three runs over hurdles before the 2015 Cheltenham Festival, and he needed every one of them. Leopardstown at Christmas, Leopardstown in January, Leopardstown in February. He was dangerous, you needed to have control of him all the time. If you changed your hands, if you let him go, he'd attack a hurdle, and he wouldn't stop, he wouldn't correct himself. We weren't on the same wavelength in any of those Leopardstown races, but we were at Cheltenham.

We knew he would be a better horse at Cheltenham, and he was. He was dynamite there, Dermot had him razor sharp, and we won the Neptune Novices' Hurdle.

I was riding for Dermot and I was riding for Charles Byrnes and I was riding for whoever else would have me. Jessica Harrington and John Queally and Tom Mullins and Henry de Bromhead and Peter Fahey and Paul Nolan. I'd say Frostie's telephone bill went through the roof. I struck up a good partnership with Mallowney for Tim Doyle, I rode him to win a couple of good races.

I started to ride a bit for Gordon Elliott too at the time. I wasn't going into Gordon's at all, not after I lost the Gigginstown job, and Davy Condon was riding most of Gordon's horses, but Gordon was always very good to me, he was still giving me a few rides.

Olly Murphy had started working for Gordon as assistant trainer. As I mentioned before, I knew Olly since he was a kid, through his dad Aiden. I always thought he was a smashing kid. So Olly started ringing me.

'Come on in David,' he would say, in his English accent.

'I'm telling you David, you need to come up. I promise you, there's some real good horses here.'

So I started going into Gordon's. It was all very relaxed, I'd go in when I could, I wouldn't go in if I couldn't. I'd call Olly. He'd be doing up the board for the following day.

'I'll be up tomorrow. Put me down for four.'

So I'd go into Gordon's and I'd be down to ride four lots. It could be a Tuesday or a Wednesday or a Friday or a Saturday. It didn't matter, I could go in when I could go in.

It was through Olly too that my relationship with Diana and Grahame Whateley developed. Olly and his dad were close to the Whateleys, and they were great owners, they had lots of good horses in training with Philip Hobbs in Britain, Menorah and Captain Chris and Wishfull Thinking and Garde La Victoire. They started to have a couple of horses with Gordon, Royal Captain and Jetstream Jack. Then Diamond King came along.

Diamond King was a great horse for me. He won two bumpers and two novice hurdles for Donald McCain before he came to Gordon, and I rode him just once before the 2016 Cheltenham Festival, in a handicap hurdle at Fairyhouse the previous November, when we finished second.

Gordon had him primed for Cheltenham, he was in some form going there in March 2016, for the Coral Cup. I was quite happy with the ride I gave him too, I had him around the inside the whole way, if there had been white paint on the inside rail I would have scraped it off with my boot.

We were only about 11th or 12th on the run down the hill to the second last flight, but I was so happy, I knew how much he had left. It was just a case of asking him for his effort at the right time. I got some run around the inside too, I was able to stay on the inside around the home turn, saving ground. I didn't ask him to pick up until we straightened up for home and even then, I didn't ask him for everything.

We made ground on the run to the final flight, I saw a stride at the last and he came up for me. We actually picked up in front at the last. Only then, only when we landed, did I ask him for everything, and he gave it all. He bounded up the hill and won by daylight.

That was magic. No Gigginstown job and still I was able to bag a Cheltenham Festival winner. I got a great kick out of that.

I did ride for Gigginstown in the Gold Cup that year. I rode Don Poli to finish third behind Don Cossack. Bryan had the choice between the two Dons, and I was always going to ride the one he didn't ride. It was a close call, they schooled at Leopardstown on the Monday before Cheltenham, and Bryan chose to ride a novice chaser in the school, with me on Don Cossack.

Don Cossack schooled brilliantly for me. Gordon was there, and I had so much fun schooling him. I knew he was going to have a big chance in the Gold Cup. As a result, Bryan chose to ride Don Cossack at Cheltenham. If I had been a bit cleverer, I would have taken him back, got him to go in tight to a couple of fences, got off him and said, nah, he won't win a Gold Cup anyway. Then Bryan might have chosen Don Poli and I could have ridden Don Cossack. But I wasn't cute enough to do that!

Ah you couldn't be doing that, and I got a good ride off Don Poli in the Gold Cup. He just kept going, that was Don Poli. He wasn't fast. He started off at one pace, and he stayed going that pace for three miles and two and a half furlongs. I was happy for Bryan, he got his Gold Cup win, and I was delighted for Gordon to get his, and for Michael and Eddie to get another one, but I was a bit sad for me.

Olly Murphy got a great kick out of Diamond King's win too. Best ride I've ever seen in my life, he said. And it was brilliant for me to hear that, it would fill you with confidence. And you're back to thinking that you were making a difference, that you were more than just a journeyman jockey. The following day, I won the Pertemps Final on Mall Dini for Pat Kelly and Philip Reynolds.

Owners were so important to me then. Owners who wanted me to ride their horses, Diana and Grahame Whateley and Philip Reynolds and Chris Jones.

Philip Reynolds owned Presenting Percy too, and Presenting Percy was a very special horse for me. He was up there with my favourite horses. For me, there were the Gigginstown horses, Mansony, Solwhit and Presenting Percy. Our son Liam's first name was going to be Percy. Not just after the horse, Peter Vaughan's dad is Percy as well, and Edelle and I just liked the name too. So now Liam's second name is Percy, Liam Percy Russell.

I won the Pertemps Final on Presenting Percy at the 2017 Cheltenham Festival, he was my only winner at the festival that year. I remember when he won a Pertemps qualifier at Fairyhouse a couple of weeks before Cheltenham, he won it off a handicap rating of 130, and the British handicapper gave him a mark of 146! He gave him a 16lb higher mark for winning a handicap by three and a quarter lengths. I thought that it was crazy, and I said as much publicly.

Now, Presenting Percy won the Pertemps Final that year, off his mark of 146, but it doesn't mean that the British handicapper was correct in giving him that mark. The handicapper is supposed to handicap horses based on what they have done, not on what they think they are going to do.

Percy was brilliant though that day at Cheltenham in the Pertemps Final, Pat Kelly had him in rare form, and he was brilliant the following year in winning the RSA Chase. I loved riding him, you were able to bide your time on him. He wasn't overly big, he didn't look like a typical chaser, but he was brave and he was brilliant to jump and he could travel.

That was a very strong RSA Chase too that year. Monalee finished second, and Monalee was top class. Al Boum Photo would have been second or third had he not fallen at the second last fence, and Al Boum Photo went on to win the next two Gold Cups. I really enjoyed that ride in the RSA Chase. Presenting Percy just kept filling himself up and, the more you'd take him back, the more confidence he'd get.

I let him move on into the lead around the home turn, and I asked him up at the second last fence. There is a very short run now on the Old Course at Cheltenham from the home turn to the second last fence, since they re-sited the second last. The fence used to be before the home turn, but they always said it was a tricky fence, on a downhill part of the track, so they moved it and put it into the home straight. There are literally about seven or eight strides now between the point where you straighten up in the home straight and the point where you meet the second last fence.

Anyway, I asked Presenting Percy up on a fairly long stride at the second last, and he came up. He was never not going to come up but, if he hadn't, I could have ended up in the stands. We won by seven lengths.

Presenting Percy was actually sent off as favourite for the Gold Cup the following year, Al Boum Photo's first Gold Cup, but he hadn't had a great run into the race, he had only run once that season beforehand, in the Galmoy Hurdle at Gowran Park the previous month.

That was some day, Thyestes Chase day at Gowran Park. There is always a big crowd at Gowran Park on Thyestes Chase day anyway, it's a massive day for Gowran, but lots of people went to see Percy too. He was such a popular horse. A lot of that was down to the horse himself, how good he was, and to the fact that he was trained by Pat Kelly, a small trainer who people didn't know a whole lot about, and to the fact that he was owned by Philip.

Philip was a popular man in his own right, and he was also the son of Albert Reynolds, who, as I said, was Taoiseach and Fianna Fáil party leader between 1992 and 1994. My dad would have been a Fine Gael man, but he always said that Albert Reynolds was a great politician.

We won the Galmoy Hurdle, and that was brilliant, but it didn't happen for Percy in the Gold Cup. He never travelled for me and he came home lame. He ran in the Gold Cup the following year too when, again, he didn't have a great run into the race. But he was actually going okay, I thought we had a chance when we turned for home, I hadn't really gone for him and he was just starting to stay on, but he got the second last fence wrong and came down.

Chris Jones had horses with Gordon and he had horses with Henry de Bromhead, and the fact that I was riding Chris's horses was a big help to me in cementing my relationship with Gordon and Henry.

I had a disaster on Zabana at the 2016 Cheltenham Festival, we were sideways on to the tape at the start of the JLT Chase when the starter let us go. A fellow smacked a long tom off the ground just behind us, Zabana got a bit of a fright, he jinked to his left and I came off.

I was gutted for Chris, and for Zabana's trainer Andy Lynch. They were brilliant about it afterwards though and, actually, strange the way these things happen but, if he had run well in the JLT Chase, Zabana might not have won the Grade 1 three-mile novices' chase at the Punchestown Festival the following month.

I rode Noble Endeavor for Chris to win the Paddy Power Chase at the Leopardstown Festival in December 2016, and I rode Mega Fortune for him to win the Spring Juvenile Hurdle at Leopardstown the following February, and I rode Mala Beach to win the Troytown Chase the following November.

I was able to keep things ticking over, without having the depth of horses to ride that I had when I was riding for Gigginstown.

But I was only ticking over. To put it into context, the season that I won my second jockeys' championship, 2012/13, my last full season in the Gigginstown job, I had 549 rides in Ireland, and I won the championship with 103 winners. The following season, half the season with the Gigginstown job, half without, I rode just 75 winners. The following season, I had just 51 winners. And in 2015/16, I had only 245 rides and just 36 winners. It was my lowest total number of rides and my lowest total number of winners since the 2003/04 season. Fewer than half the number of rides I had in 2012/13, just three years earlier, and just one-third the number of winners.

It was even more important during those years that I had winners at the Cheltenham Festival. A season with 36 winners was not a good season, but at least I had Diamond King and Mall Dini at Cheltenham. A bad year is one thing, but a bad year with no Cheltenham Festival winner is a disaster.

Chapter 17

Things were quiet enough for me now during the summer of 2015. I was truly appreciative of the support I was getting, but it still wasn't easy. Two winners in July, two more in August.

I went to Mallow on the last Sunday in August to ride a mare for Peter Fahey in the opening maiden hurdle, Meadowlands, a 50/1 shot who had a rating of 51 off the flat. We never got to the start though. Meadowlands reared up on me in the parade ring before we even got out onto the track and I came off.

I broke my arm in two places, and it was the sorest thing. Usually, when you get a fall in a race, when you suffer an injury, your adrenaline is up and you can cope with the pain. This time though, I had no adrenaline to mask the pain. And it was a proper break too, my hand was down there and my elbow was up there. There was only skin holding my arm together.

The ambulance had gone onto the track, so it took the medics a few minutes to get back, but it felt like a few hours. I got into the ambulance and I got to the hospital. I remember sitting in the hospital waiting to be seen, wincing with the pain.

Finally they called me and I got up to walk to the X-ray machine. It was only then that I realised that my foot was sore too, so they X-rayed my foot too, and discovered that it was broken as well. I was in so much pain with my arm, I didn't realise that my foot was broken too.

And then, things go through your mind, like, will I ever ride again? Is this it? It wasn't long after I had lost the Gigginstown job and I was thinking, I will be sad now if this is the end. I didn't really get the chance to prove that I was just as good a rider even without the backing of Gigginstown.

I asked the surgeon.

'Do you think that I'll be able to ride again?' I said.

'What?' asked the surgeon.

'You know, I'm a jockey,' I said. 'Will I be able to ride again?'

'I know you're a jockey,' said the surgeon. 'Of course you'll be able to ride again. We'll have you back in no time. I repair bomb victims. This is nothing.'

A switch flicked in my head. I went from feeling sad, despairing even, to feeling positive and hopeful. This is nothing, I kept thinking. We'll have you back in no time.

* * *

We were still three weeks away from Edelle's due date when she started feeling unwell, so we went straight to the hospital. Everything was fine, thank God. It was just that things were going to be happening a bit earlier than we thought they were going to be happening.

I had one ride in Downpatrick that day. I would have preferred to have had more rides, but that's the way it was in those years, and one ride was better than no ride. I would always go to Downpatrick for one ride. I would always go anywhere for one ride.

I asked the nurses in the hospital if I would be okay to go to Downpatrick, if I would have time to get there and get back before the baby arrived. It was a bit unrealistic I suppose, Galway to Downpatrick is nearly a four-hour drive. The nurses laughed at me. No chance. Things are going to be happening here fairly soon, they said.

So I phoned Frostie to tell him what was happening, I asked him to tell Jimmy Finn, the trainer of the horse I was due to ride, and to tell the Turf Club. I asked Frostie to say I couldn't ride because of personal reasons. They didn't need to know the exact details, they didn't need to know that Edelle was about to have an emergency Caesarean section.

All went brilliantly in the hospital. Edelle was brilliant, and the doctors and the nurses and the midwives were all superb, and Lily came into the world. She was three weeks earlier than we thought she would be, and she gave us a bit of a fright now, but she was fantastic, and she has been fantastic ever since.

So it had all calmed down that evening. Edelle needed lots of care obviously, she needed time to herself, she was resting, and I was lying on the bed with my feet up, Lily in my arms, everything good in the world. I started flicking through my phone, and next thing I see this headline: Youghal jockey fined €500 for no-show.

What the fuck?

There weren't many Youghal jockeys at the time.

Sure enough, I clicked into the piece, and it was me. Davy Russell, fined €500 for not turning up at Downpatrick for his one ride today.

It looked terrible, it read terribly. It was like I just didn't go all the way to Downpatrick for one ride, it was like I just didn't bother. Like it was too far to go for one ride so I just decided not to go. A no-show.

I phoned Frostie.

'Frostie, please tell me you phoned them?'

'I did,' said Frostie. 'I did all of that. I can't understand why you've been fined.'

I was so annoyed. I had done everything I should have done, I had done everything I needed to do, and still I was being fined and being put down as a no-show.

I phoned Denis Egan, the head of the Turf Club at the time. I tried to be calm, to speak calmly, but I'm sure I failed.

'Now Denis,' I said. 'That €500 fine, you can shove that wherever you want to shove it. But as well as that, I want an apology. It's not right that people will think that I just didn't bother going to Downpatrick.'

'You said it was for personal reasons,' Denis Egan said. 'Sure that could be anything.'

'I said personal reasons because the reasons are personal.'

I was livid now. I was biting my tongue.

'Sure personal reasons could be making hay.'

I took a couple of seconds.

'Denis,' I said carefully. 'It's September. Who makes hay in September?'

* * *

First day of the new National Hunt season, Down Royal, 1 May 2017, I was down to ride a horse for Gordon and Gigginstown in a conditions hurdle, Ballela Boy. It was only a five-horse race, Gigginstown had three in it, with Bryan Cooper down to ride the favourite, Monbeg Notorious. As it happened, Monbeg Notorious was withdrawn on veterinary advice, and I fully expected that Bryan would switch to Ballela Boy, and leave me without a ride in the race. That was the way it was, I had to accept it, Bryan was Gigginstown's number one rider, he had the pick of the Gigginstown horses.

I was a little surprised then, and quite happy actually, when Bryan instead switched to Bel Ami De Sivola, the other Gigginstown horse. I had never ridden Ballela Boy before. David Mullins had ridden him to win his maiden hurdle at Downpatrick the previous October, Bryan had ridden him at Downpatrick earlier that spring, Jack Kennedy had ridden him in a handicap hurdle at Fairyhouse.

He was a grand horse, Ballela Boy, a son of Golan. I settled him in second place behind a horse of David O'Brien's, Ned's Island, J.J. Slevin riding him, claiming 5lb. J.J. started riding the leader along as we got to the top of the hill with two flights to jump, so I moved up on his outside.

We moved to the front on the run down the hill to the second last flight, I gave him a squeeze, he picked up nicely for me and he jumped the second last well. A bit to his left, but he kept going forward. I could see a horse on my left, on my outside, and I could see the Gigginstown colours, I knew it was Bryan on Bel Ami De Sivola. He got to within about a half a length of me, but he got no closer. Bellela Boy jumped the last well, and we actually came away from Bel Ami De Sivola on the run to the line.

I got a lot of satisfaction out of that win. I don't know what it was, I was on the supposed second string of the Gigginstown horses, Bryan had chosen to ride a different horse, I was wearing the white cap, the second cap, he was favourite, odds-on favourite. And I won.

That was a turning point, I felt. That was me, back in favour at Gigginstown. Nobody ever said anything, there was no conversation between me and Eddie or between me and Michael, I just got the sense after Down Royal that day that they wanted me to ride their horses.

I was in a good place in my career. I was riding good horses for good people. I was riding more and more horses for Gordon, I was riding good horses for Charles Byrnes, Sea Light and Top Of The Town and Black Warrior, and I was riding good horses for Henry de Bromhead, Ordinary World and On Fiddlers Green and Deans Road and Some Plan. I won the Grade 1 Irish Arkle on Some Plan at Leopardstown in January 2017, but that was a strange one. It was just a four-horse race, and the other three horses in the race fell. That was one of just two Grade 1 winners I rode that season, but you take them all. Grade 1 wins are huge, and you take them any way you get them.

The National Hunt season now runs from May until the following April, from the day after the Punchestown Festival ends until the last day of the Punchestown Festival the following year, and the season started well. The summer rolled in and I started to ride lots of winners, 15 winners in June, 11 in July, 15 more in August. Before September started, I had almost 50 winners on the board for the 2017/18 Irish National Hunt season. To put that into context, at the same stage the previous year I had 25. The year before that, I had nine.

The 2017 Galway Plate was big for me too. Gigginstown announced just before the Galway Festival started that they wouldn't be retaining a rider anymore, that they would just be using the best available, so the rides on all the Gigginstown horses in the Galway Plate were up for grabs. They were going to have at least five runners, but I wanted to ride Henry's horse Balko Des Flos in the race, and I figured out fairly quickly that Henry wanted me to ride Balko Des Flos in the race.

Henry is a brilliant trainer, and I rode lots of winners for him. I rode point-to-point winners for him when he was getting going, and then I rode plenty of winners for him on the track.

It's the best feeling, I swear to God. When you know someone wants you to ride their horse. It fills you with confidence. It's strange but, hundreds of winners, Grade 1 winners, Cheltenham winners, Gold Cups, I still always felt that I had to prove I could still ride. So when you knew someone believed in you, that was massive. It was for me anyway. It always was.

It was a short conversation with Henry.

Me: 'I can ride Balko Des Flos.'

Henry: 'Fantastic.'

You could hear the joy in his voice.

Henry: 'That's fantastic. I think you'll really suit the horse.'

The conversations can be short when you're not wanted. (I can ride your horse if you want me to? I don't want you to.) But they can be short too when you are, and they are the nicest conversations of all.

Balko Des Flos won the 2017 Galway Plate in the rain, and there was never a point in the race where I thought he wouldn't. Before the race, I thought he would win it, and at no point during it did my opinion change. He travelled away for me great, just behind the leaders, and he jumped great. It didn't really matter when I let him go on, I could have let him go on into the lead at any stage of the race. But I waited until we were on our way down the hill to the final two fences in the dip before I let him roll. And he jumped them well – up, stride, stride, stride, up, stride, stride – and suddenly we were in front.

I sat on him for a while, didn't ask him for anything, but it didn't really matter. I gave him a squeeze as we rounded the home turn, and he picked up and bounded into the home straight and up the hill. Then I got after him and kept him going up the hill. In the rain.

I didn't feel the rain. I didn't hear another rival.

That was big for all the reasons. For me, a Galway Plate. Galway is massive, it's one of the few race meetings that make mainstream news. When I won the Galway Hurdle, on both occasions, I was all over the newspapers the following day, all over the news, all over the *Six One* news on RTÉ so that Edelle's dad could see me and say, is that your fellow? And the Plate was at least as big, maybe even bigger than the Hurdle. It was great for my connection with Henry too.

That was another turning point in my relationship with Gigginstown, I thought, Balko Des Flos's Galway Plate. I felt they wanted me to ride for them after that. I felt that the trainers wanted me, and that Eddie and Michael were happy to let me ride for them. They had no retained rider after all, and it was probably just as easy for them to let me ride for them if the trainers wanted me to ride for them. It was a great feeling to be wanted.

I was riding lots for Gordon too, and I needed to concentrate on him. I had kind of become Gordon's stable jockey. He had plenty of riders, he had four or five jockeys, and nothing was ever said, but it kind of got to the stage were I was riding the better ones.

I did have a bit of a lapse at Tramore shortly after Galway. I was riding a mare for Roger McGrath, Kings Dolly, in a mares' handicap hurdle. She got a bit of a run on me on the way to the start, she was keen. We were going down to the show hurdle, you have a look at the show hurdle before you turn back around and go back to the start, I was trying to get her to slow down, but she wasn't listening to me.

She was careering along to the hurdle and I got a bit scared that she wasn't going to stop. She did stop suddenly just before the hurdle, and I managed to stay on board, but I got a bit of a fright. I hit her a bit of a smack on her neck: don't do that again. I shouldn't have done that. It was wrong. I just wanted her to know that she shouldn't have done that, that she shouldn't do it again.

The raceday stewards didn't take any action, but there was lots of talk about it on social media afterwards, so the Turf Club referred it to the Referrals Committee just over a week later. The Referrals Committee cautioned me. There was more talk on social media, some people said I should have been suspended, so the registrar of the Irish National Hunt Steeplechase Committee invoked a review, on the premise that the punishment may have been unduly lenient, and the appeals body gave me a four-day ban. I accepted my punishment, I knew I was in the wrong. I was happy to put the incident behind me and move on.

Other than that, I was in a really happy place. I was in a great place in my career, I was in demand, I was riding good horses, and I was in a great place in my life. I was with my life partner, Lily and Finn were doing great, and we had just found out that Edelle was pregnant with Liam. Finn was born in Cork in October 2015. There was something about our first boy, born in Cork, a true rebel from birth! I used to tell him about where we would go, all the matches, all the point-to-points we would go to together. It had been a difficult year, Edelle had had a miscarriage the previous year, and that was so tough for her. The whole process. It's difficult to describe, but you are in grief. We are still in grief. There will be a tree there on the lawn out at the back of the house for years to come now in memory. We were so happy then when we learned that Liam was on the way.

Tess came along then after Liam, in June 2019. She missed both Grand Nationals. I rode on for four years after she was born, I always hoped that she would remember me riding, but I don't think she does or she will. The other three do, but I think Tess will remember more about me dancing than she will about me riding. That's okay too though. She's cute out, a little princess, but she's tough. I suppose she has to be tough. You don't get any leeway for being the youngest of four.

I always wanted kids. All my life. I always loved being around kids and I always thought about how I would be with my own kids. Even when I was younger, I always wanted to have kids, I always wanted to have my own family.

I didn't think I was riding any better than I had been riding earlier in my career, but I knew that I was wanted, and that was always so important for me. Maybe you ride better when you know that you're wanted, maybe you ride with more confidence. I don't know. But how do you ride with confidence if you're not in demand? And how are you going to be in demand if you're not riding with confidence?

I was a little older too, maybe with a little more perspective, which maybe comes with age. I'm not sure. I was just content, settled, relaxed. People started to say I was riding well. It's mad. You ride a few winners, and people start to say that you're riding well, therefore you must be riding well. I didn't feel that I was riding any better than I ever rode, I definitely wasn't doing anything different, I always rode the same way, always tried to get the horse to do as well as he or she could do, but people seemed to start to appreciate what I was doing, how I rode, the patient approach.

When you're riding in a race, the easiest thing in the world to do is to get down and start driving. As soon as you feel the horse coming under pressure, start riding him along. Anybody can do that. And people watching have no issue with that, because you're being seen to be making an effort. But often, as I mentioned before, it isn't the right thing to do, it isn't the way to get the horse to achieve his or her best possible position. You burst the horse, you run out of petrol, he won't finish. Best to give him a chance, wait until you feel the power coming back, then get him going again, hope that, when the power comes back, you have enough time to pick up at least some of the pieces, to get the horse to run on to pass a few of your rivals, sometimes even all your rivals.

A.P. McCoy ruined it for all of us. He was brilliant at it, he'd be riding away, busy away, getting a horse to go forward. Whatever it was about A.P., he could be riding away and the horse would keep responding. You'd never let him off, you could never let A.P. off into a clear lead, even if you thought he was going too fast, because even if it looked like he was doing too much too early, he never was. Horses kept finding for him. He was a master at that. He was unique.

A.P. always talked about the importance of not bullying a horse, not forcing it to go faster than it could earlier than it could, but of convincing the horse that it wanted to run for you. There's a big difference. For A.P., his way was to ride away, to be busy on a horse's back, and his way was better, because it was visible. And, because he was champion jockey in Britain 20 times in a row – 20 times in a row! – his way was seen as being the best way. My way was always different, I would be quieter, but still trying to achieve the same result, still trying to convince a horse that he wanted to run for me.

I used to get a lot of stick for that on social media, for not making enough of an effort. But that's because many people on social media didn't understand what I was doing. But I wasn't riding for them, I wasn't riding *to be seen to be trying* to achieve the best possible position. I was riding to *actually try to* achieve the best possible position. At least the stewards seemed to understand, I was never done for stopping a horse in my life. Never. Not once. I didn't always get it right, but I always rode to try to achieve the best possible position, I always tried to do the right thing in a race, the thing I judged to be the right thing at the time.

I watched the movie *Ford v Ferrari* there recently, with Matt Damon and Christian Bale, and I found it fascinating. There's a quote in the film by Matt Damon, he talks about a point, at 7,000 RPM, where everything fades. The machine becomes weightless, he says. For me, riding horses, it's similar. It's all about the revs. You have to get to the number of revs where a horse is comfortable, but go beyond that and it's too much. If it's going too fast you blow the engine.

With cars, you have computers, monitors. Everything is measured and recorded. With horses in a race, you have the jockey. That's it. And judgement. Experience. The jockey has to know where a horse is comfortable, when it's going at optimum speed, the point beyond which the revs are too high and you will burn out the engine.

* * *

Everything clicked that season, 2017/18. I hit a sweet spot in my career. I was riding good horses in good races, and I was riding winners. Lots of winners. I had been over to Britain during the summer to ride John Constable for Evan Williams and Dai Walters in the Swinton Hurdle at Haydock and in the Summer Handicap Hurdle at Market Rasen, and we won both races.

I won the Troytown Chase in November on Mala Beach for Gordon and for Chris Jones, and, on Hatton's Grace Hurdle day at Fairyhouse in early December, I won the Drinmore Chase on Death Duty and the Porterstown Chase on Presenting Percy, a six-year-old, a novice, carrying top weight. I had two Grade 1 winners at Leopardstown that Christmas, both for Gordon: Apple's Jade for Gigginstown in the Christmas Hurdle – I had never ridden Apple's Jade in a race before – and Mick Jazz for George Mahoney in the Ryanair Hurdle.

I won the Dan Moore Chase on Doctor Phoenix and the Boyne Hurdle on Diamond Couchois and the Winning Fair Juvenile Hurdle on Mitchouka, all for Gordon. That was my 100th winner of the season in Ireland, Mitchouka in the Winning Fair Hurdle. I had ridden 100 winners or more in a season only three times before that, and there I was, on the last Saturday in February, over two months still to go in the season, with 100 winners on the board. I went to Naas the following day and I rode two more winners, Hardline and Doctor Phoenix. That was 102, and I was miles clear in the jockeys' championship. Paul Townend was my nearest pursuer on 65. I was able to coast to the championship then, I could have been crowned champion jockey long before the season ended at Punchestown, and that was brilliant. Champion jockey again, for the third time.

Through all of this though, Mam wasn't doing too well. She had been sick for a while and, in the last four or five years, her quality of life hadn't been great. She never complained though, she never felt sorry for herself.

The week before she died, there was a big freeze in Ireland and lots of snow. I remember I was around home, trying to keep things going, trying to prevent the pipes from freezing. But there wasn't much to be done on the farm, and there was no racing, so it meant I was able to spend lots of time with Mam in the hospital. I really cherished that time.

I had decided that I wasn't going to go to Cheltenham that year, I had decided I was going to stay with her, spend as much time as I could with her. Then, on Saturday 3 March, at 4.44pm, she passed away.

I have always had a thing with numbers on the clock, when the same digits line up. 11.11pm, 5.55am, 2.22pm. I often seem to look at the clock when the numbers are lining up. Anyway, Mam passed away and I looked at the clock. 4.44pm. There's nothing in it, no meaning or anything, I just smiled when I saw it.

Mam was an unbelievable person. The upbringing she gave us, we had so much freedom, but, at the same time, we had so much security, and we knew where the boundaries were. We knew too that she was always there for us. She was a constant in my life, a continuous comfort.

She was always busy, always doing something. During the day, she had all the kids to mind and all the paperwork to do for the garage. In the evening, she'd be in the room there, on the phone to her relatives. She was originally from Kells, and she'd be on the phone to them there all night long, catching up, while at the same time sewing a button on a shirt or fixing a pair of trousers on her sewing machine or darning a sock. This would be an old sock now that should have been thrown in the bin years ago, but Mam would be in there fixing it, making it right.

Her funeral was unbelievable. She was loved by so many, respected by everyone. She never had a bad word to say about anybody, and that was reciprocated. I was kind of blown away by the crowds, by the people who came. Everybody from the town, every person Mam ever came in contact with, and lots and lots of people from racing. Everybody was there for her. It was all very humbling.

I think of her all the time. Like, when something good happens I think, Mam would have loved this. When something happens with the kids, birthdays, Communions, when they ride a clear round on their ponies.

Or when I was on *The Late Late Show*. Mam never missed *The Late Late Show*. She would have got some kick out of me being on it. Or winning a big race. She never watched me riding, she was always too worried, she was always concerned that something would happen to me. She never watched my races live, but she watched them afterwards, when she knew I was okay, and she got as big a kick out of my wins as anybody got.

Or flowers. Mam loved flowers. Especially daffodils. Any time I see daffodils I think of Mam.

I did go to Cheltenham that year, I rode four winners and I won the Leading Rider award. Maybe Mam had something to do with that too.

I won the RSA Chase on Presenting Percy on the Wednesday, and then the Thursday was just one of those days. Delta Work in the Pertemps Final, Balko Des Flos in the Ryanair Chase, The Storyteller in the Plate.

I didn't think Delta Work would win the Pertemps. I had ridden him at Leopardstown just over a month earlier and he had run well, he had finished fourth. But he was only five, it was a big ask for a five-year-old to win a Pertemps Final. Only one five-year-old had ever won the Pertemps Final before that, a race that was first run in 1974, five years before I was born, and no five-year-old has won it since.

We just got up too. I switched to the near side of Gordon's other horse Glenloe on the run to the final flight, we jumped the obstacle well and he was strong up the hill. We just got up by a nose from Glenloe in the end, a 1–2 for Gordon with just two runners in a 23-runner race, one of the most competitive staying handicap hurdles on the calendar.

Balko Des Flos was just very good, Henry had him in rare form and he won well. That was the first time a Gigginstown horse had won the Ryanair Chase, and Michael got a good kick out of it. He had been trying for years to win it, so it was nice to be able to ride his first Ryanair Chase winner for him. He hasn't won it again since so, 20 years of the Ryanair Chase, and Balko Des Flos is still Gigginstown's only winner of the race.

Then there was The Storyteller in the Plate, just over an hour after Balko Des Flos. The Storyteller was always very brave over hurdles, and he had been competing in good novice chases that season, so it was a great move by Gordon to run him in a handicap at Cheltenham that year. I just hunted him around, along the inside and not too far off the pace.

I got a lovely run around the whole way. He got into a rhythm from early, and his jumping was very good, accurate and fairly effortless. We stayed on the inside until the run down the hill to the third last fence, when I took him off the rail to go around Richard Johnson on Village Vic, who was fading. We got a bit crowded for room at the second last fence, and he got in tight, but he had lots of energy left. He started to pick up on the run to the last, and I was thinking, meet this right and we'll win.

We did meet it right, he flew the fence and landed running. Only Jamie Bargary on Splash Of Ginge was in front of us, over to my left, but I knew we had him. Then the right-hand rail stopped and The Storyteller started to hang to his right. It's understandable, a big old hill in front of you, crowds on both sides of the rails and a wall of sound hitting you in the face. Come on now though. I tried to straighten him up, reins in my left hand, whip in my right.

He keeps going right, but he keeps going forward. I can see Splash Of Ginge over to my left, well away from us to my left, and he is definitely behind us. There's the width of the track between us, but we're in front, me and The Storyteller, and that's all that matters.

Three winners on the day, four at the meeting, and leading jockey at the Cheltenham Festival.

That was the 13th Cheltenham Festival in a row at which I had ridden at least one winner. It started with Native Jack in the Cross-Country Chase in 2006, and it ran all the way to Balko Des Flos in the Ryanair Chase in 2018. It was nice to have got to 13.

I didn't ride a winner at the 2019 Cheltenham Festival, it just didn't happen for me, so the run was broken, but I was back in 2020 with three: Envoi Allen, Samcro and Chosen Mate.

Samcro was obviously a high-profile horse, he was always highly regarded at home, but he had his issues, and it was a great training performance by Gordon to get him back to win the Marsh Novices' Chase at Cheltenham that year. We just got up to beat Melon by a nose.

That was the first time I had ridden Samcro in a race, so it was brilliant to win on him, to win a Grade 1 race at the Cheltenham Festival on him. As well as that, it brought up Gigginstown's 100th Grade 1 win, so it was nice to be a part of the achievement of that milestone.

Envoi Allen was a Rolls-Royce of a racehorse. I loved Envoi Allen. He could have been anything if he had got a clear run at it. He had won his only point-to-point and he had won his four bumpers the previous season, Jamie Codd had ridden him in all four. I had ridden him to victory in his three novice hurdles earlier in the 2019/20 season, he just did everything so effortlessly. We expected he would win the Ballymore Novices' Hurdle easily at the 2020 Cheltenham Festival, and he duly did.

Chosen Mate was a little different, we thought he had a big chance all right, but it was the Grand Annual, a really competitive two-mile handicap chase. Again though, Gordon had him in unbelievable form, and he stayed on well up the hill to come clear of Gordon's other horse in the race, Eclair De Beaufeu.

That was my 25th Cheltenham Festival winner. I didn't know it at the time, but it was also my last.

Chapter 18

I love the Grand National. I have always loved the Grand National. It was always the race that did it for me.

There was so much about it for me as a kid, the big fences, different to others, big spruce fences, and unique, with names, Becher's Brook and the Canal Turn and The Chair. There was no other race in the world that I knew of that had names on the fences. The number of runners, so many horses in one race. The spectacle of it.

I remember the Grand Nationals when I was growing up. West Tip and Richard Dunwoody. Mr Frisk winning it in the fastest time, beating Red Rum's time. Seagram beating Garrison Savannah, when it looked like Garrison Savannah was going to complete the Gold Cup/Grand National double. And still no horse has done that double since Golden Miller in 1934.

And I was all about the Grand National at home. When Dad would cut the grass, we had quite a big garden so there'd be a lot of grass, and we'd gather up all the grass. It was pure torture gathering all the grass, but it was worth it because we'd be able to use the grass to make the fences, Grand National fences, just so we could jump over them and kick the tops off them, like the horses did with the big spruce fences in the Grand National. When I was riding my pony, I was riding him in the Grand National. When I was jumping over

MY AUTOBIOGRAPHY

planks and poles on Thunder, I was jumping the Grand National fences.

I didn't know I was riding Tiger Roll in the 2018 Grand National until declaration time, two days before the race. I knew I would be riding something for Gordon, and Gordon had three in the race, so I was happy to ride whatever Gordon would put me up on. All the way through my career, when I had picked horses myself, when I had the choice of one horse over another, I had often got it wrong, so I was happy to let Gordon pick for me. Gordon had always picked the right one for me. It didn't always work out, but it was always the right one for me going there on the day. He had never put me wrong.

Tiger Roll wasn't really a special horse for me before the 2018 Grand National. He was special in the sense that, after I had lost the Gigginstown job, he was the horse I got back on at Cheltenham in 2014 and won the Triumph Hurdle, on the day I won the Gold Cup. That was obviously a very special day, and he was a big part of that. But he disappeared for me fairly quickly after the Triumph Hurdle. I rode him in the Champion Four-Year-Old Hurdle at Punchestown that year, the month after we had won the Triumph Hurdle, but I didn't ride him again in a race after that. Not until I got up on him for the 2018 Grand National.

He stayed over hurdles the following year, Bryan Cooper rode him in most of his races. Jack Kennedy actually rode him to win his beginners' chase at Ballinrobe in May 2016, Donagh Meyler rode him to win the Munster National in October 2016, and Lisa O'Neill rode him to win the National Hunt Chase at the Cheltenham Festival in 2017. His next win was in the Cross-Country Chase at the 2018 Cheltenham Festival, when Keith Donoghue rode him. But he had 10st 13lb to carry in the Grand National, and Keith couldn't do 10st 13lb.

You'd never look at Tiger Roll though and say that he was a Grand National horse. He was a small horse, 15.3hh, no more, and he wasn't great to jump. He didn't have a great technique. He had his own way of doing things, and he was clever, but you'd worry for him. Like, you'd never track him in a race over fences. You wouldn't want to be in behind him going over a fence. I would never have sent him over fences in the first place if he had been mine, I never really saw him as a steeplechaser, but Gordon, obviously, the trainer that he is, the eye that he has, he obviously saw something in him.

We went to Cheltenham four months earlier, in December 2017, for the Cross-Country Chase at the December meeting. I was set to ride Bless The Wings in the race, Keith Donoghue was set to ride Tiger Roll. We schooled the pair of them over the cross-country course the day before the race when we were over there, and Tiger Roll couldn't get the hang of it at all. After the third attempt over the Cheese Wedges, the obstacle just in front of the stands, after he had sprawled on the ground again, I said to Keith, ah here, we'd better stop. This isn't working.

In fairness to Keith, he got him around in the Cross-Country Chase the following day, he got him over the Cheese Wedges and the Aintree fence, where he really wasn't good at all, and all the other obstacles, and they finished fifth. Bless The Wings was great that day, he jumped super for me and he stayed on well to win nicely.

As I mentioned before, the Grand National had never been a lucky race for me. I had my first ride in the race in 2003, the year Monty's Pass won it. I was riding for Ferdy Murphy at the time, and I rode Ballinclay King for him, but we never travelled, he never jumped, he broke a blood vessel actually and I ended up pulling him up before we had gone a circuit, before The Chair.

I rode Takagi in it the following year for Edward O'Grady. We were actually going okay, they went very fast up front, but I was happy with where we were and how we were going, back in the field. The winner Amberleigh House was behind us when we got to The Chair, but Takagi left his hind legs in the ditch and flung me out over his head, drove me into the ground. I remember that well, my neck was shocking sore afterwards.

I went through years without ever really going close in the National. I completed on Joes Edge in 2006, finished seventh behind Numbersixvalverde. And in 2016 I thought I was going to win it. As I mentioned before, I was travelling so well on Morning Assembly. He did everything easily. Across the Anchor Bridge crossing and around the home turn, and we moved into second place, just The Last Samuri and a loose horse in front of us. Then it all went to pieces. He just emptied. It was like, when we hit the home straight, he just ran out of petrol.

Rule The World won the National that year. As I said, I could have ridden Rule The World, the Gigginstown horse trained by Mouse Morris, who was ridden by David Mullins in the end. I turned him down in order to ride Morning Assembly. I thought Morning Assembly had a better chance of winning the race.

He didn't.

I finished third on Saint Are the following year. He ran on into third. I was riding him along from a long way out and I never really thought we were going to win. Strangely, even though Morning Assembly finished eighth and Saint Are finished third, I thought I went closer to winning the race on Morning Assembly than I did on Saint Are. Saint Are just kept going, he did well to finish third.

Back in the 2000s, when I had my first few rides in the Grand National, I started to think I couldn't really win it. I wasn't going close, I was never really in with a chance. I loved riding in the race though, I loved riding over the fences, I always wanted to ride in the race, but winning it seemed like a long way off. Then I rode Morning Assembly, he gave me such a good spin for so long, and then I finished third on Saint Are, and I started to think, actually, winning it is closer to reality than I used to think.

A friend of mine did tell me back in the 2000s that I was going to win the Grand National some day. It was after I had finished seventh on Joes Edge or after I had finished ninth on Chelsea Harbour, he said, you'll win it at some stage. You can't say that though. You can't tell someone they're going to win the Grand National. Not someone with my record in the race at that stage anyway! He said he just thought, the way I rode, that it was well suited to the Grand National. I wasn't sure if that was a good thing or a bad thing!

Grand National day 2018, I had two rides before the big race. I rode Better Getalong for Nicky Richards in the Grade 1 Mersey Novices' Hurdle, he never travelled, and I rode Petit Mouchoir for Henry de Bromhead and Gigginstown in the Grade 1 Mersey Novices' Chase. He ran really well. It developed into a match from the second last fence between us and Diego Du Charmil and Harry Cobden, and they just got the better of us.

There were two more races after that before the National, but I wasn't involved so I just stayed in the weigh room, watched the races, got myself ready. Paddy Brennan was always beside me in the weigh room at Aintree. And Brian Hughes. I remember saying to Paddy, I'd want to have two back protectors going out to ride this fellow.

I wasn't very hopeful, I didn't think my prospects of winning the Grand National on Tiger Roll were very high. He was small, not your typical Grand National horse. I knew he had his own way of getting over his fences, but I could still remember his attempts at the Cheese Wedges at Cheltenham. If he couldn't manage the Cheese Wedges, how was he going to get over The Chair?

There was a notion going around that I didn't want to ride him, but that was never the case. I wasn't desperate to ride him, but it wasn't that I didn't want to ride him either. I was never asked. I was happy to go with whatever Gordon thought I should go with, and that was just the way it was. Nobody gave me the choice. I was just declared on him at declaration stage, and I was happy to go with that.

I tried to convince myself that he didn't have much of a chance. Any time I went into the Grand National thinking I had a chance, it all came to nothing. So I'd be talking my chances down, to myself and to anyone who would listen. The gap between the race and my flight home was short enough, so I was saying to myself, if I fall at the first fence – and there was a good chance that I would fall at the first fence – at least I would make my flight home, no problem. That was the way I tried to look at things in my mind. That if I could set my expectations low, I couldn't be too disappointed if things didn't go well.

The parade ring at Aintree before the Grand National was busy. It always was. There's always so much going on, it's the Grand National, the most famous horse race in the world, and all that goes with it. There were 38 runners that year, so 38 horses, 38 trainers, 38 sets of owners, 38 jockeys leaving the weigh room and going into the parade ring, looking for their trainers.

Gordon had three runners, Daryl Jacob was riding Ucello Conti and Jack Kennedy was riding Bless The Wings, so we all gathered together. You just want to get on with it though at that stage, all the photos are taken, you just want to get up on the horse and get out of the parade ring, away from everything, down to the start. They talk about last-minute instructions, but there's no need. I have my plan in my head and, anyway, it's a horse race, it's the Grand National, anything can happen. You can't go out with a rigid plan in your head. You have to be able to adapt to circumstances as the race happens around you.

I was always like that, for every race, not just for the Grand National. You'd do your homework, you'd do your preparation, you'd know your horse and you'd know your opposition. Ruby's horse goes forward, Barry's horse jumps to his left, Paul's horse has never been over the distance before and might not stay. So you have all the information in there, but it doesn't mean you have a set plan. You know in your head what you want to do, but you also have all the information so that you can change as things change around you. And you do it by instinct, because you have all the knowledge. You have to act quicky and react sharply. If you have to think about things before you can decide what to do, it's too late, the opportunity is gone, the race is over.

The closer I got to the race, to any race, the more focused I got. I tried to not listen to anybody. I had my plan in my head, I knew what I was going to do, and I tried not to be influenced by what somebody else would say.

I'd get into a zone before a race. It didn't matter if it was the Grand National at Aintree or a maiden hurdle at Thurles, I'd always be focused before a race. Block everything out. I'm sure I came across as rude to some people, but I didn't mean to be rude. I was just in the zone. In Thurles, you have to walk through the crowd to get to the parade ring, and I'm sure I went past some people as they tried to engage with me. That's just the way I was. An armed guard could be trying to stop me and I wouldn't have noticed.

The odd time I'd stop. Sign an autograph for a kid or something. That was always important to me, to be good to the kids. And if I stopped on my way into the parade ring, it delayed the time I was in the parade ring, and that was only a positive. I never enjoyed that time in the parade ring before a race, and owners there, excited about their horse running. Understandably so, absolutely. But then looking for selfies in the parade ring before the race, looking for me to pose for selfies before I go out to ride in a race. That never made any sense to me.

I didn't mind Pat Healy or Caroline Norris or somebody taking a photograph from the side, a photo of me without asking me to pose. That was always fine. But posing for photos before going out to ride your race? Nah, I wasn't into that.

I never apologised for that either, I wouldn't, I never thought I needed to. I was there to do a job, to ride a horse in a race for an owner and a trainer and, in order to do that job to the best of my ability, I needed to focus. That was what worked for me, that's what was successful for me, so I could never apologise for it.

And when I was younger, I used to not speak to the lad or the girl who was leading up my horse. Not a word. I was just trying to focus. That might have come across as rude too, and I used to get annoyed with them when they would try to talk to me, but that was just because I was in the zone. The most important thing to me was to give the horse the best ride I could, not to exchange pleasantries.

I got better at that in later years, and I'm glad that I did.

Gordon knew how I was, he totally understood, he knew to leave me to my own devices, and it was great for me to know that he had that type of confidence in me. And before the Grand National, in the parade ring before the Grand National, all the talking was done anyway. Gordon went over the plan for Bless The Wings again with Jack, and he went over the plan for Ucello Conti again with Daryl. Then he turned to me and he just said, you know what you're doing.

Strange the effect that something so small can have on you, but it meant a lot to me. It gave me more confidence. Even at that stage of my career. Maybe especially at that stage of my career. That Gordon Elliott thought enough of me to leave me off, do what I wanted to do, in the Grand National. That he had that level of confidence in me.

The bell went for the jockeys to mount, and I headed over to Tiger Roll, Louise Magee leading him up. Gordon obviously had three in the race, Jack and Daryl had to be legged up too, so Michael O'Leary came over to Tiger Roll with me and legged me up. That meant a lot too. I don't know if that was Michael's plan, or if that's just the way it happened, but he had five runners in the race, he could have legged up any or all of the other four, so I thought it was good of him to leg me up. It was like I was the main character in the movie. That gave me a lot of confidence too.

So I'm focusing now, on Tiger Roll's back, Louise leading us, on our way around the parade ring before going out onto the course, and I'm trying to block everything out. I do hear the commentator over the Tannoy though, he's name-checking every horse as each one goes out, and he comes to Tiger Roll:

'The smallest horse in the race, ridden by the oldest jockey in the race.'

I had a bit of a laugh with Louise about that.

It was good to get out onto the track though, get away from it all, just me and Tiger Roll. I wanted to show him the first fence, but I also wanted to get a good position at the start, and if you are late arriving down at the start, you won't get your position. I decided it was important to show him the fence, then I could take my chances with getting a position.

He was looking around him as we went down to the first fence to have a look at it. He was paying attention. I could feel him looking at the fence as we approached it, pricking his ears, examining it. I liked that, I liked that he seemed to notice the difference.

He pricked his ears again as we stopped at the fence. A big spruce fence, towering over him. He'd have to jump it, so it was important that he got a look at it. He'd have to jump 29 other similar fences too, some of them even bigger than this one. I gave him a pat on the neck and took him away from the fence. I didn't want to stay there too long, I wanted to get to the start early, get my position. The start in the Grand National is so important.

There aren't any real rules at the start of the Grand National, or at the start of any National Hunt race. It's different in flat races, in flat races you have stalls and you have your draw, and you go into the stalls and you all start in a straight line. In National Hunt races, jumps races, you start behind a tape. It's like the difference between a 100-metre race, in which you have lanes and starting blocks, and a cross-country race, where you all line up and you elbow the other fellow out of your way and get ready for when the starter says go.

I just wanted clear sailing to the first fence. I didn't want any horse to be in front of us. I didn't want to be in front, not necessarily, I just wanted Tiger Roll to have a clear sight of the fence.

In Grand Nationals past, I used to get worked up about where I wanted to be, on the outside at the start, middle to outside at Becher's Brook, angling towards the inside at the Canal Turn. You had to be on the inside at the Canal Turn, you had to be on the inside at Foinavon. That hadn't served me so well though. I had never won it. Forget that. I just wanted a clear view of the first obstacle, get over the first fence safely and take it from there, see where we were.

We started to group up in front of the stands as start time got closer. We walked towards the Water Jump, away from the starter, and I was in the front rank, around the middle. We turned as a group and started to walk towards the starter and the other horses started to join the bigger group, like little drops of mercury being sucked into the bigger pool. Tiger Roll and I retained our position in the centre, just behind the front rank.

Most of the horses started to jig-jog as we moved as a group around the corner that goes away from the stands and started to face up to the starting tape. They knew something was up, they could sense it. Heart-rates up, horses and jockeys. We were in the front rank and in the centre, perfect, Jack Kennedy to my right, Danny Cook to my left. The starter put his yellow flag up. He waited until we got a little closer, then he released the tape:

'Come on then!'

Chapter 19

Winning the Grand National, what was that like? People asked me then, people ask me now. I don't know how to describe it really. I didn't know then, and I still don't really know.

It's like, something you've been aware of your entire life. Something you knew about before you knew that you knew anything about anything. Something that's so far away that it's not really within reach, it's not within your reality. It's something other people do. Something you see on television.

It's like, for a young fellow or a young girl who spends his or her time studying planets, studying space, getting on a rocket and going to the moon.

The Grand National was that big for me. Riding in the Grand National, winning the Grand National. It was like going to the moon. It was like getting to the top of Mount Everest and sticking a flag in the ground.

Mam was on my mind. She was on my mind a lot then, she is never too far away from my mind, but this was just a few weeks after she had passed away. I looked up to the skies, I put my hands up to heaven. Martin Budds too.

Luke Harvey from ITV was suddenly alongside me with a microphone in his hand. He was talking, shouting, he asked me something and put the microphone up to my face.

'I was afraid he wouldn't take to it,' I said. 'Because he's very economical with his jumping. Keith Donoghue has done a wonderful job with him.'

I didn't know what to say. In the moment. I was just after winning the Grand National, millions watching, a microphone in front of my mouth. I thought of Pat Smullen.

'This one's for P. Smullen,' I said. 'Luke. This one's for Pat Smullen. I was speaking to him the other morning. The man is as tough as nails. This one is for Pat.'

The microphone was still there in front of my face. Luke asked me something else.

'I don't know what to say,' I said.

Because I didn't.

It's a fairly long walk in from the racecourse, down the chute, under the stands and back in towards the winner's enclosure, but it flew. It wasn't long enough. I would have loved a bit more time to try to take everything in. Gordon was over to my right, Louise at Tiger Roll's head. All the noise and all the crowds and all the fanfare. Barry Geraghty grabbed my hand before we got into the Number 1 spot. He was still in his silks, still in the J.P. McManus colours he had worn on Anibale Fly. I didn't know it at the time, but he had finished fourth. I didn't ask him. I should have asked him.

I wanted to see Michael. I was looking for Michael. And then, just as we arrived into the winner's enclosure, before I dismounted, I felt this pat on my knee and there he was. He reached up to shake my hand, and I leaned down and gave him a hug. I meant it too. He grabbed the sides of my helmet with his two hands and gave me a kiss on the cheek.

I dismounted and opened the girth and slipped the saddle off Tiger Roll's back. I was concerned that I had to weigh in. The result isn't official until you weigh in, prove that you came back in with the same weight as the weight you went out with. There's so much going on, all the crowds, all the hustle-bustle, I was thinking that anything could happen. A piece of lead could fall out of your saddle and then you weigh in light and then it's all for nothing. Strange the things that go through your head. You have to remember to weigh in. So I took my saddle over to the scales and I weighed in, 10st 13lb. Exhale.

After that, pandemonium. Everybody wants a piece of you. It's understandable, the Grand National is the most famous horse race in the world, and you're just after winning it. Cameras everywhere, microphones everywhere, people grabbing your arm, people talking to you, shouting at you, asking you questions.

Just shows you, the difference between winning and not winning. The previous year, when I had finished third on Saint Are behind One For Arthur, nobody wanted to talk to me.

I didn't make my flight home! The flight, the one I thought I would make if we fell at the first fence, that flight left without me. I wanted to get home though, I didn't want to be in Liverpool that night. The evening is all a bit of a blur to be honest, but Michael arranged a different flight home for us and we ended up getting back to Ireland and I ended going to a party in Skreen with Gordon. That was some craic. I don't drink, but I was just high on the day.

I went racing the following day, and that was a mistake. I was fucked, I could barely open my eyes, I should have taken the day off, but I had committed to riding at Tramore the following day back before I had won the Grand National. I rode a double, I won the first race on a mare of John Kiely's, Decision Time, and I won the second on Monatomic for Gordon and Gigginstown. I wasn't good on either horse though, I only just got home on Monatomic, we just held on to win by a short head. Two horses had passed us three strides after the line.

I got beaten on Lieutenant Colonel and I got beaten on a horse for Terence O'Brien in the handicap chase, Consharon Boy. I was on auto pilot. I wasn't any help to any of the horses I rode that day. I shouldn't have gone racing. I should have taken the day off.

That's the thing about racing: it keeps on rolling. There's no pause, no let-up. You win the Grand National, and there you are, riding at Tramore the following day. It would be like winning the Champions League on Saturday evening and playing a match on Sunday morning.

If you win the All-Ireland, that's it, season over. You take time out, you get the time to take it all in, to appreciate what you've just achieved. You go around the schools with the Liam MacCarthy Cup, you take the time to celebrate. You're not back at training the following day.

We did go around the schools with the Grand National trophy though, and that was brilliant. I loved being around the kids, and they all seemed to get a great kick out of it. But I had to fit that in around my riding. There was no point where we took time off to properly celebrate it and look back and appreciate it all. No time to recharge before we had to get going again.

Of course, I could have taken the time off myself, allowed racing to go on without me, but that wasn't my way. That was never my way. If racing was going on, I wanted to be riding. If there was a race to be run and a race to be won, I wanted to be in it with a chance of winning it. I was always like that. In point-to-points, at the racecourse, I never wanted to be sitting in the weigh room watching on as a race was being run.

It's the same with the end of the season. The Irish National Hunt season ends at Punchestown every year these days. The last day of the Punchestown Festival is the last day of the National Hunt season. It's good the way it is now, it's far better than it used to be until the late 1980s, when the season used to end at the end of the calendar year, right in the middle of the real National Hunt season. (Somebody should have told Michael O'Leary that it had been changed before 2013.) But even now, the champions are crowned, champion owner, champion trainer, champion jockey, the dials are set back to zero, and you're off again. You're riding at Tipperary five days later.

We had some evening the following evening though. In Summerhill, Gordon's local village. The crowds. I couldn't believe the crowds. As I was driving down the road, getting close to the village, I was thinking, I'm never going to be able to get through these crowds. Then a Garda spotted me, recognised me, and suddenly he was on the case, escorting me, moving people out of the way to make a path for me to get down the street.

Walking down the street, I felt like a king. All the people were there to see Tiger Roll. It was amazing how popular he became, he was that type of character, the little terrier, the little tiger who had scaled the big fences and won the Grand National.

It was unrehearsed too. Gordon just brought Tiger Roll into Summerhill and the people came. You couldn't have rehearsed it, the village just exploded. A lot of my uncles and aunts on my mam's side live in Meath, and they all came, so it was great to see them there. But the atmosphere the whole evening was brilliant.

When the dust settled a little, the realisation dawned on me that I had won the Grand National, and that was massive for me. It was a bit different to winning the Gold Cup. When I won the Gold Cup, a weight was lifted off my shoulders. The Gold Cup is the pinnacle of the sport, the best horses all carrying equal weights. It's all about class, and the best horse, the best staying chaser in any given year usually wins the Gold Cup. Top-class horses and top-class jockeys win the Gold Cup, and I desperately wanted to win it.

Winning the Grand National was different to winning the championship too. I really wanted to be champion jockey. Again, like winning the Gold Cup, the best jockeys become champion jockey. The clue is in the title. If I had got to the end of my career without being crowned champion jockey, I'm sure I would have felt unfulfilled, I'm sure there would have been a gaping hole in my sense of what I had achieved as a National Hunt jockey.

Equally, if I had got to the end of my career without winning the Grand National, I would have been disappointed. Of course I would have been. It's massive for me that I won it. But I wouldn't have been as disappointed as I would have been if I hadn't won the Gold Cup or if I hadn't been crowned champion. The Grand National is the most famous horse race in the world, but it's a handicap. The better the horse, the more weight that horse carries. In theory, all horses carry weights that give each horse just as good a chance as – no better than, no worse than – every other horse in the race.

There used to be 38 or 39 or 40 runners in the Grand National every year – the maximum field size was reduced to 34 in 2024 – so, as long as you had a ride in the race, you had just one chance in 38 or 39 or 40 of winning it. You need to get on the right horse, and then you need everything to go right for you in the race, because so much can go wrong. It's a big ask.

Some of the best jockeys in National Hunt racing never won the Grand National. John Francome was one of the best National Hunt jockeys ever, he was champion jockey in Britain seven times, and he never won it. Peter Scudamore was champion jockey eight times and he never won the Grand National. Richard Johnson has ridden more National Hunt winners than any other jockey with the exception of A.P. McCoy, he won the Gold Cup twice, but he never rode the winner of the Grand National. Frank Berry never won it, Charlie Swan never won it, and they were each crowned champion jockey in Ireland nine or 10 times.

You'd see old footage of Grand Nationals past, and you'd be looking for yourself in the race. You'd have to look fairly closely at the 2003 Grand National, my first, when I pulled Ballinclay King up after a circuit. You might see yourself for a few fences on Joes Edge or on Chelsea Harbour, or travelling well on Morning Assembly before weakening. You were always a bit-part player though, part of the supporting cast at best. You were never the central character.

Next thing you know, you've got the lead role.

I grew up watching Grand National movies. I loved *National Velvet*, a young Elizabeth Taylor winning the Grand National. And *Champions*, the Bob Champion story, horse and rider coming back from the brink and winning the National. That one was real, fact is more incredible than fiction sometimes, and John Hurt was brilliant as Bob Champion. That was a fantastic movie, a fantastic story.

For me, at the start of my career, to just have a ride in the Grand National was huge. But there was no reason why I shouldn't have won a Grand National. I had ridden winners over the Grand National fences before, just not in the Grand National. It was just a case of finding the right horse, the right parts, and them all fitting together.

If I had won the race early in my career, it might not have meant so much. I was on the back nine when I won it. I was on the last three or four holes actually and, when I won it, it meant the world.

It meant the world to Gordon too. He had won it before, in 2007, 11 years earlier with Silver Birch. But he said that a lot of it passed him by at the time. Gordon was only starting to make his way as a trainer in 2007. Amazingly, as I mentioned before, he hadn't had a winner in Ireland when he won the Grand National for the first time. He'd had three or four winners in Britain, but he didn't have his first winner in Ireland until the month after he won the Grand National with Silver Birch.

It was some performance by a young trainer, to send a horse out to win the Grand National before he'd had a winner of any kind under Rules in his own home country. But Gordon is an extraordinary trainer, and he always said that he'd love to win the Grand National a second time, that he would appreciate it more if he did, and I was delighted I was able to ride that second winner for him.

The fact that it was for Gordon meant lots to me too. We have always had a very strong connection. I was effectively his stable jockey, his number one rider, and I was very much a part of the team. That was so important to me.

Tiger Roll was important to our kids too. Finn loved Tiger Roll from the start. He wouldn't go to bed without seeing the video, or without me telling him the story of Tiger Roll. I remember him waking up in the middle of the night shortly after the Grand National, he was very upset, so I took him down to the sitting room and we sat on the couch and I got my phone out and we watched Tiger Roll. Edelle came down, wondering how it had all gone so quiet, she came into the sitting room and there we were, Finn and me, lying together on the couch, watching Tiger Roll.

When Lily started jumping fences on her pony, it was always about Tiger Roll. Or if any of them was upset about something, come on, we'll watch Tiger Roll! It always cheered them up, Tiger Roll was always great for them.

Tiger Roll was great for me too.

Chapter 20

'The young fellow is dying to get a go in a pony race,' Peter Vaughan said to me.

The young fellow was his son Paddy, great young fellow, lovely little rider.

'Leave it with me,' I said.

I phoned Paddy Kennedy to ask if he knew if there was anything he could do for young Paddy Vaughan. There was a meeting the following Sunday up in Meath, and Paddy told me to bring him along, that he should be able to get a ride or two for him. Paddy was true to his word, he got young Paddy Vaughan a ride.

That was the first time I saw Paddy Kennedy's young brother Jack ride in pony races. He had six or seven rides that day, and he had five or six winners. They were all different types of rides too. He made the running on one, he dropped another in, he sat second or third on another. He rode them all. No matter what he did, the end result was the same on all but one of his rides.

He was such a lovely young fellow too, Jack. Quiet and unassuming, but he had this air about him. He was quiet, but he wasn't lacking in confidence. He was unassuming, but he wasn't timid. It's a very difficult balance to strike, but he managed to strike it. There was this air of a young fellow who was at ease with life, but who knew where he was going and who knew exactly how he was going to get there.

Jack started to text me. He started to tell me that he was going to be a jockey, and that he loved the way I rode. His mother and father called me soon enough afterwards. Lovely people too. They asked me if Jack should go to Gordon's. I said definitely, there's no better place for him to go, but before he goes to Gordon's, he should go to Tommy Stack's. He's light enough still, he can still ride on the flat. Now, he may not get a ride at Tommy Stack's, he may not ride a winner, or he may ride a thousand winners, but it will be a brilliant place for him to go for experience. Tommy is just a brilliant man, and he loves giving apprentices an opportunity.

Jack won the Dingle Derby on Coola Boula in 2014, then he moved to Tommy Stack's and then to Gordon's. He had his first ride on a racecourse for Gordon at Clonmel in May 2015, and he rode his first winner a couple of weeks later on a horse of Pat Flynn's, Funny How, in a handicap on the flat at Mallow. That was just Jack's sixth or seventh ride on the racecourse.

In July 2015, he won a big handicap on the flat at the Galway Festival on Clondaw Warrior for Willie Mullins. In November 2015, he won the Troytown Chase at Navan on Riverside City for Gordon and J.P. McManus, and he rode a treble on the same day.

What Jack has achieved already in his relatively short career to date is quite remarkable, but it is not surprising. Anyone who knew him back then would have fully expected him to be hugely successful as a jockey. He has it all, that quiet demeanour of his is reflective of his riding style. Quiet and relaxed, horses run for him. He has ridden 11 Cheltenham Festival winners already, including winning the Gold Cup on Minella Indo and, in April 2024, he was crowned champion jockey in Ireland for the first time.

Jack never really asked me for advice. I'm sure he knew I was there to give him advice if he needed to ask me, but he didn't need to. He always seemed to know what he was doing. He was always just a shockingly talented rider, and a great fellow, from a lovely family.

From the day he arrived at Gordon's, it was always likely he was going to be number one rider there at some stage. He was happy to bide his time though. I never really discussed it with Jack, or with Gordon, but the understanding always was that, when the time was right, he would take over.

He kind of rode as number two behind me for a few years and, any time I got injured, he effectively rode as number one. As he got more successful, he never changed, he still had the same laid-back demeanour. And he was never on at me or on at Gordon that he should be number one. He just kept riding away, riding well, riding winners. He knew the time would come for him to take over as number one, we all knew that time would come and I figured that, when it did, we would all know it.

* * *

It's one thing winning the Grand National, but it's another thing now going back and winning it again. Before the 2019 Grand National, no horse had won back-to-back renewals of the race since Red Rum won it in 1973 and in 1974.

From the moment Tiger Roll crossed the winning line at Aintree in April 2018 though, a head in front of Pleasant Company, Gordon's aim with him was to go back and win the race again in 2019. Same plan as last time, he said: Cross-Country Chase at Cheltenham in March, Grand National at Aintree in April.

Tiger Roll made his debut the following season in the Cross-Country Chase at Cheltenham's November meeting, and he ran really well in that, staying on well to take fourth place. The Cross-Country Chase at Cheltenham in November is a handicap, so he was conceding weight to all his rivals, and it was a good run on his first run since he'd won the Grand National.

Keith Donoghue rode him there, and Keith rode him again when he won the Boyne Hurdle at Navan in February, springing a 25/1 shock. And Keith was on board again when he won the Cross-Country Chase back at the Cheltenham Festival in March 2019. He was brilliant that day, Gordon had him in brilliant form going into the race and he won by over 20 lengths. I couldn't wait to get back on him again at Aintree.

The handicapper had raised Tiger Roll's handicap mark by 9lb since 2018. It was perfectly understandable, he had won the Grand National, even if he had only got home by a head. The Grand National weights are published in February and, unlike in any other race, if you win a race after the weights have been published, you don't have to carry a penalty. If the handicapper had had the evidence of his Cross-Country Chase win at Cheltenham in March, he probably would have given him more weight.

Anibale Fly was in the race, he was the top-rated horse, he was rated 5lb higher than Tiger Roll. He was carrying top weight of 11st 10lb, so we were set to carry 11st 5lb, and that was fine.

It could have all ended at the first fence though. Vintage Clouds jumped right across in front of us and came down. We didn't miss him by much. Tiger Roll saw him all right but, if he had been a fraction of a second earlier, we would have had nowhere to go and we would have been on the ground with him.

After that, pretty much everything went to plan. Tiger Roll was low over his obstacles again, he just skimmed through them. He recognised it all, figured it all out in his head again very quickly, and he loved it. It appeared as if he was really enjoying himself.

No drama at Becher's this time, he sailed out over it and landed easily. He was a bit awkward at Foinavon, the ground came up to meet him a little more quickly than he had anticipated, as is often the way at Foinavon. He juttered a bit, we lost a little ground, and we were squeezed out on the run to the Canal Turn, but we switched to the inside, he jumped the fence well and we were back travelling again.

Over The Chair, where Magic Of Light made a bad mistake and Paddy Kennedy did well to remain on board, over the Water Jump and we moved to the inside – I channelled my inner Arthur Moore – as we headed for the bend that would take us away from the stands, one circuit down, one to go.

The more the race developed, the more my confidence grew. He just did everything so easily, he was just enjoying it all. He nodded a little on landing over the fifth last fence, and he was a bit long at the fourth last and nodded again. They were the only worries, and they were small.

Magic Of Light led to the home turn under Paddy Kennedy. We were along the inside, running away, so I allowed him move up on the inside of Ruby Walsh and Rathvinden and move into second place. And like the previous year, I was just thinking, don't go too early. I sat upsides Paddy on Magic Of Light over the second last fence. I sat still as Paddy rowed away on his mare. I saw a stride at the final fence and I gave him a squeeze. He came up lovely as Magic Of Light made a mistake beside us. So we were in front, again. In front in the Grand National, like we were in front in the 2018 Grand National, history in sight.

I sat still though. I didn't go for him. Remember last year? This was different though, I didn't have to wake him up. I gave him a shake as the Elbow approached, around the Elbow and into the final 200 yards. Tiger Roll seemed to know better now too, he saw the Water Jump all right, but he didn't think he was done when he did. He kept going all the way to the line.

Remarkable. Extraordinary. Another Grand National. The first dual winner since Red Rum. History in the making and we were a part of it.

* * *

Seamus Murphy called me one Friday in early May 2019.

'Can you do 10–10?' he asked.

'Can I do what?'

'Can you ride at 10st 10lb,' asked Seamus.

'I can,' I said assuredly.

'Can you get yourself to Auteuil on Sunday to ride Carriacou in the Grand Steeple-Chase de Paris?'

The Grand Steep is a massive race in France. It is effectively the French Gold Cup, run, as it is, over three miles and six furlongs at Auteuil in the middle of May, and worth around €400,000 to the winning owner.

I had always taken a keen interest in the race, and I loved the water jump, La Rivière des Tribunes, about three times as wide as the water jumps in Britain, that you jump in front of the stands.

I remembered The Fellow when I was a kid, François Doumen's horse who won the Grand Steep in 1991, then went over to Britain, to Kempton, and won the King George the following December, and the December after that. Then he went back to Britain in 1994, to Cheltenham, and won the Gold Cup.

The Fellow's full brother Al Capone also won the Grand Steep, six years after his brother, and First Gold won it in 1998, two years before he won the King George at Kempton. First Gold was bought by J.P. McManus and he won the Punchestown Gold Cup in 2003 as a 10-year-old.

I had only ever ridden at Auteuil once, I rode Solwhit to finish second to Gemix in the French Champion Hurdle there in June

2013, so I was a little surprised to get the call to ride Carriacou. I had always said I would love to ride in the Grand Steep though, so I was delighted to get the ride.

Carriacou was Jonathan Plouganou's ride, but he was riding the favourite in the race instead, Bipolaire. I was really grateful though to Seamus and to Carriacou's trainer Isabelle Pacault for entrusting the ride to me.

It had been a real international week for me. I was over in Percy Warner Park in America the previous Saturday to ride a few horses for Gordon. Chief Justice finished fourth in the Champion Hurdle, and Stooshie finished second in the handicap hurdle, and I won the maiden hurdle on Markhan.

I got to Auteuil early on Sunday morning and walked the track. It was as impressive as I had remembered it, more impressive than it looked on television. I liked the track, I figured it was just a case of getting a horse settled, getting him to relax, so that's what I did with Carriacou. We moved to the front at the second last fence and, when I asked him to pick up on the run-in, he picked up well and won nicely.

That was brilliant. I was delighted to just get to ride in the race, so to win it was unbelievable. It was fantastic to get to add the Grand Steeple-Chase de Paris to my CV.

* * *

October 2020, and we thought that Doctor Duffy was going into the Munster National with a real chance of winning it. He had won his beginners' chase at Kilbeggan and he had won the Mayo National at Ballinrobe during the summer, and he had run a big race to finish third in the Kerry National at Listowel just three weeks earlier.

It all happened fairly quickly. We were off and running towards the first fence, we got a nice start, we were in the front rank, we had a clear sight of the first fence. He just jumped a bit to his right at the first fence, he collided with Conor McNamara's horse in mid-air, he became unbalanced and he couldn't get his landing gear sorted before the ground came to meet us.

I knew it was bad straight away. I got fired into the ground, head first, and I could feel the pain straight away. I had weird pains in different parts of my body. I actually thought I had broken my shoulder, that was where I felt the greatest pain, and I felt like a firework had gone off in my thumb. I felt like my thumb had exploded. I had numbness in different places, but I could move my fingers and my toes so I knew I was okay.

This was during Covid, Edelle was watching on the television with the kids. She saw me fall, and she immediately fired the children out of the room. She phoned the track, but couldn't get anybody. She phoned Gordon, but Gordon wasn't there. What with Covid, nobody was there. She phoned Jennifer Pugh, Adrian McGoldrick. She phoned Kevin O'Ryan, but he wasn't there either. She was going mad, she couldn't get any news. Then Rachael Blackmore called her. Rachael got Edelle's number, she knew she'd be up the walls. He's gone to hospital, Rachael told Edelle, but he was moving his fingers and his toes.

At least that.

As it turned out though, I had broken one vertebrae, crushed another and dislocated another. I was lucky it didn't get my spinal cord. The doctors told me I was very lucky, that I was in the 10% of people who suffer that injury who are able to walk again.

Rehabilitation was long and it was painful. They had to fuse two vertebrae together, and then they had to stretch me out so they could pop the other one back into place. So they drilled two holes in my head and lay me on my back, and they hung buckets of water off it in order to stretch me out. They added more water in order to add more weight and stretch me out more. The pain was almost unbearable, I'll never forget it, I remember roaring with the pain.

I always had pains in my legs, in my hips, tightness, soreness. Getting to the races, getting in and out of the car. And when they started stretching me, the pain was at its most severe in my hips.

I was screaming so one of the nurses came into me.

'Where do you feel the pain?'

'In my hips,' I said, wincing.

'That's fine,' she said.

It wasn't fine.

'Once it's not in your neck, you're all right.'

I put all my effort into my rehabilitation. Every ounce of me went into getting back riding. All the exercises, all the physio, all the doctors, all the people who were helping me. Sean Deegan was brilliant, he's a super physio. I used to go to him in Clonmel at least once a week, often twice a week. Sean went beyond what was necessary. I was so focused. It was all I was doing. All I wanted to do was get back riding. I couldn't drive, so I was walking and cycling everywhere. Me and my neck brace.

Some people were asking me if I was going back riding, some people were telling me I would be crazy to go back riding, that I should walk away while I still could. Lots of people were talking about my retirement, but I wasn't one of them.

I didn't want injury to retire me. I couldn't let an injury retire me. Above everything else, when I was going out, I wanted to go out on my own terms. I wanted to stop riding when I wanted to stop riding, not when an injury said I should. I wasn't sure if that might mean recovering and coming back for one ride so I could retire on my own terms, but I was determined to get back.

The doctors in the Mater Private were brilliant. Not only will you get back, Dr Joe Butler told me, but your neck will be stronger than ever.

He was right. I was fit, I felt strong, and I was back riding out at Gordon's the following January. I wasn't ready to race ride at that point though. I was still having difficulty raising my head to look out over the horse's ears. When you're riding, you're standing in the irons, your back is straight, so you have to tilt your neck backwards in order to be able to look forward. I couldn't do that.

I remember schooling a horse at Gordon's around that time, and pulling the horse up before the final hurdle in the school, because I couldn't lift my head enough to see that there was another hurdle left to jump.

I didn't get back race riding until September 2021, almost 11 months after my fall in the Munster National. It happened quite quickly in the end. I was riding out at Gordon's one morning in September, and I felt great. All the movement was back, I had no restrictions. So I told Gordon, put me down for whatever you want at the weekend.

My return was fairly seamless. I just slotted back in. I won the Daily Star Chase at Punchestown on Galvin a month after I returned, and I won the Troytown Chase at Navan in November on Run Wild Fred. And I won the two big Grade 1 staying chases in Ireland that winter.

It was great to win the Savills Chase at Leopardstown over Christmas on Galvin, we just got home by a short head from the Gold Cup runner-up A Plus Tard. It was great to win the Irish Gold Cup too the following February back at Leopardstown on Conflated. We just went around the inside, saving ground. Conflated always jumped a little to his left, so it made sense to go around the inside. I kicked him on at the third last fence, and they just couldn't catch us.

I got a great kick out of that, and I got a massive kick out of winning the Mersey Novices' Hurdle at Aintree that April on Three Stripe Life, who was owned by my good friend Kenny Haughey. I had always liked Three Stripe Life, ever since he was a young horse in Gordon's and, before he made his racecourse debut at Navan in

January 2021, I suggested to Kenny that he should buy him. Kenny has been a big supporter of mine for years, and we continue to work together. So it was brilliant to see Three Stripe Life realise the potential we saw in him then, it was fantastic to ride him to victory in a Grade 1 race.

Chapter 21

'Hey Gordon,' I said.

'Yeah?'

'My next winner will be my last.'

'Right.'

That was it. That was the extent of the chat. Mid-December 2022 and I knew the time was right. I had come back from injury, I had come back so I could retire on my own terms. I was sharing the rides at Gordon's with Jack, we were kind of joint number ones at Gordon's, Jack had the horses he rode, I had the horses I rode, but that wasn't sustainable. By definition, there can only be one number one, and it was dawning on me that, very soon, it was going to be Jack. He was ready. Jack was always ready. It was time for me to get out of the way, I figured. Let Jack off, let him be the number one rider at Gordon's, let him kick on. His time had come. He had waited long enough.

Gordon declared six horses at Navan the following Sunday, the Sunday before Christmas, and he declared me on every one of them. He put Jack on none of them, but Jack was going to the meeting too, the understanding being that, once I rode a winner, I would announce my retirement and Jack would take over on the rest of Gordon's runners.

Surely one of them would win.

Just shows you though, the best-laid plans. Navan was abandoned, so the plan had to be shelved. There was another meeting in Ireland on the day, Thurles, but Gordon had just one runner there, Liberty Dance, in the listed mares' novices' hurdle. Gordon told me to go and ride her, he said I could ride everything from then on until I rode a winner.

So, plans changed, I went to Thurles for one ride, one bullet, not knowing if it was going to be the final ride of my career or not. Liberty Dance had a big chance in that listed hurdle, she was sent off as favourite and she always travelled well, just up on the outside of the leader, Rocco Belle. I let her move to the front as we turned for home, we jumped the second last in front, and she picked up well. We came away from the rest of them, jumped the last well, and she kept on strongly up the run-in to win nicely.

It was a strange feeling pulling up. I took my gum shield out as we walked back down after pulling up and put it into my cuff. Bryan Cooper on The Model Kingdom, who had finished third, shook my hand. People seemed to know. There was a hum around the enclosures as I was coming back in, there seemed to be more people there than would normally be at a Sunday afternoon meeting at Thurles during the winter.

It was very nice, coming back into the winner's enclosure. Edelle was there with the kids, Jaimee was there, my dad was there, my sisters and brothers were there. I don't really know how they all ended up there. I didn't go around telling everyone, if I win on Liberty Dance today I'll be retiring. What if she didn't win? Everybody would have made all that effort for nothing. Then the next day, if I ride a winner today, I'll be retiring. No winner? Well, the next day then.

I was delighted they were all there though. It was lovely to come back into the winner's enclosure and see them all. It was nice to go out at Thurles too, a real National Hunt meeting, where I had ridden so many winners in the past. It was good to do it on a mare owned by Tim O'Driscoll, I had ridden plenty of winners for Tim, and obviously on a mare who was trained by Gordon.

Lots of people said lots of very nice things about me on the day. Lots of people asked me what I was going to do next. I said I didn't know, because I didn't. I had retired though, that was clear in my head. I didn't think I would be back race-riding less than a month later. And I definitely didn't think that, a little further down the road, I would be dancing in front of hundreds of thousands of people.

* * *

I said no initially. *Dancing with the Stars?* I couldn't imagine anything worse. Away from horses, away from racing people, inside in a studio for hours on end, for weeks on end, practising a dance.

I wasn't a star and I couldn't dance.

I'm not sure why or how I changed my mind. Edelle was a big part of it. She thought it would be a good thing for me to do, bring me into contact with different types of people, people from walks of life that I would never encounter in the ordinary course of events, try something new. She thought that getting outside my comfort zone would be a good thing as opposed to a bad thing and, you never know, she said, you might even enjoy it!

I didn't enjoy it at the start. Going up to Dublin, away from Edelle, away from the kids, away from the horses, spending hours in a studio, staying in Dublin for a couple of nights. It was intense, it was all-consuming.

But there were great parts of it even from the beginning. Meeting all the people was fantastic. Everybody from different walks of life, people I would never encounter in the ordinary run of things. It was brilliant to talk to everybody, get their stories, their perspectives, their opinions. Their take on life. And all the contestants, we were all in the same boat. Some of them were different to me, in that some of them could actually dance, but everyone was out of their comfort zone.

My partner Kylee Vincent was brilliant. She was so easy to work with, she simplified everything. She was so encouraging. If I wasn't getting something – and there were many times when I wasn't getting something! – she was so patient, always understanding, always reassuring. It was a joy to work with her. When I had a little wobble towards the end of the second week, when it was all getting very difficult and I was thinking of chucking it all in and going back to Youghal, she encouraged me to stay. I may not have stayed had it not been for her.

I'm so glad I stayed too. It was brilliant, a once-in-a-lifetime experience. To spend the whole week practising a dance, and then to perform it, in all the gear, a two-minute dance that took hours and hours of preparation, six hours a day, and then to perform it on Sunday night, in front of an audience with hundreds of thousands of people watching you on television. And then the worry that you'd be voted out, and the joy when you weren't. It was an extraordinary experience.

I was afraid I would be voted out the first week and, when I wasn't, I relaxed into it a bit. I thought there was a very real possibility that I would be voted out on the first week, and I would have hated if I had. Every week I was still in after that was a bonus.

The lads got big into it at home. All the kids got a big kick out of it, Lily and Finn and Liam and Tess. Jaimee got into it too. Edelle loved it, she came up for the show a couple of times. You had to be over 16 to go to the shows, so the kids couldn't go, but they came up for one afternoon of rehearsals. They loved that.

The whole town of Youghal got behind me. The downside was that I was away from home for longish stretches at a time, and I hated that. I hated being away from Edelle and the kids. Even so, I was delighted every time I got through another round. I suppose my competitive spirit kicked in at some stage. I was a 50/1 shot to win *Dancing with the Stars* at the start but, by the time semi-final night rolled around, the Saturday before the 2024 Cheltenham Festival, I was a 7/2 shot.

I have to say, I was a little disappointed when I was voted out. Nobody likes going out in the semi-final. We did a gothic Viennese waltz dressed as skeletons (the kids loved that!), we got 27 points, but it wasn't enough. We ended up in a 'dance off' with David Whelan and Salome Chachua, and we lost that. I was sad to leave but I knew I had given it my all. It was a fantastic experience, all of it, from beginning to end.

There was a silver lining too. The semi-final was on the Sunday before Cheltenham. If I had got through to the final, I wouldn't have been able to go to Cheltenham, I would have been in rehearsals all week. So I was able to get on a flight early on Monday morning and get to Cheltenham. I was there on Monday and Tuesday, for the first day of the festival. I wasn't riding there of course, but I hadn't missed a Cheltenham Festival in years, so it was nice to be able to go, to go back even when I wasn't riding. Then I flew back to Dublin on Tuesday evening, rehearsed for the rest of the week for the group dance on the Sunday, did the group dance on the Sunday evening and said goodbye to everybody.

* * *

The second Sunday in the new year, 8 January 2023, three weeks after my retirement from the saddle, I was driving up the road with Robert Widger and a few ponies when Gordon rang.

'Are you at Naas?' asked Gordon
'What?'
'Are you at Naas?' he asked again.
'No I'm not. I'm . . .'
'Could you be here by two o'clock? Jack's after getting injured.'

It was desperate for Jack. He had broken his leg four times before that. This was his fifth leg-break, when poor Top Bandit had fallen in the novices' chase earlier on the day. Gordon was wondering if I could get there in time to ride Irish Point in the Grade 1 Lawlor's of Naas Novice Hurdle.

I couldn't. But I did start to think, if I could, or if I had been at Naas, I would have ridden him all right.

I wasn't going to go back easily, I was going to have to be asked. And I wasn't going to be going back to be a bit-part player.

'Here, come on in on Monday will you?' Gordon said.

There was nothing more said after that, that's typical in racing, but I knew what was coming. It was really nice to go back into Gordon's. All the lads seemed to be delighted to see me. Are you coming back? And all the good horses there. I had a look at the board, and I was down to ride everything, all the good ones. Horses I wouldn't normally ride out.

There wasn't really a decision to be made. My last ride, Liberty Dance at Thurles, was on 18 December. That was only about three weeks earlier. If you were injured or suspended you could have been out for longer. Gordon wanted me to ride for him, and all the good horses were there for me to ride. I was helping Gordon out and I was getting to ride lots of good horses in lots of good races. The decision to go back was an easy one.

Chapter 22

The second day of the 2023 Dublin Racing Festival was the big day for me. I was riding Mighty Potter in the Grade 1 Ladbrokes Novice Chase that day, and I was riding Irish Point in the Grade 1 Tattersalls Ireland Novice Hurdle, and I was riding The Goffer in the Leopardstown Chase.

Irish Point finished fourth, he ran well, he was always going to improve for it. But the other two won.

Mighty Potter in particular was impressive. He was brilliant, he won as easily as he liked, and they put him in at a short price for the Turners Chase at Cheltenham on the back of that run. It was all very exciting.

I was so happy, riding out of my skin, good Dublin Racing Festival, lots to look forward to during the build-up to Cheltenham.

My last ride on the day was on The Tide Turns in the Liffey Handicap Hurdle. He ran well to a point, he travelled well across the top of the track and into the home straight, but he just tired from there, he couldn't get any closer to the leaders.

He was a beaten horse as we approached the final flight, I just thought we would pop the last and he could run on up the hill, complete the race. But he got the final flight wrong, and he kind of slithered to the ground. It was the easiest fall you could ever hope to have. It was like he eased me down onto the ground. I was like a Hollywood stunt man, I swear to God. The Fall Guy wouldn't have done it so well. Then a horse came behind us and got me. His knee just caught me in the back.

It was such bad luck now. There was only really one horse behind us as we fell but, despite his best efforts to avoid me, he got me properly, like a hammer hitting you square on the small of your back.

I was winded, I couldn't get up at first, then I got up. I always got up if I could. You wanted people to know you were okay. It was sore in the ambulance and I thought, ah I'd better go and get this X-rayed. I had broken two transverse processes in my back. They're like the wings of your vertebrae.

It was sore now. It wasn't sore enough to stop you riding, but it was sore enough to make you sore. I took a bit of time off, I just wanted to be good for Cheltenham. I rode a winner at the Leopardstown meeting in early March, the last National Hunt meeting of the season at Leopardstown, Fils D'Oudairies in the Anton O'Toole Hurdle, and I was third on Present Soldier in the next race. And I rode Irish Point to win the Grade 3 Kingsfurze Hurdle at Naas on the Sunday before Cheltenham. I was all set.

The problem with Cheltenham is that it is so intense. That's also the beauty of it, but the intensity exposes any flaws. If you are not a hundred per cent, if you are not completely ready, fully prepared, you are going to get found out. It's multiple rides one day, multiple rides the next day, multiple rides the next day, multiple rides the next day. You could ride two or three one day no problem, then have a day or two off. Then two or three or four the next day, then two or three days off. You don't have that option during the Cheltenham Festival, and it's the multiple rides on consecutive days that catch you.

I was grand on the first day at Cheltenham. Perfect. The Goffer ran okay in the Ultima Handicap Chase, and Zanahiyr ran okay in the Champion Hurdle, he kept on for me to finish third behind the superstar Constitution Hill, and Queen's Brook ran okay in the Mares' Hurdle. Like Zanahiyr she just stayed on to take third place behind Honeysuckle and Love Envoi in a race I never really thought we were going to win.

I thought the week would get better but, actually, it got worse.

I didn't ride Gerri Colombe in the Brown Advisory Chase on the Wednesday. I was never riding him, he was always Jordan Gainford's ride. He was beaten a short head, he just didn't catch The Real Whacker. I felt for Jordan. It's back to the same story, when you get beaten a short head, you can always look back on the race and say, if I had done this, or if I hadn't done that, it might have made the difference of the short head.

Galvin gave me a great spin in the Cross-Country Chase, the race developed into a match between me and Keith Donoghue on one of Gordon's other horses, my old friend Delta Work. I thought we had him when we landed over the last, but Delta Work loves that hill and he was just stronger on the run up to the winning line.

Mighty Potter was an odds-on shot in the Turners Chase, the first race on Thursday, but we couldn't get it done. I got a lot of stick for that ride, we finished third behind Stage Star, who made all the running, but we were never travelling. He just didn't feel like the horse who had won the Grade 1 novices' chase the previous month at Leopardstown. I knew we were beaten going to the first fence. In the end, I thought he did well to keep on as bravely as he did to finish third.

Teahupoo could only finish third too in the Stayers' Hurdle later in the day. That was frustrating as well. I had ridden Teahupoo to win the Galmoy Hurdle at Gowran Park six weeks earlier. That was my first time to ride him in a race, and he can be a difficult ride. I didn't think we were going anywhere in that race, so I had to get after him but, when I did, he was set alight, and we ended up winning the race by half the length of the home straight.

He probably had a harder race there than he needed to have, over an extended three miles on soft to heavy ground at Gowran Park in January. And that probably told at Cheltenham.

He wasn't giving me the same feel at Cheltenham. I still thought we were getting there, but you don't want to hit the front too soon, because he idles when he gets into the lead. So we're getting there and we're getting there. But then, when I make to go upsides Dashel Drasher, he moves across in front of me. I shift to go the other way, and he moves across in front of me again. So we've had momentum checked and we have to start again. Next thing I know, Sire Du Berlais is finishing off like a train on the far side, and we still can't get past Dashel Drasher.

I am convinced that, if Dashel Drasher hadn't moved across in front of me, we'd have won. As it was, the stewards on the day promoted us to second place, but we were demoted again to third place after the Dashel Drasher people appealed. It didn't really matter than much to me, we hadn't won the race. They were arguing over the difference between second and third, a bald man arguing the case for a comb. I didn't care. We weren't going to be promoted to first. Gordon did win it though with Sire Du Berlais.

I was in pain on the Friday morning, but I didn't feel like I couldn't ride. Going to the final flight in the County Hurdle, I thought Pied Piper was going to win. Everything had gone smoothly through the race, I had produced him to join the front rank on the run to the last, and I saw a stride. He flew the obstacle, he took it in his stride. The problem was that he stumbled a bit on landing.

I gathered him up, got him balanced again. By the time I had though, Favoir had joined me on my right-hand side, he had probably gone about a head up. We had the length of the run-in to find that head, all the way up the hill to the winning line, but we couldn't. We went down by a head, by the bob of a head.

I felt like screaming.

I rode Search For Glory in the Albert Bartlett Hurdle, but he was never travelling, and I pulled him up before the final flight.

I was due to ride Conflated for Gordon and for Gigginstown in the Gold Cup, but I didn't feel up to it. The pain was just too great, I didn't think it would be fair to the horse, or to Gordon or to Michael or Eddie. I told Gordon as much, and he said fine. Sam Ewing rode Conflated (he ran a massive race to finish third behind Galopin Des Champs and Bravemansgame) and I headed for the airport.

That's it, I thought. That's my days as a jockey at the Cheltenham Festival done. That's my days as a jockey done.

* * *

I was genuine. Done. Game over. Good night and God bless. No fanfare, just finished at Cheltenham and done, out the door, finished as a jockey.

I didn't ring Gordon over the course of the next few days, and Gordon didn't ring me. I just kept my head down and got on with things at home. The way I saw it, Gordon had my number if he wanted me to ride for him at Aintree. Not in a bad way, I just didn't want to be foisting myself upon him if he didn't want me.

Then the week before Aintree, I got a call from Busty, Ian Almond, one of Gordon's top people.

'We're schooling a couple of horses on Wednesday,' he said. 'Come in.'

'Ah fuck it Busty,' I said. 'I don't know.'

There was a bit of a pause on the other end of the phone.

'Do you know what you'll do now,' said Busty then. 'Come in here on Wednesday, school one or two horses, then go to Aintree, ride one or two Grade 1 winners, then sail off into the sunset.'

It was so good of Gordon. He didn't want my career to end like that, with a whimper, on the final day of the Cheltenham Festival, my final ride on Search For Glory in the Albert Bartlett Hurdle, pulled up before the final flight. He was right. It wouldn't have been good. I didn't really care at the time, I didn't really think about it too deeply. I just got on with it. That's a thread that has run through my entire career. But I'm sure I would have cared later.

I was very happy going back to Aintree, and I was looking forward to riding Gerri Colombe and Irish Point in the Grade 1 races. They were both trained by Gordon and they both raced in the Robcour colours of Brian Acheson, and they both went to Aintree with big chances. Gerri Colombe was on the Friday, the first race on the Friday, the Mildmay Novices' Chase, and he was dynamite. I had never ridden Gerri Colombe in a race before, but he did everything I expected him to do, he did everything I hoped he would do.

Harry Skelton kicked clear on the mare Galia Des Liteaux on the run into the home straight, but I knew I had loads of horse underneath me and loads of time to make up the ground. I just allowed him to make up his ground on the outside, I didn't even have to ask him, we moved up on the outside of the leader and we jumped into the lead at the second last fence. Then I asked him to pick up and we came away on that big open run from the second last fence to the last at Aintree, pinged the final fence and stayed on well.

That was a great feeling, a massive relief. I didn't really realise how big a relief it was until I was pulling up after crossing the winning line. It was my first winner since I had ridden Irish Point to win the Kingsfurze Hurdle at Naas on the Sunday before Cheltenham. Lots had happened between the two, Cheltenham and everything, but it was really nice to come back into the winner's enclosure, on a horse with Gerri Colombe's class, after a Grade 1 race.

Irish Point was on the Saturday, Grand National day, just over two hours before the Grand National. Irish Point was very good too. We started off well back in the field, he settled lovely for me, and we started passing horses. He moved up nicely in behind the leaders early in the home straight, I took him towards the outside after we had jumped the second last flight and, when I did, he picked up well. We hit the front on the run to the final flight, jumped that obstacle nicely and he kept going really gamely up to the winning line.

I stood up in my irons and punched the air when we got there. I don't know, I didn't really think about it, I didn't really think that it might be my final winner. I just felt relieved, exhilarated, excited, another winner at Aintree, an exciting horse, another Grade 1 win. It meant an awful lot. It was my 61st Grade 1 win, and it was win number 1,576 in my career, after more than ten thousand rides.

I rode Galvin in the Grand National just over two hours earlier, but there was no fairytale ending. Of course, it was too much to hope for. I thought Galvin had a chance in the race actually, but it all went wrong at the first fence. We were a little further back than I wanted to be on the run to the obstacle, we got a little crowded as we jumped it, Galvin went to his left, and I came off him on the right. It was just one of those things.

It's the Grand National. Big fences. Anyone's race can be over at the first.

That's how the race rolls.

My final ride was in the final race that day, in the bumper on Grand National day 2023, on Pour Les Filles. It was nice to go out on a horse trained by Gordon, and it was fitting too to go out on a horse owned by Kenny Haughey. It was like a link between my past and my future.

I was happy to walk away though, happy to walk out of Aintree that evening, Grand National evening 2023, on my own, unaided, all limbs intact, all faculties in operation. I was happy to get a flight back to Cork, get back to Youghal, and go home to Edelle and Lily and Finn and Liam and Tess. I know how lucky I am.

The life I had as a kid, that carefree life, always doing, always up to something, knowing where the boundaries were, and yet, knowing that, if there was mischief around, you were allowed to find it. I want that for them.

People asked me then what I was going to do, given that my career as a jockey was over, and I said I didn't really know. They still ask me now. I suppose I'm doing it. I'm around with the kids, working on the farm, working with the horses, buying a few, selling a few, breeding a few. Always something to do with horses.

I haven't thought about it too deeply though. I'm just getting on with it.

Acknowledgements

I have so many people to thank. My family have been brilliant, in everything. They have been with me through the highs and lows, the ups and downs. Real life.

I owe so much to my wife Edelle. She might not know much about racing, but she knows me better than anyone else knows me, and I am continually and deeply grateful to her for always supporting me, for being such an amazing wife and a fantastic mother to our four children.

My children, Jaimee, Lily-Marie, Finn, Liam, Tess. Now I have the chance to spend more time with them, to be with them more, and I am so thankful for that. To spend time together on the farm or when they ride their ponies or when they are showjumping at the weekends. This was not possible when I was racing. They're brilliant. They make me laugh.

My parents, my siblings Finnuala, Eimear, Aileen, Sean, Diarmuid. They gave me incredible backing from the very start. My parents gave us this marvellous upbringing, they supported me from the very beginning, they were the foundation for the person I became, the person I am today. They instilled values in me that mean the most to me and which I hope to pass on to my own children. Values that mean that the daily grind becomes a beautiful fulfilment, where I can go home and share my passion with them.

My aunts, my uncles, all my cousins all over the world.

There are far too many owners and trainers to mention. From the first to the last trainer and everyone in between. Special mention, though, to Gordon Elliott, Charles Byrnes, Arthur Moore, Ferdy Murphy, Mick O'Brien, Tom O'Mahony. I wouldn't have turned professional without their support and guidance.

They all had a huge influence on my career.

All the doctors and surgeons, the medical staff, the Order of Malta, who work tirelessly and give their time voluntarily, on both sides of the Irish Sea. A special mention too to Dr Adrian McGoldrick and Dr Jennifer Pugh. Also, my physiotherapists, especially Sean Deegan who kept me together.

My two agents, Frostie Kelly, who was with me through thick and thin from very early in my career, and Kevin O'Ryan, a brilliant person who took over from Frostie when he retired.

The boys and girls in the weighroom, amateur and professional. It is a unique setting, the camaraderie the undercurrent to the rivalry, and all the characters that make the weighroom the fantastic environment that it is.

I'm also very fortunate to have a close-knit group of trusted friends with whom I am just myself, with whom I can have a real laugh. Special mention to Peter Vaughan, a confidant, always there for a post-race chat and support and to my brother-in-law Colman Walsh, always there for me.

Horse Racing Ireland and the Irish Horseracing Regulatory Board, still the Turf Club to some, who run our sport to the best of their ability.

All staff involved in the everyday running of our racing yards, who work so hard and give such long hours. They sometimes don't get the recognition that they deserve, but they are at the core of our sport and our industry. It couldn't work without them.

The point-to-point committees throughout the country, volunteers, the fence stewards, who work tirelessly for the love of our sport. Their enthusiasm is infectious. They truly are the life and blood of our sport.

Bill Esdaile and all at Square In The Air for all the advice and support, and the professional guidance that they have given me.

My sponsors: Star Sports, the Star newspaper and Citipost.

Everyone at Bonnier and Eriu, Deirdre Nolan and Lisa Gilmour, but for whom this book would not have been possible.

Donn McClean. I always thought if I ever produced a book, I would love Donn to work with me. We worked hard together on this book, there were long meetings, long hours and lots of travel. Thank you for listening Donn and for researching dates and results. Also to Rachel, your support to Donn was ever present in putting this book together.

Finally, to the racegoers, the people from Ireland and Britain and from all over the world who follow and support our sport. Without you, none of this would have been possible.